FAMILY THERAPY

FAMILY THERAPY
A Nursing Perspective

Imelda W. Clements, R.N., Ph.D.

Associate Professor
Academic Director of Graduate Mental Health Nursing
Vanderbilt University School of Nursing
Nashville, Tennessee

Diane M. Buchanan, R.N., M.S.N.

Assistant Professor
Psychiatric Mental Health Nursing
University of Ottawa School of Nursing
Ottawa, Ontario

A WILEY MEDICAL PUBLICATION
JOHN WILEY & SONS
New York · Chichester · Brisbane · Toronto · Singapore

Cover design by Wanda Lubelska

Library of Congress Cataloging in Publication Data:
Main entry under title:
Family therapy.

  (A Wiley medical publication)
  Includes index.
  1. Family psychotherapy. 2. Psychiatric nursing.
I. Clements, Imelda W. II. Buchanan, Diane M. III. Series.
[DNLM: 1. Family therapy—Nursing texts. WY 160 F198]
RC488.5.F334   616.89′156   81-13129
ISBN 0-471-08146-9   AACR2

Printed in the United States of America

10 9 8 7 6 5 4 3 2 1

Contributors

Joan Soulier Adams, R.N., M.S.N.
Assistant Professor
Department of Nursing
Murray State University
Murray, Kentucky

Bertram Bandman, Ph.D.
Professor
Philosophy Department
Long Island University
Brooklyn, New York

Elsie L. Bandman, R.N., Ph.D., F.A.A.N.
Professor
Hunter College Bellevue School of Nursing
City University of New York
New York, New York

Ruth Belew, R.N., M.S.N.
Instructor
Jewish Hospital School of Nursing
Cincinnati, Ohio

Eva Benson, R.N., M.S.N.
Quality Assurance Coordinator
Holderman Memorial Hospital Veterans' Home
Yountville, California

Marion Fitzsimmons Briel, R.N., M.S.N.
Clinical Specialist
Zepf Community Mental Health Center
Toledo, Ohio

Jane Kreplick Brody, R.N., M.S.N.
Instructor
School of Nursing
Fondulac College
Philadelphia, Pennsylvania

Diane M. Buchanan, R.N., M.S.N.
Assistant Professor
Psychiatric Mental Health Nursing
University of Ottawa School of Nursing
Ottawa, Ontario

Gloria Weber Calhoun, R.N., M.S.N., R.N.C.
Private Practice, Huntsville, Alabama
Doctoral Student, School of Nursing
University of Alabama
Birmingham, Alabama

Imelda W. Clements, R.N., Ph.D.
Associate Professor
Academic Director of Graduate Mental Health Nursing
Vanderbilt University School of Nursing
Nashville, Tennessee

Deane L. Critchley, R.N., Ph.D.
Professor
Graduate Nursing Program
University of New Mexico
Albuquerque, New Mexico

Linda Dumat, R.N., M.S.N.
Certified Member, I.T.A.A.
Clinical Specialist
Veterans' Administration Medical Center
Murfreesboro, Tennessee

Francesca Farrar, R.N., M.S.N.
Assistant Professor
Belmont College School of Nursing
Nashville, Tennessee

Marjorie Fox, R.N., M.S.N.
Training and Motivational Consultant
Nashville, Tennessee

Ethel Hines-Battle, R.N., M.S.N.
Clinical Specialist
Veterans' Administration Medical Center
Murfreesboro, Tennessee

Anita Turner Kinslow, R.N., M.S.N.
Instructor, School of Nursing
Middle Tennessee State University
Murfreesboro, Tennessee

Ann Kleine-Kracht, R.N., M.A.
Instructor
Bellarmine College
Louisville, Kentucky
Doctoral Student, School of Nursing
University of Indiana
Indianapolis, Indiana

Paul Kleine-Kracht, J.D.
Attorney-At-Law
Spaulding, Cato, Kleine-Kracht & Ames
Louisville, Kentucky

George A. Lee, R.N., Ph.D.
Instructor
Deaconess Hospital School of Nursing
St. Louis, Missouri

Mary Jane Macey, R.N., M.S.N.
Associate Professor of Nursing
Vanderbilt University School of Nursing
Doctoral Candidate at Peabody College
Nashville, Tennessee

Judith Maurin, R.N., Ph.D.
Associate Dean
Graduate Nursing Program
University of New Mexico
Albuquerque, New Mexico

Susan A. Morgan, R.N., M.S.N.
Associate Professor of Nursing
Assistant Dean for Student Affairs
Vanderbilt University School of Nursing
Doctoral Candidate at Peabody College
Nashville, Tennessee

Perry M. Nicassio, Ph.D.
Associate Professor of Psychiatry
Vanderbilt University Medical Center
Nashville, Tennessee

Nancy Nygaard, R.N., M.S.N.
Doctoral Candidate, School of Nursing
University of Texas at Austin
Austin, Texas

Florence Roberts, R.N., Ph.D.
Associate Professor
School of Nursing
Vanderbilt University
Nashville, Tennessee

Gloria Russell, R.N., M.S.N.
Assistant Professor
School of Nursing
Tennessee Technological University
Cookeville, Tennessee

Carol A. Seeger, R.N., M.S.N.
Doctoral Student
Department of Mental Health and Community Nursing
University of California at San Francisco
San Francisco, California

Shirley Smoyak, R.N., Ph.D., F.A.A.N.
Professor
Graduate Nursing Program
Rutgers—The State University of New Jersey
College of Nursing
New Brunswick, New Jersey

Susan Thomas, R.N., M.S.N.
Clinical Specialist
Middle Tennessee Mental Health Institute
Nashville, Tennessee

Margaret McAvoy Trimpey, R.N., M.S.N.
Director of Nursing
Moccasin Bend Mental Health Center
Chattanooga, Tennessee

Susan Van Gee, R.N., M.S.N.
Clinical Specialist
Indiana University Medical Center
Indianapolis, Indiana

Beverly Young, R.N., M.S.N.
Clinical Instructor
Ohio State University School of Nursing
Columbus, Ohio

Carroll Young, R.N., M.S.N.
Ambulatory Liaison Instructor
Vanderbilt University Hospital
Nashville, Tennessee

Mary Ann Woodward-Smith, R.N., M.S.N.
Clinical Specialist
Veterans' Administration Medical Center
Nashville, Tennessee

Deborah Williams, R.N., M.S.N.
Administrator
Allen County War Memorial Hospital
Scottsville, Kentucky

Debra Gooden Woosley, R.N., M.S.N.
Coordinator
Therapeutic Center
Santa Rosa Mental Health Center
Milton, Florida

Foreword

One of the most significant advances in the clinical practice of nurses in the past quarter of a century has been their participation in the development and use of family therapy. Since the mid-1950s graduate programs in psychiatric–mental health nursing have been training professional nurses in this psychotherapeutic modality. In this book, many of the contributing nurse-authors have completed such graduate psychiatric–mental health nursing programs and continued to practice family therapy; and herein they share insights from their practice.

This book adds substantially to the scientific knowledge that nurses can use to understand phenomena observed in family therapy interactions. That same knowledge can be used to decide the therapeutic interventions to help families resolve their difficulties. A highlight of this work is the presentation of succinctly defined concepts with illustrations of their applicability to clinical data.

The importance of scientific theory to a family therapist cannot be over-emphasized. The interactions of diverse parts, processes, and patterns of a dysfunctional family system are complex; and understanding them has required new theories, which are quite unlike concepts that illuminate individual behavior. Theories that are most useful in family therapy provide explanations of the dynamics of sequences of network interactions, the reciprocal influences among members toward pattern-maintenance, and the effects of these patterns. These theories are still being evolved.

There are many theoretical, legal, and ethical issues related to family therapy, which this book places in a nursing perspective. Nurses who engage in family therapy need this information in order to practice in a fully responsible manner.

Family therapy is of recent origin; consequently, the conceptualizations of the structure and method for conducting family psychotherapeutic sessions vary greatly. The authors have presented a selection of models that are currently being tested by family therapists. Nurses who practice family therapy should study and compare the various conceptual models to enrich their approaches to their work with families. The search for the single, most effective model for family therapy continues, and nurses are participants in that inquiry.

As a mode of treatment, family therapy holds great promise. When the role of "mentally ill patient" is ascribed to an individual family member and that person is hospitalized and treated separately, other members of the family are unlikely to consider their participation in the dysfunction of the "sick" person. By contrast, when the family system as a unit is the object of inquiry and treatment, the difficulties of the "identified patient" are seen as a system effect that can be modified. Nurses who work in psychiatric hospitals have observed that patients who are discharged following individual treatment are often readmitted to the hospital shortly after returning to their homes. It can be said that, despite treatment, they could not survive the subtle (and sometimes overt) dysfunctions of the family system. On the other hand, when the entire family is the unit of treatment, there is a possibility for simultaneous change in a favorable direction for all members of the family.

This book sets forth a broad range of information and illustrates many productive reasons for nurses to practice family therapy. It demonstrates the capability of nurses not only as practitioners of family therapy but also as contributors to the clarification and enrichment of knowledge and method for this form of treatment.

Hildegard E. Peplau, R.N., Ed.D.

Preface

It has been a quarter of a century since nurses first became involved in the form of psychotherapy that deals with the family. Since then, family therapy has evolved into a respectable treatment form and has received recognition as being a necessary response to psychosocial disorders. As family therapy has grown and changed, so has nurses' involvement in it. Family therapy has gained a degree of sophistication. Nurses are practicing family therapy in private and public institutions and in private practice. They are involved in research related to families and family therapy. As well as being necessary components of graduate psychiatric–mental health nursing programs, the concepts and benefits of family therapy are now introduced at the baccalaureate level. The volume of articles published by nurses on family therapy has multiplied, yet no major texts have appeared to date. This collection of contributions by mental health nurse clinicians attempts to fill this void.

This text includes a historical view of family therapy, gives an operational approach to a number of family theory concepts, provides comparison and contrast studies of several concepts, and provides the means by which the nurse can effectively intervene in therapy sessions with maladaptive families. It is not our intention to develop an extensive book of family concepts or theory but rather to provide the basis for family therapy intervention rationale. The emphasis is on the teaching/learning process used to identify the dynamics in a given family and to define the operational components in order to have a rational intervention in the actual family. A nurse using this book can select a concept, observe how it is used within a theoretical framework, and then assess how to deal with it in a family therapy session.

The book is divided into five parts. Part I reviews the historical development of family therapy. The qualifications and certification prerequisites for a practicing nurse family therapist are identified, and the value of family therapy is explored. The nurse's role in family therapy is examined. Such components as legal aspects and bioethics are discussed. Part II discusses the various models of family therapy, the family structure model, the transactional analysis model, the communication model, and the behavioral model, with special emphasis on the general systems model. The scientific aspects of family therapy are drawn together by Parts III and IV, written by mental health nursing graduate students during their clinical coursework in family therapy at the Vanderbilt University School of Nursing. Part III provides operational definitions for, and examples of, a variety of concepts related to family therapy. These concepts have, for clarification purposes, been placed in groups using as headings Barnhill's eight dimensions of family mental health and pathology of: role reciprocity, generational boundaries, individuation mutuality, perception, communication, flexibility, and stability.* Part IV shows the linkage of concepts through comparison and contrast of a number of standard family concepts. Part V demonstrates the nurse therapist's purposeful use of self in applying family concepts through the use of the nursing process to relieve dysfunctional communication patterns in ongoing family therapy sessions. The nurse therapist's approach to the family as a living system is that of teaching healthy communication skills. Tools for family assessment and evaluation of the therapist's work are also included in this section.

With the need for accountability in all facets of health care, family therapy, although relatively young, should also offer quality client care. The plan of this book provides material for nurse practitioners already working in family therapy. It is by questioning and critiquing family therapy and its concepts, by developing valid theoretical approaches, and through continued documentation of this knowledge that nurses can be assured that they can provide quality family therapy.

I. W. C.
D. M. B.

---

* L. Barnhill, Healthy family systems. *The Family Coordinator,* January 1979, 94–100.

Acknowledgments

Of all those who helped and encouraged us in the development of this book, we especially wish to mention the following people:

Jim Simpson from John Wiley & Sons, whose warm interest encouraged us throughout this project.

Grayce Sills, who gave generously of her time and expertise in reviewing the original manuscript. Her constructive criticisms assisted greatly in refining the chapters.

Colleagues and students who have shared our ideas and challenged us to refine our thinking. Particularly, we thank Margie Gale and Lorraine Papa, who helped formulate content and assisted in the initial editing, and Florence Roberts, for the final reading.

Ann Sanders and Pat Kovalcheck, whose assistance helped ensure that the manuscript met high editorial standards.

And special thanks to each of our families, whose support and faith in our efforts spurred us on to the publication of this book.

I. W. C.
D. M. B.

Contents

PART V
CLINICAL PRACTICE

FAMILY THERAPY

Part I

HISTORICAL ASPECTS: THE NURSE THERAPIST

1

Family Therapy Origins

Ruth Belew and Diane M. Buchanan

Family therapy has evolved as a matter of course from treatment of the individual in the psychoanalytic era, to group therapy in the interpersonal era, to family therapy in the systems era. Brodkin, however, sees family therapy as having evolved from two crises: "the identity crisis of the individual" and the "crisis of order in a pluralistic social setting" (1).

The family as a unit of communication, relating feelings and dealing with change and problems, has existed since the beginning of humanity. The family that needs outside help to deal with problems to the extent seen today is a modern day phenomenon caused by many of the historical, sociological, and psychological changes of this century. The psychosocial changes of the past 60 years have often resulted in a strong conflict between meeting the needs of the individuals within a family and meeting the needs required to maintain a functioning family.

Family therapy is defined here as that therapeutic modality that has the family as its unit of treatment. The family is viewed as an organismic whole, and the treatment is of the impaired functioning of the family system. The essence of family therapy deals with a natural group, the family, whose members have a history, present, and future of interacting with one another. Members include parents, children, significant relatives, and any other people who are important to the family function.

THE FAMILY THERAPY MOVEMENT

The movement toward family therapy began in the late 1940s and early 1950s when a number of therapists began treating whole families. Before this, the individual was the focus of diagnosis and treatment. The shift to family orientation was gradual and involved many contributing factors.

Early Development

The pioneers in family therapy became involved in the family movement through their research in schizophrenia, which was well funded by the government in the postwar period. They observed the family of the schizophrenic person and the interactions that occurred.

Nathan Ackerman, considered the founding father of family-centered therapy, originally started treating the entire family with the intent of alleviating stress in an individual member of a family, usually a child. He initially worked with the child, then began seeing the child and mother together. Ultimately his therapy extended to include the entire family. Ackerman became aware of the intricate interweaving of the identities of the individual and the family and used home visits by the staff as part of his break with traditional treatment as early as the 1940s. This early phase of development has been described by Brodkin as "saving the individual, family style" (1).

Ackerman came to the family movement with a psychoanalytic background in child psychiatry. It had become apparent that something was missing in traditional psychoanalytic therapy. The ill person had been removed from the environment in which the illness developed. When he found that satisfactory therapy was difficult without benefit of healthy family relationships, he moved toward the theory that a person could be made well within the family setting in which he became ill (2). This idea was enhanced by the government-supported child guidance movement and the surge of research in schizophrenia.

Ackerman considered the development of family therapy a historical necessity. He stated the reason for this as:

> the recognition of certain weaknesses in traditional forms of psychotherapy, the evolution of the theory of personality, and the quest for a new synthesis in the theory of psychotherapy, new developments in the behavioral sciences, changing conceptions of mental illness, and the crisis of family instability induced by social change (3, 4).

Other therapists began to recognize the complexities of the family and the need for therapy specifically geared toward this social system.

Virginia Satir's theory and practice of family therapy developed from her evaluation of communications with other family members concerning the patient she was treating. This evaluation revealed the significance of family interaction and its relationship to the treatment of the individual (5).

Jay Haley's shift to a family orientation evolved from his work with

Gregory Bateson and John Weakland on a research project dealing with communication of schizophrenics. In 1953, their observations of family behavior offered new insights into the causes of family problems. At the same time, Haley noticed a relationship between changes in the patient and changes in the family. With the idea that the family contributed to the etiology of the pathology of the patient, Haley theorized that the individual would benefit from family therapy (6).

While performing therapy and consultation primarily with hospitalized schizophrenics, Don Jackson observed a common cycle: a person is hospitalized, improves with therapy, is returned home, but soon is readmitted to the hospital. Jackson wondered about this cycle and the changes that occur in family members when a patient changes in treatment. His observations prompted his earliest paper on the family, "The Question of Family Homeostasis" (7).

Murray Bowen believed the family therapy movement developed through an effort to produce more effective treatment methods for severe emotional problems. The factor that distinguished his involvement in the family movement from previous family work was an alteration in the basic treatment process (8). The development of Bowen's family theory originated from his family research study in which schizophrenic patients and their parents lived together at the National Institute of Mental Health (NIMH), Bethesda, Maryland. His observations of family relationships suggested that the family was the unit of illness.

FAMILY THEORIES DEVELOPED

Early development of family therapy dealt with attempts to save the individual through the use of the family structure. In the 1960s, a number of sociological changes began to threaten the very existence of the family, thus changing the focus of the family therapist. Brodkin describes this second phase as "fighting for the embattled family" (1).

It was during this phase that nursing involvement in family therapy became more apparent, and nurses were given recognition as family therapists. Public health and mental health nurses realized that emotional disturbance in one member often indicated disturbance within the family system, thus changing the focus to family-oriented nursing care (9). As more therapists became committed to the concept of family therapy, conceptual frameworks and theories were developed. Attempts to categorize and explain observations of family interaction and the factors that seemed to contribute to change in the family resulted in an overabundance of jargon stemming from the various theoretical backgrounds of those involved and in a lack of consensus regarding a specific theoretical model. Brodkin suggests that family therapy, rather than being a therapeutic technique or theoretical model, is a paradigm (1). This may be expressed as involving an ideological movement that encompasses a variety of theoretical frameworks emerging from various disciplines.

Psychological theory, learning theory, and group theory have all had a place in the development of family therapy theories. One of the conceptual frameworks most frequently associated with family theories is the *systems* theory (see Chapter 10), drawn from the physical sciences. The systems approach views the family as a system that changes when any one part of the system changes.

Ackerman maintained that family therapy had not reached a sufficient level of development for it to be called a systems approach to pathology; however, he admitted that the general systems theory was the major theoretical thrust in the field (4). The use of a systems framework resulted from a need for family therapists to describe and conceptualize family relationships in terms understandable to treatment. The terminology of psychoanalytic therapy that existed at this point was based on the individual and was not applicable to the whole family. According to Haley, the systems theory was popular because it could handle interacting factors in a self-correcting way (10). Even though all theorists did not subscribe to the systems approach as a model, early proponents were the communications group of Bateson, Weakland and Haley, and Bowen's group. The family systems theory of Bowen originally focused on concepts linked to psychoanalysis and schizophrenia and then to a broader theory of emotional dysfunction. As the systems theory was being adapted to families, each therapist was on his own in conceptualizing his observations, bringing to the literature a potpourri of new terminology and a redefinition of some terms already in existence. For example, Weakland redefined the term *double bind* as meaning interactional or "the circular causal explanation of any family member's disorder" (1) rather than as viewing the patient as the victim of a dysfunctional family.

New Therapy Models

Structural therapy (see Chapter 6) is exemplified by Minuchin who frequently induces and capitalizes on crises. He uses the unstable family situation to change and restructure the family (11). Bowen's style of therapy progressed to modifying the disturbed family structure by working with the two most important members in the family and using the therapist as a third person in a therapeutic triangle. The theory is that if the two primary members can resolve their difficulties and alter their behavior, then the other members will follow in a similar manner.

Operant classic and observational learning principles provide the theoretical basis for *behavioral family therapy*. As discussed more fully in Chapter 8, the problem behaviors exhibited in the family are the targets of clinical intervention. The family members are helped by the therapist to learn how to exert independent control over maladaptive behavior, first by achieving experimental control over the overt problem behavior and then by changing the maladaptive behavior in the natural behavior.

Watzlawick and Haley contributed significantly to the development of the *family communication model*. This approach, discussed more fully in Chapter 9, involves the therapist initiating and directing new patterns of communication between family members.

The *transactional analysis model* is the preferred theoretical framework and treatment approach by some family therapists. As indicated in Chapter 7, this psychodynamic theory developed by Eric Berne in the 1950s evolved into a growth model focusing on the client's strengths (12). It lends itself to the treatment of pathological family systems by providing a concise framework within which the therapist can view what is happening in the family.

TODAY'S CHALLENGE

The options of family life-styles that evolved through the 1970s brought "an era of ambiguity" (1) and further development in family therapy. Many people are no longer certain of a stable family, and therapists have the dual challenge of preservation of the individual and support of mutuality (11). The future of family therapy is by no means "fixed" but will continue to be altered, modified, and redefined in order to meet the needs of our changing society.

LEGITIMIZATION OF THE CONCEPT AND METHODS

In order to spread the word and legitimize a new form of health care, there are a number of necessary processes. These include receiving acceptance by the professional organizations, researching worthwhile theories and ideas and reporting relevant results, and taking part in the educational system.

The move toward professional acceptance began when William Menninger urged the Group for the Advancement of Psychiatry to form a committee on the family. Through this committee several papers describing family-schizophrenia research were presented at the 1957 meeting of the American Orthopsychiatric Association. As further acceptance was gained and other therapists reported their findings, funding for family therapy research expanded, and family therapy programs were included in university graduate curricula.

Writing, as well as research, originated with the work done on schizophrenia. The bibliography section of this chapter has a more complete listing of the literature. Bateson and Jackson's development of the theory of double bind led to the publication of the article "Toward a Theory of Schizophrenia," 1956 (13). R. D. Laing in *The Divided Self*, 1959, referred to the schizophrenic family's communication problem of denying and negating the patient's experience as "mystification" (14). In 1965, Theodore Lidz and his colleagues at Yale University identified confusion of roles among members of schizophrenic families (15). Lyman Wynne at NIMH was involved in describing the identity formation in families of schizophrenic patients and coined concepts such as pseudomutuality (16). Murray Bowen, also at NIMH, wrote his observations and termed the fusion of family identities as *family ego mass* (17).

The writing and research in the 1960s showed a move away from schizophrenia, such as Satir's *Conjoint Family Therapy* in 1964 (5) and *Families of the Slums* in 1967 (18). They reflected the concern of therapists during this era for saving the family. Haley's writing reveals that at this time research showed concern for the stages of family development as a crucial factor in the development of symptomatology (10). Likewise, crisis intervention gained recognition as reported by Lansley in 1968 (19).

In the 1970s the research and publications expanded to include the variety of optional family situations. The effects of divorce on the family, individual spouse and children, were examined, as well as single families and blended families. The ramifications of trying to protect the needs of the individual as well as the family were evident in journals and texts concerned with family therapy. The journal *Family Process* (first published in 1962) and the *American Journal of Orthopsychiatry* were two prominent publications reporting the theories and research of this period. Concomitant to the increased involvement of nurses in the field, the late 1960s and 1970s brought a rapid increase of publications by nurses on the topic of family therapy (9).

As Haley stated, it takes about 20 years for a new concept to enter universities at the teaching level (10); thus, it was during the 1960s and 1970s that family therapy entered graduate level education. This was probably aided by the action-oriented generation of clinicians of the 1960s. Therapists had become more interested in bringing about change in the family rather than singularly dwelling on helping individuals gain insight into their problems. One difficulty was how to teach family therapy. As many methods for performing family therapy evolved as there were theories, and students were asked to adapt to a different focus—that of the family— rather than focusing on the individual as learned in earlier programs.

Research and writing in the 1970s reflected the interest in developing training programs that extended their scope to family theory and therapy. Nathan Epstein, Duane Bishop, and Sol Levin developed the McMaster model of family functioning (20), which was based on 20 years of research and practice with families. It is a conceptual model using the systems theory, which is clinically useful, teachable, and provides a framework that therapists can use to conceptualize their work with families. Laurence Barnhill in "Healthy Family Systems" (21) reviews and then integrates concepts of the healthy family. He describes the need for family therapists to be trained to recognize and use a variety of family theories and concepts. With this knowledge, therapists can intervene at any point in a family's health cycle, based on the needs of that specific family. In the 1979 article by Karl Tomm and Lorraine Wright, "Training in Family Therapy: Perceptual, Conceptual and Executive Skills" (22), an outline is presented of family therapy skills aimed at providing a more precise focus for training therapists. The ongoing literary challenge is to clearly define family therapy theories in a manner that can be researched, provide accountable treatment models, and provide a means of teaching future clinicians.

AN ADDENDUM

In any historical review of family therapy it is important to consider the major centers in which the concepts and theories have developed. The following is an attempt to highlight some of the centers and groups recognized as having shaped and chronicled the evolvement of today's concept of family therapy.

The Palo Alto Group

In 1952 Gregory Bateson received a grant to study and research human communications. Jay Haley and John Weakland joined in this effort. Don Jackson, then a supervising psychiatrist in residency programs, began working on the project as consultant and clinical supervisor in 1954. The development of the systems model as related to human behavior and to the family was a result of their combined efforts.

As the project declined, Jackson formed the Mental Research Institute (MRI) in 1959. Virginia Satir joined Jackson and found herself at the center of the family movement. She brought together her ideas with those at MRI and later published the book *Conjoint Family Therapy* (5). In 1962, when the Bateson project formally ended, Haley, Weakland, and Watzlawick became associated with the MRI group. By the end of the 1960s, Satir was director of Esalen Institute in California, Haley had moved to the Philadelphia Child Guidance Clinic, and Jackson was dead.

National Institute of Mental Health

In 1961 Murray Bowen published results of the pioneering research he had done with schizophrenics and their families. Bowen's work had actually begun in Topeka, Kansas at the Menninger Clinic where the main focus was around mother-child symbiosis. In 1954 Bowen moved to the National Institute of Mental Health and began his landmark project. Bowen hospitalized whole families for observation with the purpose of gathering information on the family as a unit of illness. The direct observation of family interactions led to a new form of therapy focused on saving the family and was an important step in family-oriented theory.

The Ackerman Institute for Family Therapy

Nathan Ackerman founded The Family Institute in 1960. This was the period when family therapy was further developed and introduced into clinical programs and into the mainstream of the psychiatric field. The institute was the first organization of its kind specifically dedicated to the treatment and study of the family. In its beginning, a small clinic was set up to treat families referred to Ackerman. He would interview the family and then transfer them to a staff member, remaining available as a supervisor/consultant. As the institute grew, the name was changed to The Ackerman Institute for Family Therapy.

The Colorado Group

In 1964, Don Langsley and David Kaplan began an NIMH-supported project along with Frank Pittman III, Kalman Flomenhaft, and Carol De Young at the Colorado Medical Center in Denver. The aim of the project was to determine if people in an acute crisis could be maintained outside the hospital setting by using a brief family therapy approach.

Other groups or centers involved in forming today's concepts of family therapy include The Philadelphia Group, consisting of Salvador Minuchin, Jay Haley, and Ross Speck; the Eastern Pennsylvania Psychiatric Institute, where Ivan Boszormenyi-Nagy, James Framo, David Rubinstein, and Gerald Zuk were located; and the Tavistock Institute of Human Relations in London, through which R. D. Laing and Rhona Rapoport were working. This by no means includes all the therapists involved in the formation of family-oriented therapy, and many of those mentioned have moved to other locations. However, it does provide an overview of the names most frequently encountered in reviewing the origins of family therapy.

SUMMARY

In its brief history, family therapy has moved through several phases, influenced by psychosocial changes in our society; it has been built on the knowledge and skills stemming from a variety of backgrounds. One of the recurring approaches to family therapy is the use of the systems theory, evident in several of the theories as well as in research and in training new therapists. As long as family therapists continue to explore and share their ideas concerning this ever changing field, family therapy will keep abreast of current psychosocial changes and will continue to meet the needs of both the individual family members and the family unit.

REFERENCES

1. Brodkin, A. Family therapy: The making of a mental health movement. *American Journal of Orthopsychiatry*, 1980, *50*, 4–17. Reprinted, with permission, from the *American Journal of Orthopsychiatry:* copyright 1980 by the American Orthopsychiatric Association, Inc.

2. Ackerman, N. W. Interlocking pathology in family relationships. In S. Rado, & G. Daniels (Eds.), *Changing concepts in psychoanalytic medicine*. New York: Grune & Stratton, 1956, pp. 135–50.

3. Ackerman, N. W. The family in crisis. *Bulletin of the New York Academy of Medicine,* March 1964, *40,* 171–187.

4. Ackerman, N. W. The future of family psychotherapy. In N. Ackerman et al. (Eds.), *Expanding theory and practice in family therapy*. New York: Family Service Association of America, 1967, pp. 3–16.

5. Satir, V. *Conjoint family therapy*. Palo Alto, Calif.: Science and Behavior Books, 1964.

6. Haley, J. The family of the schizophrenic: a model system. *The Journal of Nervous and Mental Disease,* October 1959, *129,* 357–374.

7. Jackson, D. The question of family homeostasis. *Psychiatric Quarterly Supplement,* 1957, *31,* 79–90.

8. Bowen, M. *Family therapy in clinical practice*. New York: Jason Aronson, 1978.

9. Smoyak, S. Family therapy. In F. L. Huey (Ed.), *Psychiatric nursing 1946 to 1974: A report on the state of the art*. New York: American Journal of Nursing, 1975, 36–49. (Monograph)

10. Haley, J. A review of the family therapy field. In J. Haley (Ed.), *Changing Families*. New York: Grune & Stratton, 1971, pp. 1–12.

11. Minuchin, S. *Families and family therapy*. New York: Harvard University Press, 1974.

12. Berne, E. *Games people play*. New York: Grove Press, 1964.

13. Bateson, G., Jackson, D., Haley, J., & Weakland, J. Toward a theory of schizophrenia. *Behavioral Sciences,* 1956, *1,* 251–264.

14. Laing, R. D. *The divided self*. London: Tavistock Publications, 1959.

15. Lidz, T., Fleck, S., & Cornelison, A. *Schizophrenia and the family*. New York: International Universities Press, 1965.

16. Wynne, L., Rykoff, I., Day, J., & Hirsch, S. Pseudo-mutuality in the family relations of schizophrenics. *Psychiatry,* 1958, *21,* 205–220.

17. Bowen, M. Family psychotherapy. *American Journal of Orthopsychiatry*, 1961, *31*, 40–60.
18. Minuchin, S., Montalvo, B., Guerney, Jr., B. C., Rosman, B., & Schumer, F. *Families of the slums*. New York: Basic Books, 1967.
19. Langsley, D., Pittman, F., Machotka, P., & Flomenhaft, K. Family crisis therapy—Results and Implications. *Family Process*, 1968, *7*, 145–158.
20. Epstein, N., Bishop, D., & Levin, S. The McMaster model of family functioning. *Journal of Marriage and Family Counseling*, 1978, *4*, 19–31.
21. Barnhill, L. Healthy family systems. *The Family Coordinator*, January 1979, *28*, 94–100.
22. Tomm, K., & Wright, L. Training in family therapy: Perceptual, conceptual and executive skills. *Family Process*, September 1979, *18*, 227–250.

BIBLIOGRAPHY

Bowen, M. The use of family theory in clinical practice. *Comprehensive Psychiatry*, 1966, *7*, 345–374.

Foley, V. *An introduction to family therapy*. New York: Grune & Stratton, 1974.

Guerin, P. Family therapy: The first twenty-five years. In P. Guerin (Ed.), *Family Therapy*. New York: Gardner Press, Inc., 1976, pp. 2–22.

Jackson, D., & Satir, V. A review of psychiatric developments in family diagnosis and family therapy. In N. Ackerman et al. (Eds.), *Exploring the base for family therapy*. New York: Family Services Association of America, 1961, pp. 29–51.

Laing, R. D. Mystification, confusion, and conflict. In I. Boszormenyi-Nagy, & J. Framo (Eds.), *Intensive family therapy*. New York: Harper & Row, 1965, pp. 343–63.

LaPerriere, K. Family therapy training at the Ackerman institute: Thoughts of form and substance. *Journal of Marital and Family Therapy*, July 1979, *5*, 53–58.

Lidz, T., Cornelison, A., Fleck, S., & Terry, D. The intrafamilial environment of the schizophrenic patient. II. Marital schism and marital skew. *American Journal of Psychiatry*, September 1957, 114, 241–248.

Massie, H., & Beels, C. The outcome of the family treatment of schizophrenia. *NIMH Schizophrenia Bulletin*, Fall 1972, *6*, 24–36.

Pittman, F., Flomenhaft, K., & De Young, C. Cleaning house. In J. Haley, & L. Hoffman (Eds.), *Techniques of family therapy*. New York: Basic Books, 1967, pp. 361–471.

Satir, V. Conjoint family therapy: Fragmentation to synthesis. In G. Gazda (Ed.), *Innovations to group psychotherapy*. Springfield, Ill.: Charles C Thomas, 1968, pp. 256–271.

Weakland, J., & Greenberg, G. Don D. Jackson's contributions to group therapy. In L. Wolberg, & M. Aronson (Eds.), *Group therapy 1977: An overview*. New York: Stratton Intercontinental Medical Book Corporation, 1977, pp. 5–13.

Zuk, G., & Rubinstein, D. A review of concepts in the study and treatment of families of schizophrenics. In I. Boszormenyi-Nagy, & J. Framo (Eds.), *Intensive family therapy*. New York: Harper & Row, 1965, pp. 1–31.

2

The Nurse as Therapist

Gloria Weber Calhoun

It is important for the nurse who wishes to practice as a family therapist to know the skills and qualifications needed to practice in this specialized area of advanced nursing. Nursing has long been involved with families in all settings—the home, hospital, institution, or other health care agencies. Involvement with families requires proficiency in many roles, the nurse being care giver, teacher, counselor, consultant, liaison person, and resource person. In researching the literature there are few published articles on this aspect of nursing care. Only in the last 25 years have a growing number of articles devoted to nursing's association with the family been written. Hildegard Peplau's book, *Interpersonal Relations in Nursing* (1), was one of the first publications to state the importance of the nurse working therapeutically with families. In this book, she emphasizes the importance of the nurse helping the family members differentiate themselves from each other and from the nurse.

This was the beginning of some remarkable changes in psychiatric mental health nursing and other mental health professions. The emphasis of nursing practice is now focusing on short-term treatment models that are based in the community rather than in long-term care institutions. A significant number of sociocultural changes make it necessary for nurses to address the broadening scope of their practice. This includes the skills necessary to become an effective family therapist.

Most of us are familiar with the changing sociocultural forces that have affected us during the last 50 years. Society has become more mobile, especially with the trend to move from rural to urban areas. The rapidly accelerating divorce rate has led to questions about how families function and why some marriages succeed or fail. Women are returning to the work force in large numbers, creating needs for adequate child-care facilities. This problem, in addition to the strain felt from the dual roles of motherhood and career, has created more stress in some families. Inflation has produced more money-related problems. Because the nurses have traditionally worked in different settings, they have many opportunities to work with families experiencing the difficulties associated with illness, financial problems, and the concomitant stress of family dysfunction.

The concept of family therapy originated in the mid-1950s (2). At that time Bateson et al. (3) had published information on a new concept called the *double bind theory*. About the same time Wynne (4) and his colleagues at the National Institute of Mental Health used the concept of *pseudo-mutuality* to describe a family who attempts an appearance of agreement and well-being while sacrificing individual growth and identity within a rigid family system. Other pioneers in family therapy include Nathan Ackerman (5), Murray Bowen (6), Virginia Satir (7), and John Bell (8). These early theorists and clinicians supported the argument that family therapy is based on systems theory. They described the family as a delicately balanced system that is continually changing and simultaneously struggling to maintain its homeostasis.

These changing concepts and knowledge base gave new perspectives to the nurse practitioner. Not only was the nurse becoming a respected member of the interdisciplinary treatment team, but also another dimension of nursing care was being developed, that of family therapy. In 1969 Smoyak stated that:

> Since human beings are socialized within family systems to play their future societal roles, it is necessary to seek an understanding of the various styles and workings of these intricate systems as they affect cognitive and emotional development of their members (9).

She also declared that nurses need to identify and operationalize the family dynamics contributing to the inadequate and/or destructive functioning among family members, if nurses are to work therapeutically with distressed families. As a pioneer nurse in family therapy, Smoyak encouraged nurses to close the gap between theory and practice through nursing intervention research. She stated:

> The search for understanding in the family field ought to take the direction of operationalizing recurring family dynamics so that the nurse can generate family theory and develop appropriate intervention strategies.

She encouraged every nurse therapist to develop an awareness about what the nurse does not know about family therapy and then to investigate and share data with other nurses regarding which interventions were therapeutic and which ones were not (10).

Many other psychiatric nurses have studied at various schools of family therapy. These nurses are sharing their observations and conclusions. Many documented and well-written findings on family therapy are now authored by nurses.

QUALIFICATIONS FOR A NURSE FAMILY THERAPIST

The ANA division on psychiatric mental health nursing (11) recommends that the minimum educational preparation for the role of a psychiatric nurse is a baccalaureate degree in nursing. Following this basic nursing preparation, it is the nurse's responsibility to assess his/her level of competency and to identify continuing education needs in order to provide services requiring various levels of expertise such as family therapy. A study conducted by the ANA statistics department completed in early 1979 found that "nurses who hold baccalaureate and higher degrees are more likely to be performing functions that are part of the expanded scope of nursing practice than those with diplomas or associate degrees" (12).

This study also stated that nurses with a higher level of education, especially nurses with master's and doctoral degrees, performed specific responsibilities in the expanded scope of nursing practice such as:

> developing therapeutic plans, (and) instructed and counseled patients and families in health promotion and maintenance, implemented therapy and had primary responsibility for providing follow through on patient care (12).

The ANA division of psychiatric and mental health nursing practice asserts that a minimum of a master's degree preparation is necessary for the development of skills and expertise necessary to be an effective family therapist. Family therapy is a complex process and can be difficult. It requires many skills, preparation, and experience. This additional preparation can increase the nurse's confidence as well as her knowledge. There are many adequately prepared nurses of all backgrounds who have the basic skills to provide informal counseling services to the patient and family. This service focuses primarily on providing support, preparation, and education. This is different from the practice of psychotherapy, which the ANA defines as "a formally structured contractual relationship between the therapist and client(s) for the explicit purpose of affecting change in the client(s)" (11).

Family therapy falls within this more structured context. In addition, family therapy involves a comprehensive understanding of family dynamics, psychopathology, family concepts, therapeutic interventions, personality development and adaptations, family games, issues of power, influence and control, boundaries, systems theory, and awareness of the therapist's personal issues affecting the therapeutic process. A family therapist must be an empathic communicator and give clear directives. This therapist must have the skills to think strategically, develop proficiency in diagnosing a sequence and structure, and must be able to design a direction that will produce positive change.

A variety of techniques can be used within the framework of family therapy, including group process techniques, family sculpting, transactional analysis, psychodrama, gestalt therapy, behavior modification, encounter group techniques, and psychoanalytic theory. There are many case presentations and theories regarding these schools in the literature.

Besides a well-prepared educational background, the nurse should also have a repertoire of behaviors adaptable to many situations. In order to provide a wide range of therapeutic approaches, the family therapist must sometimes appear to be authoritarian, or helpless, or grim and serious, or even at times playful. The nurse must know how to nurture as well as fight (fairly). Above all, it is important for the nurse to be comfortable with herself. This takes an astute awareness of what she is feeling, thinking, and doing during the therapy session. The nurse must understand the dynamics and importance of the counter-transference phenomenon, the unresolved conflicts within the nurse that may result from interaction with a particular client. The nurse also needs to be aware of any conflicting cultural backgrounds, values, beliefs, or life-styles that may be interfering with the therapeutic process. The nurse needs to know when she is experiencing anxiety, anger, guilt, or other feelings toward the patient and why. The therapist should also be aware of when she is doing most of the "work" during a session. Is the client sitting back and not taking responsibility for understanding the problem issues? Is the client doing a fair share of the problem-solving process and generating alternatives? Many times a novice therapist becomes convinced that the client has little resources or strengths to make appropriate changes and will attempt to take charge and institute changes for the client. This promotes dependency on the part of the client toward the therapist. There are nurses and other mental health professionals who enter the mental health field to forget about or to work on their personal problems through interaction with patients. They have a need to be needed. The professionals invest a lot of their ego into getting clients well so they can feel better about their own self-worth. These two situations create much conflict and disappointment in the therapist and can result in nontherapeutic interactions. If these nurses understand that this may be an ongoing personal issue, they may consider going into therapy themselves. It takes ongoing determination and commitment to improve expertise through advanced training, continuing education, consultation, research, and clinical supervision.

In order to protect the rights of the consumers and patients, the ANAs division of nursing practice (13) has developed standards for psychiatric nurses that provide some elements of control in the practice as well as assurance to the public that the profession will provide quality of service to all. The direct nursing care functions as developed by the division of nursing practice may involve "individual psychotherapy, group psychotherapy, *family therapy* and sociotherapy." These standards of psychiatric nursing practice pertain to all nursing practice settings and should maintain the "characteristics identified by these Standards if patients are to receive a high quality of nursing care."

Standards number IV and number X specifically address themselves to the needs of the family. Standard IV states: "Individuals, families and community groups are assisted to achieve satisfying and productive patterns of living through health teaching." This standard invites the nurse to use every interaction to promote understanding of mental health problems and to develop methods of coping with them. Standard X states: "The practice of individual, group or family psychotherapy requires appropriate preparation and recognition of accountability for the practice." This standard asserts: "the potential of the nurse to function as a primary therapist is evaluated . . . accountability for practicing psychotherapy is recognized and accepted." This standard assumes that the nurse will have adequate knowledge of "growth and development, psychopathology, psychosocial systems and small group and family dynamics." Included in this standard is the assumption that further supervision, consultation, and other learning opportunities will be used to develop needed knowledge and skills.

The issue of credentialing is certainly visible in nursing today. Credentialing exists primarily to benefit and protect the public but is also a relevant factor in determining accountablity and competence. In a discussion of the "Study of Credentialing in Nursing" presented at the ANA Advisory Council (12), Ms. Ira Gunn stated: "Credentialing is a key to the fulfillment of (nursing's) potential. Whoever controls credentialing controls the profession and occupation of nursing."

One procedure for credentialing is a formal review of professional achievement called certification, developed and conducted by the division on psychiatric and mental health nursing of the American Nurses Association (14). Certification is an intense, time-consuming process that assesses the nurse's knowledge and demonstrated clinical expertise. It requires passing a written examination and documentation and description of the candidate's practice and practice setting. Certification by the ANA is available for two categories of psychiatric mental health nurses: (*1*) General certification for nurses without graduate education, and (*2*) Specialist certification, for nurses whose preparation includes master's and higher degrees. Acquiring certification can be very rewarding in terms of the personal satisfaction resulting from passing a rigorous examination and evaluation. Other certification options for the nurse in family therapy are through the International Transactional Analysis Association (ITAA) and the American Association of Marriage and Family Therapists. These two organizations have rigorous clinical supervision requirements.

SUPERVISION AS AN ESSENTIAL COMPONENT OF TRAINING IN FAMILY THERAPY

Supervision can be an invaluable aid for learning family therapy. Therapy is a personal encounter, and a therapist can only learn it by actually doing it. Therapy cannot be learned just by reading about it, by hearing lectures, or by having discussions. The best way for learning family therapy is by conducting it under the close supervision of a qualified and experienced therapist. Supervision can be done with audio or audiovisual tapes of the session. It can also be done behind a one-way mirror with the supervisor closely monitoring and ready to give immediate feedback or options regarding the therapist's behavior during the session (via telephone, etc.). The Philadelphia Child Guidance Clinic uses this method to give the therapist feedback regarding his behavior and its relationship to his selective perception. An economical way to train and supervise is in a group. This way many more ideas about what to do are available to the supervisee and his/her peers. This arrangement encourages role playing of difficult clinical cases. Some schools, such as in transactional analysis training, advocate the use of personal therapy for supervisees as an integral part of the supervision process. B. Gaoni and M. Neumann (15) define four stages in the supervisory process from the point of view of the supervisee:

1. The teacher/pupil relationship
2. Apprenticeship
3. Focus on the intrapsychic and interpersonal problems of the supervisee to aid in the development of his or her "therapeutic personality"
4. Mutual consultation among equals

At this fourth stage "supervision becomes an exchange of openness, advice, and experience between equals, though one is more experienced than the other" (15) . A most effective type of supervision results from the support offered by the group. This can be structured so that the supervisee receives positive information first. The group shares what they like about the session, then gives options and/or constructive feedback. It is hoped that this protective environment will keep the supervisee from being defensive against criticism. Instead the supervisee will feel free to accept feedback from a "caring position" of the group and learn more in the process.

It is the responsibility of the supervisees to state clearly in the contract with the supervisor and the group what they want from the supervision session. This will involve an indepth awareness of strengths and weaknesses as well as clearly stated goals and objectives that the trainees desire in the learning process. If the nurse is in private practice, there may be a tendency to become isolated from contact with peers, from feedback, and from intellectual stimulation and growth. Staying involved in an ongoing supervision relationship(s) will prevent isolation and its concomitant problems.

Progression of Independent and Collaborative Nursing Practices

Because psychiatric nursing is practiced in a wide variety of settings, it is essential for nurses to have the skills necessary to collaborate with other disciplines. Collaboration involves teamwork, planning, and coordination with the other people caring for the same client. This involves an understanding and appreciation for the concept of synergism among the team members. Synergy implies that each person has unique and valuable contributions to offer a working group, thereby enhancing the quality of service. Nurses have many valuable skills to bring to the interdisciplinary team. Nurses bring with them a sound knowledge of anatomy and physiology, diagnoses of illness and wellness, pharmacology, growth and development problems, emotional factors accompanying illness and stress, and prevention of illness. Many therapists do not have this broad background and can use the nurse as a helpful resource person.

There continues to be a strong trend for nurses to establish autonomous practices. This may involve a joint practice setting in which the nurse is associated with a clinical psychologist, psychiatrist, or other mental health professionals. A joint practice with a licensed psychologist, psychiatrist, or physician will provide the nurse more opportunities to receive third party insurance payments. If the nurse chooses to practice collectively with other nurses or by oneself in private practice, the reimbursement from third party payors is much more difficult. A recent report (16) written by the Council of Specialists in Psychiatric and Mental Health Nursing cites that one major reason for the underuse of psychiatric nurses is "the scarcity of third party reimbursement for their services, both in organized service settings and in private practice." This council also states that "psychiatric and mental health specialists certified by the professional organization meet established criteria for competence and should be eligible for third party reimbursements." This lack of reimbursement makes it difficult to compete for clients in the private sector. A fact sheet (17) developed by the ANAs division on psychiatric and mental health nursing practice based on a 1977 survey states that it is financially difficult for mental health agencies and clinics to employ psychiatric and mental health nursing specialists because their services are not directly reimbursable. In this survey 67% of the respondents provided direct patient services but less than 3% received third party payments for services provided. This lack of third party reimbursements prevents psychiatric/mental health specialists from providing services in rural areas where there are a few salaried positions that can support the position of a nurse. In addition, the requirement of a physician to supervise a nurse if reimbursement is to be made, restricts the nurse from practicing in an area that needs services but has no physician. It is apparent that people needing mental health services require a wide range of qualified providers, such as psychiatric/mental health nurses. At the present time insurance coverage narrowly restricts and limits the type of service provider for whom the consumer may be reimbursed. Appropriate insurance coverage is needed that will provide accessibility to qualified psychiatric/mental health nurses who are willing to provide needed services to the community. There is now a gradual trend for third party reimbursement funding to shift from government agencies to the private sector.

Establishing a private practice can be difficult, but it is helpful if the nurse has established a competent area of expertise that is recognized in the community. In order to do this, it may be necessary for the nurse to be highly visible in the community, speaking before groups or conducting workshops. In addition, the development of unique marketable skills such as family therapy will make it easier to get referrals from the community. The best advertisement is a satisfied client, however.

An adequate referral network is necessary for the establishment and maintenance of a private practice. This can be promoted through a sense of professional loyalty and collegiality among nurses. Professional loyalty requires adherence to a set of standards and values as determined acceptable by the professional organization, such as the American Nurses Association. These values and standards can provide a source of external support and continuing validation of the nurses' professionalism. This is closely related to collegiality in which a personal bond is also established. Nurses need to become aware of the standards of practice acceptable to family therapy, then find out who are qualified and competent practitioners. Nurses need to refer to each other! Nurses in all settings should become aware of the need to refer to a nurse colleague when certain family problems surface in their work. The effective use of a referral system among nurses promotes collegiality, professional loyalty, and is a useful power strategy.

SUMMARY

In order for nurses to develop fully into competent family therapists, they must translate their "professional potential" into action. This will involve establishing an inventory of skills and becoming increasingly aware of their deficiencies. This will also involve having a strong sense of personal and professional identity, of feeling confident and positive about themselves and where they are going (18). Other criteria necessary for developing competence are: critical thinking, assuming responsibility for actions, a consistent search for increased knowledge and information necessary for up-to-date expertise, and a willingness to risk new and innovative approaches based on sound scientific rationale. This requires drive, imagination, and thoughtful planning, and it cannot happen without energy and enthusiasm. When these phenomena do occur, the self-development that occurs with being an effective family therapist is both fulfilling and satisfying.

REFERENCES

1. Peplau, H. *Interpersonal relations in nursing*. New York: G. P. Putnam and Sons, 1952.

2. Satir, V., Stachowiak, J., & Taschman, H. *Helping families to change*. New York: Jason Aronson, 1975, p. 24.

3. Bateson, G., Jackson, D., Haley, J., & Weakland, J. Toward a theory of schizophrenia. *Behavioral Science*, 1956, *1*, 251–264.

4. Wynne, T., Rycoff, I. M., Day, J., & Hirsch, S. I. Pseudomutuality in family relationships of schizophrenia. *Psychiatry*, 1958, *21*, 205–220.

5. Ackerman, N. Interlocking pathology in family relationships. In S. Rado, & G. Daniels (Eds.), *Changing concepts of psychoanalytic medicine*. New York: Grune & Stratton, 1956, pp. 135–150.

6. Bowen, M. A family concept of schizophrenia. In D. Jackson (Ed.), *The etiology of schizophrenia*. New York: Basic Books, 1960, pp. 346–372.

7. Satir, V. (Ed.). *Conjoint family therapy*. Palo Alto, Calif.: Science and Behavior Books, 1964.

8. Bell, J. *Family group therapy*. U.S. Public Health Monograph (No. 64), Washington, D.C.: U.S. Government Printing Office, 1961.

9. Smoyak, S. Threat: A recurring family dynamic. *Perspectives in psychiatric nursing*, 1969, *7*, 267–268.

10. Smoyak, S. (Ed.). *The psychiatric nurse as a family therapist*. New York: John Wiley & Sons, 1975.

11. American Nurses Association Division of Psychiatric Nursing, *Statement on psychiatric mental health nursing practice*. Kansas City: ANA Pub. Code PMH-3, 10m, 1976, p. 9.

12. American Nurses Association. Credentialing: A call for action and cooperation. *The American Nurse*, II, June 20, 1979, 5.

13. American Nurses Association. *Standard psychiatric mental health nursing practice*. Kansas City: ANA Pub. Code PMH-1, 1973.

14. American Nurses Association. 1977 National sample survey of registered nurses. *The American Nurse*, May 1979, *11*, p. 1.

15. Gaoni, B., & Neumann, M. Supervision from the point of view of the supervisee. *American Journal of Psychotherapy*, 1974, *28*, 108–114.

16. Council of Psychiatric and Mental Nursing Specialists. Reimbursement for services of psychiatric and mental health nursing specialists. Unpublished study for the American Nurses Association, 1979, p. 2.

17. American Nurses Association. *Fact sheet on clinical specialists in psychiatric and mental health nursing.* 1980.

18. Pardue, S. Translating professional potential into action. *Image,* February 1980, *12,* p. 17.

BIBLIOGRAPHY

Goulding, M., & Goulding, R. *Changing lives through redecision therapy.* New York: Brunner/Mazel, 1979.

Haley, J. *Problem solving therapy: New strategies for effective family therapy.* New York: Harper Colophon Books, 1978.

Leininger, M. (Ed.). *Contemporary issues in mental health nursing.* Boston: Little, Brown & Co., 1973.

Morewitz, J. *Family therapy and transactional analysis.* New York: Jason Aronson, 1979.

Morrison, E. Aspects of supervision in psychiatric nursing. In C. Kneisl, & H. Wilson (Eds.), *Current perspectives in psychiatric nursing.* St. Louis: C. V. Mosby, 1976.

Sager, C., & Kaplan, H. (Eds.). *Progress in group and family therapy.* New York: Brunner/Mazel, 1972.

Sedgwick, R. The family as a system: A network of relationships. *Journal of Psychiatric Nursing and Mental Health Services,* 1974, *12,* 17–20.

Yalom, I. *The theory and practice of group psychotherapy.* New York: Basic Books, 1975.

Zak, G. H., & Boszormenyi-Nagy, I. *Family therapy and disturbed families.* Palo Alto, Calif.: Science and Behavior Books, 1967.

3

The Value
of Family Therapy

Ethel Hines-Battle

The nurse, as well as other psychiatric workers or therapists, usually encounters the family following crisis or conflict between spouses, generations, or extended members. Traditionally, therapy has been offered to the member who has been labeled *patient*. Whether intervention was on an inpatient or outpatient basis, the patient was involved in individual therapy or group therapy for patients with similar problems. Although this practice continues, many therapists today are increasingly interested in family therapy as an alternate method of intervention. The psychological treatment of whole families is derived from numerous theoretical persuasions and methodologies based on psychodynamic theory, communication and systems theory, or social learning/behavioristic theory. However, as with all forms of therapy, family therapy must ultimately address itself to the question: is it of any value when compared with other treatment modalities? If so, what accounts for the benefits?

INDIVIDUAL, GROUP, AND FAMILY THERAPY

Family therapy is differentiated from individual therapy by the location of forces perceived to be predominant in determining inner personality and behavior patterns. Although practitioners of individual therapies do not deny contributory environmental factors, internal events or intrapsychic mechanisms are considered to be dominant in a person's development.

23

Symptoms result from inner conflict and, whether behavioral or psycho-analytic, therapy is structured to change behavior or resolve conflict. The assumption is that changes in the individual are unopposed or resistant to environmental or external pressures. Individual therapy neither stresses nor influences change in the environment. Transference to the therapist is a key determinant in individual psychoanalysis, and the patient reveals and discusses his problems with one person who is not usually a part of his living environment.

> The fact that the individual therapist structures treatment in such a way that contact with the patient's interpersonal environment is avoided is a logical extension of his belief that treatment ought to change the way the patient handles certain aspects of his own internally organized behavior (1).

Other individual approaches may include client-centered, behavioral, or gestalt therapies, but their common concern is intrapsychic phenomena.

Conversely, practitioners of family therapy believe the dominant forces in personality to be external with the family playing the major role in managing and regulating the interpersonal life of its members. The impact of family system characteristics is viewed as highly coercive and transgenerational. Symptomatology is associated with a dysfunctional family system. Thus, the family therapist aims to improve the level of functioning for the whole family and to promote healthy intergenerational relating.

Group psychotherapy, as an alternative to family therapy, is based on the premise that the group provides an opportunity for patients/clients to share and resolve mutual problems or conflicts in a structured setting. This method is distinguished from individual psychoanalysis by greater emphasis on sociological factors in the form of group interaction and on intellectual comprehension of behavior. Transference may be of the patient-to-patient or patient-to-therapist type and affords the "possibility that the entire group will provide a kind of 'catharsis-in-the-family' with an accompanying resolvement of conflicts and the displacement of parent love on to new objects" (2). As with individual therapy, group therapy may be based on any of several conceptual models, but, ultimately, group interaction is expected to offer patients the opportunity to compare problems and use the group experience to formulate new modes of behavior that will prove valuable in social adjustment. To some, group therapy may be viewed as the compromise between the polarities of individual and family therapy and is held in wide acclaim as the treatment of choice to treat large numbers of patients/clients at one time. However, if only one individual family member participates, he may return to the family environment and find adjustment difficult if other members remain dysfunctional.

In family groups, the emotional problem or conflict involves the entire family, not just the sick member. The greatest dividend for the therapist is the opportunity to observe family interaction and use knowledge of family relationships to guide therapeutic efforts. Also, research has shown that patients tend to perform differently in family groups than in patient groups. When patient/family group sessions were compared with conventional patient groups, verbal activity and interaction were significantly higher with little silence among the family members. Not only was the quantity higher but the quality—as indicated by evaluative statements, mirror imaging, and problem solutions—was also significantly higher. The data suggested that family presence stimulated and encouraged rather than inhibited the discussion of threatening areas (3). Similarly, differences in words and actions of married couples were noted when the spouses were in separate and joint groups. In separate groups, husbands and wives said one thing about each other but their actions in joint sessions were contradictory to what was verbalized in the group (4).

In no way is there an intent to imply that individual and group treatment are without merit. In fact, the literature reveals numerous contraindications to family therapy (5–8). Nevertheless, therapists are faced with the decision of choosing the most effective treatment modality. Clarkin, Frances, and Moodie (9) proposed a model of differential therapeutics to guide the clinician in selecting family treatment as opposed to individual, marital, sex, or hospital treatment. In the event that hospitalization is required, Boyd (10) suggests that the individual therapist's goals and the family therapist's goals need not be mutually exclusive but can be enhanced by communication among all involved.

The Efficacy of Family Therapy

Research in Family Therapy.   The efficacy of family therapy as a treatment modality has prompted proponents to establish success criteria and pursue research endeavors to support their claims. The difficulty encountered in quantifying the benefits of family therapy is well known, and methodological issues in outcome research have been well documented elsewhere and need not receive lengthy detail here (11–15). Among the main themes of critics of evaluative reports are (*1*) the successes were self-reports by the patient or families who were in treatment, (*2*) nonrandomized sampling procedures were used, (*3*) there was no adequate control group, and (*4*) reliable pretherapy and posttherapy measures were lacking. However, if all clinical innovations were to await optimal research conditions, progress would falter. As with other ambitious clinicians and investigators, many family therapists and researchers have strived to minimize the methodological limitations and have perceived clinical outcome as indicative of a trend. They have proceeded to collect and report data with the hope of developing more definitive interpretations and theory.

Family Therapy versus Traditional Approaches.   One effort undertaken by Ro-Trock, Wellisch, and Schooler (16) demonstrated that family therapy was more effective than individual therapy for hospitalized adolescents who were diagnosed *schizophrenic reaction adolescent adjustment*. Among the 14 subjects treated in individual therapy, six (43%) were rehospitalized within 3 months of discharge, while none of the adolescents who had received family treatment required readmission during the same period. In keeping with the concept of family homeostasis, the investigator suggested that the untreated families may have reinduced psychiatric dysfunction among the recidivists. Improved family communication and earlier community adjustment (return to school or work) were additional indices of success.

Using the readmission rate as a measure of success, Esterson, Cooper, and Laing (17) reported the results of conjoint family and milieu therapy with 42 hospitalized schizophrenic patients. The use of tranquilizers was reduced, and no individual psychotherapy was conducted. The average length of stay for the patients was 3 months, and within 1 year of admission all were discharged. The readmission rate of only 17% was significantly lower than the national trend for patients treated with traditional methods. Among the 83% who were not readmitted, 72% of the men and 70% of the women had attained social adjustment to the extent that they were able to earn a living during the year following discharge.

Juvenile delinquency traditionally has been a problem dealt with by individual therapist, church groups, or the legal system. The efficacy of family therapy as a preventive measure was explored by Klein and Alexander (18) and compared with available treatment modalities. The families of 86 delinquents were randomly assigned to a behavioral family systems intervention program, a client-centered program, a no-treatment group, or a church-sponsored eclectic-dynamic family counseling program. As an evaluation of secondary prevention six to 18 months following termination of therapy, the percentages of recidivism among the juveniles assigned to the short-term behavioral family system program were 47% among the client-centered group, 70% among the eclectic-dynamic group, and 50% among those who received no treatment. The percentage of court involvement due to delinquency among siblings was used to evaluate primary prevention 2½ to 3½ years after therapy. Twenty percent of the siblings in the family group required court involvement, while the percentages of referrals among the client-centered and eclectic-dynamic groups were 59% and 63%, respectively. Forty percent of the siblings who had no treatment required court involvement. Although process changes in family interaction (tertiary prevention) were not measured for the church-sponsored group, the high rate of recidivism and sibling court involvement suggest that the quality of family intervention may have been a factor.

Case Reports

On the premise that individual problems, pathology, or crises do not occur without affecting all members of the family, therapists have expanded the gamut of mental and physical pathology, maladaptation, dysfunction, and crises for which family involvement is advocated. Following his observation that family therapy proved beneficial for certain behavior and emotional difficulties that were resistant to drug or individual therapy, Jaffe (19) proposed a connection between physical illness and psychological or family distress. A middle-aged female who had breast cancer did not respond to chemotherapy. After the secondary gains of her illness were identified, family therapy was initiated and her response to medical treatment improved.

Tiller (20) alludes to family psychopathology and interactional disorders as being prominent among tiqueurs. Brief analytically oriented outpatient therapy was used in treating an 8-year-old girl with a history of multiple tics. Drug therapy was not used, and the patient remained asymptomatic for 9 months after family therapy was terminated. The same patient previously had been treated with drug therapy only to have the symptoms return following cessation of therapy. Tiller suggested that a principal factor in the successful outcome was the early stage of symptoms before psychotherapeutic intervention was begun. Rigid symptom and relationship patterns had not formed, and the psychological problems of the family were identified early so that the family could be assisted in modifying its transactional patterns within a therapeutic setting.

As early as 1930, the correlation of ulcerative colitis and emotional disturbance was explored, and in some instances individual psychotherapy was considered concomitantly with surgical or medical procedures. This case report of a variation in psychotherapy involved the parents of a 14-year-old girl who was the patient. Although the patient was not included in the conjoint therapy, ten sessions with the parents resulted in continued remission of the ulcerative colitis during the 1 year posttherapy follow-up. Identification of the parents' behaviors which fostered continuation of the daughter's symptoms provided the basis for implementing change (21).

Shapiro and Harris (22), recognizing the pessimistic attitudes toward individual therapy for deaf patients with psychological problems, initiated family therapy for a 17-year-old girl. In addition to her deficiency in language and communication skills, the patient lacked insight, was impulsive and prone to rage, and had poor motivation for therapy on an individual basis. As with many families of the deaf, guilt, rage, disruptions in communication, denial of deafness, and parental conflicts were observed. By identifying the patient's behavior as being representative of the family's difficulties, the therapists helped the family improve overall interaction and eliminate communication patterns that previously led to misunderstandings and misinterpretations.

Implications for the Family

Assuming that outcome data demonstrate that family intervention not only keeps patients out of mental institutions but also enhances functioning in the family and community, what are the implications for families? One axiom of family therapy is that every family member living together or every important person in the environment who influences family behavior should be included in the treatment. The basic tenet is that if only one member is treated, other members who remain dysfunctional may not only sabotage the effects of treatment but also continue maladaptive behaviors that can be communicated to the next generations. Thus, families not only are important in creating problems, but also can be instrumental in solving them.

The Hospitalized Patient and His Family.   It is usually after the family perceives coping methods to be a failure that a *patient* is presented for hospitalization or therapy. If the patient is hospitalized, in most instances the family harbors feelings of guilt, anger, hostility, anxiety, or even denial, which ultimately are detrimental to the patient. Casual or fleeting contact with the family during these periods of crisis may reduce anxiety but does little to reduce tension created by reentry of the patient to the system, nor does it identify the dynamics that maintain the illness. Many patients involved in individual, group, or other forms of therapy that exclude families eventually must return to the social system in which they became ill, and early statistics have shown that 50% of first-admission schizophrenics who return to their families of origin are readmitted within 1 year. Emotional involvement with any key member of the family seems to be the major contributor to rehospitalization (17). Strong correlations have been found between expressed emotion (EE) of relatives and relapse among schizophrenic patients and depressed patients (23, 24). Expressed emotion by family members included critical comments about the patient and his illness, hostility, and emotional overinvolvement. When families ranked high on the EE scale, it could be predicted that the schizophrenic member would have a relapse during the 9-month period following discharge. It would appear advantageous to identify families who are high risk and attempt to modify detrimental attitudes through family therapy.

Although the emphasis was on patient-to-family contact rather than therapy, Bingham (25) found that hospitalized patients made greater gains and were more motivated to leave the hospital when positive family contact was maintained. Similarly, Gould and Glick (26) found better posthospital functioning and fewer symptoms among schizophrenics whose families were present during the course of hospitalizations whether they had been involved in family therapy or not. If mere regular visitation produced such encouraging results, the implications for family inclusion in the treatment process seem evident if family ties and integration are to be maintained.

The optimal therapy would avoid hospitalization and the reentry crisis. Social isolation and disorganization usually experienced by patients who are removed from a familiar environment possibly could be reduced if there were less need to adjust to an institutional milieu of other sick or hopeless people. Needless to say, family intervention directed at prevention of hospitalization not only lends itself to maintaining the system in the home environment, but also results in greater cost effectiveness. The economic impact, as well as social and psychological factors, should be taken into consideration when the decision is made to hospitalize a family member rather than to explore alternatives.

Patient Groups versus Family Groups. Research has shown that when family members are present in patient groups, discussions of real events and family problems are more spontaneous and, by using methods of releasing tension, the usual depression that prevails in conventional groups is not evident (3). When patients can relate to family, the need for transference to the therapist or other patients is diminished, and efforts can be directed toward relating with family members. Moreover, the expected role of the patient in conventional groups is one of being sick, helpless, and dependent, whereas in family groups the patient is expected to interact on a mature and equal level. Thus, it appears that family involvement in patient groups is productive because family issues and problems are discussed and mediated among all affected members. If group process and content are altered by the presence of family members, the defects in the system become clear and can be examined by the therapist. The verbalized problems in individual or conventional group sessions take on new meaning and interpretation once the behavior is observed in the family setting. It has been suggested, however, that during periods of interaction, husbands and wives tend to obscure introspection and lose objectivity in viewing themselves. Consequently, additional separate group sessions sometimes seem indicated (4).

Physical Illness and Family Relationships. Physical illness has been purported to be the outcome of stabilization and repetition of a dysfunctional behavior pattern and chronic stress in family relationships. Hence, present day conceptualization of psychosomatic illness incorporates the systems point of view and focuses on the sick person within the family rather than the sick person as an individual. The open systems family model (27) proposes that a psychosomatic crisis has two phases. During phase I, the turn-on phase, emotional reaction by a child to family conflict triggers physiological symptoms. Phase II, the turn-off phase, is a return to the level of functioning before the precipitating event. The successful evolution through the turn-off phase is contingent on the involvement and feedback processes from other family members. The child's symptoms may be perpetuated by the role symptomatic behavior plays in conflict avoidance within the family. Whether the symptom selection is determined by physical illness or by family idiosyncrasies, family response is a major factor in rewarding, maintaining, and using the pathology. The association of secondary gain and poor response to treatment for physical illnesses have led to observations of potential gains for all family members. Illness may serve as a control mechanism without the person owning up to the unconscious actions or may help the caring spouse or other members show affection in a way that would otherwise be more uncomfortable. Thus, efforts to treat the ill person alone are frequently undermined by other well-meaning relatives.

Symptomatology and the Family Interaction. Biochemical or genetic factors have not been totally ruled out as contributors to physical or mental illness. However, family studies have suggested interactional variables that can serve as predictors of certain pathological outcomes. Symptoms may become evident in a variety of pathological and behavioral manifestations and have been related to system input.

In addition to physiological vulnerability, the child who is prone to psychosomatic illness typically belongs to a family that is characterized by enmeshment, overprotectiveness, and lack of conflict resolution (27). In a summary of family research on drug abuse, Harbin and Maziar (28) found consistent reports of an overprotective, indulgent mother and a father who was either absent or emotionally distant. Family dynamics of other psychiatric patients have been found to have similar overtones. Some of the earliest observations of family relations and symptoms were reported by therapists working with schizophrenics. Premorbid history was usually correlated with the location of family dominance. Among men, a submissive father and dominant mother typically characterized the family constellation of the group with poor premorbid history, whereas families in which fathers were dominant and the mother submissive characterized the group with good premorbid history (29). Also contributing to premorbid history was the degree of conflict between the parents. More conflict was observed among the poor premorbids. Unresolved family difficulties in early life have been studied as psychological antecedents of cancer. In a study of male medical students, those who developed malignant tumors reported significantly less closeness to parents than did their classmates who were controls (30, 31). The list of symptoms correlated with family interaction has increased during the past 2 decades. Although the findings have contributed to knowledge about the family, the complexity of human habits and patterns of relating compounds the problem of reversing long-term methods of interacting. Other variables such as culture, socioeconomic status, rural or urban environment, and religion of the family have been cited as determinants of family interaction and should be considered before families are labeled pathological. Much research is still necessary before definitive cause and effect can be identified. Although consistency has been found in some reports, findings in other replications have proved contradictory. Bringing family members together in a neutral setting with the therapist as mediator provides the opportunity for further observation of responses and reactions within the system and gives some indication of role expectations and adjustive mechanisms.

Implications for Nursing

The family point of view goes beyond individual pathology; the behavior is influenced by the group or social context in which it occurs. Similarly, that same social group or family is portrayed as a potential resource for strength and support for the patient. Thus, the nurse is in the precarious position of relating to the family to gain cooperation in the treatment process while at the same time remembering that the family contributed to the patient's pathology.

When hospitalization of the patient is required, the nurse can decrease the family's anxiety and guilt and keep them involved to plan for the patient's reentry. The structure of the family and its influence on the patient's behavior should be assessed before intervention is planned. The family may present itself for symptom relief but may become resistant to more extensive change either in the individual patient or in the family structure. In crises, symptomatic relief may be obtained and the family may not return for further therapy, but the crisis intervention should be considered therapeutic in that the desired result was produced at that particular point. It should be kept in mind, however, that early intervention is considered to be more powerful than later intervention when the pathology has become more ingrained.

In too many instances therapists plan and proceed with therapy assuming that the patient is displeased with his maladjusted level of functioning and wants to change. They further assume that the patient's social environment is equally displeased with the patient's poor functioning and assume any change to be an improvement. When therapy based on those assumptions is implemented, ambivalence and resistance are often encountered. Recognizing that change can be maintained only if supported by those in the environment, the therapist should (1) consider the patient's total social climate when intervention is planned, (2) assess the kinds of changes that the family may accept or reject, and (3) soften the shock of therapeutic change by establishing support systems that include the family (32).

Although physical illness has been described as being the outcome of repetitive maladaptive behavior and chronic stress in family relationships, other intervening variables (such as constitutional predispositions, weak organs, individual methods of handling stress, beliefs, and expectations) lie between family process and physical illness. Thus, establishing cause and effect is not as valuable as identifying interactional patterns that give some indication to the secondary gains of all involved, especially when other therapies continue to fail as symptoms persist (19).

It is up to the nurse to select a method of intervening with particular families with varied categories of problems. By assessing the structure of the family and its influence on the patient's behavior, effective intervention can be planned. As will be seen in succeeding chapters of this book, a wide variety of approaches and concepts is available to the nurse who accepts the challenge of intervening with whole families. Systems theory provides a framework for the conceptualization of behavior within the family and offers the nurse a better understanding of the family approach as compared to individual therapy.

More research is needed on the processes within the family that produce pathological behavior so that a more systematic and scientific approach can be developed and documented as an effective modality. Realistically, family therapy cannot cure all of the pathology the nurse may encounter, but it is family therapy's success in comparison to other modes of treatment that ultimately must be demonstrated.

SUMMARY

This chapter emphasizes the value of family therapy and differentiates it from individual and group therapy. Proponents of individual approaches are concerned with intrapsychic phenomena, whereas group psychotherapy places emphasis on sociological factors in the form of group interaction and intellectual comprehension of behavior. Conversely, practitioners of family therapy perceive forces in personality to be located externally and purport that emotional problems and conflicts involve the entire family, not just the designated sick member. Since the family is a rule-governed and change-resistant transactional system, treating the designated patient with no plan for family inclusion undermines the treatment process. In spite of the usual methodological difficulties inherent in clinical research, investigators have demonstrated that family therapy is equal to or superior to other treatment methods as a means of intervening in a variety of pathological conditions. The encouraging results of family therapy carry many implications for the family and for nursing. For families, the decrease in the rehospitalization rate of a member not only maintains the system, but also reduces the reentry crisis as well as the financial burden. Moreover, by identifying the secondary gains of physical or psychosomatic illness, families can learn healthier ways of relating that can be transferred to the next generation. In addition to reducing the family's anxiety and guilt when a patient is presented for treatment, the nurse can assess the structure and interactional patterns of the family to plan appropriate intervention.

REFERENCES

1. Robinson, L. R. Basic concepts in family therapy: A differential comparison with individual treatment. *American Journal of Orthopsychiatry,* 1975, *132,* 1045–1048.

2. Wender, L. The dynamics of group psychotherapy and its application. In M. Rosenbaum, & M. Berger (Eds.), *Group psychotherapy and group function.* New York: Basic Books, 1963, pp. 211–217.

3. Harrow, M., Astrachan, B. M., Becker, R. E., Detre, T., & Schwartz, A. H. An investigation into the nature of the patient–family therapy group. *American Journal of Orthopsychiatry,* 1967, *37,* 888–899.

4. Westman, J. C., Carek, D. J., & McDermott, J. F. A comparison of married couples in the same and separate therapy groups. *International Journal of Group Psychotherapy,* 1965, *15,* 374–381.

5. Ackerman, N. W. (Ed.), *Treating the troubled family.* New York: Basic Books, 1966.

6. Offer, D., & VanderStoep, E. Indications and contraindications for family therapy. In M. Sugar (Ed.), *The adolescent in group and family therapy.* New York: Brunner/Mazel, 1975, pp. 145–160.

7. Walrond-Skinner, S. Indications and contra-indications for the use of family therapy. *Journal of Child Psychology and Psychiatry and Allied Disciplines,* 1978, *19,* 57–62.

8. Wynne, L. C. Some indications and contraindications for exploratory family therapy. In I. Boszormenyi-Nagy, & J. Framo (Eds.), *Intensive family therapy.* New York: Harper & Row, 1965, pp. 289–322.

9. Clarkin, J. F., Frances, A. J., & Moodie, J. L. Selection criteria for family therapy. *Family Process,* 1979, *18,* 391–403.

10. Boyd, J. H. The interaction of family therapy and psychodynamic individual therapy in an inpatient setting. *Psychiatry,* 1979, *42,* 99–111.

11. Sigal, J. J., Barrs, C. B., & Doubilet, A. L. Problems in measuring the success of family therapy in a common clinical setting: Impasse and solutions. *Family Process,* 1976, *15,* 83–96.

12. Slipp, S., & Kressel, K. Difficulties in family therapy evaluation: I. A comparison of insight versus problem-solving approaches. II. Design critique and recommendations. *Family Process,* 1978, *17,* 409–422.

13. Riskin, J., & Faunce, E. E. An evaluative review of family interaction research. *Family Process,* 1972, *11,* 365–455.

14. Wells, R. A., & Dezen, A. E. The results of family therapy revisited: The non-behavioral methods. *Family Process,* 1978, *17,* 251–274.

15. Wells, R. A., Dilkes, T. C., & Burckhardt, N. T. The results of family therapy: A critical review of the literature. In D. H. L. Olson (Ed.), *Treating relationships.* Lake Mills, Iowa: Graphic, 1976, pp. 499–615.

16. Ro-Trock, G. K., Wellisch, D. K., & Schooler, J. C. A family therapy outcome study in an inpatient setting. *American Journal of Orthopsychiatry,* 1977, *47,* 514–522.

17. Esterson, A., Cooper, D. G., & Laing, R. D. Results of family-orientated therapy with hospitalized schizophrenics. *British Medical Journal,* 1965, *2,* 1462–1465.

18. Klein, N. C., & Alexander, J. F. Impact of family systems intervention on recidivism and sibling delinquency: A model of primary prevention and program evaluation. *Journal of Consulting and Clinical Psychology,* 1977, *45,* 469–474.

19. Jaffe, D. T. The role of family therapy in treating physical illness. *Hospital and Community Psychiatry,* 1978, *29,* 169–174.

20. Tiller, J. W. G. Brief family therapy for childhood tic syndrome. *Family Process,* 1978, *17,* 217–223.

21. MacLean, G. An approach to the treatment of an adolescent with ulcerative colitis: Conjoint therapy of the parents. *Canadian Psychiatric Association Journal,* 1976, *21,* 287–293.

22. Shapiro, R. J., & Harris, R. I. Family therapy in treatment of the deaf: A case report. *Family Process,* 1976, *15,* 83–96.

23. Brown, G. W., Birley, J. L. T., & Wing, J. K. Influence of family life on the course of schizophrenic disorders: A replication. *British Journal of Psychiatry,* 1972, *121,* 241–258.

24. Vaughn, C. E., & Leff, J. P. The influence of family and social factors on the course of psychiatric illness. *British Journal of Psychiatry,* 1976, *129,* 125–137.

25. Bingham, W. Community contacts improve prognosis. *Mental Hospitals,* 1960, *11,* 27.

26. Gould, E., & Glick, I. D. The effects of family presence and brief family intervention on global outcome for hospitalized schizophrenic patients. *Family Process,* 1977, *16,* 503–510.

27. Minuchin, S., Baker, L., Rosman, B. L., Liebman, R., Milman, L., & Todd, T. C. A conceptual model of psychosomatic illness in children. *Archives of General Psychiatry,* 1975, *32,* 1031–1038.

28. Harbin, H. T., & Maziar, H. M. The families of drug abusers: A literature review. *Family Process,* 1975, *14,* 411–431.

29. Garmezy, N., Farina, A., & Rodnick, E. H. Direct study of child-parent interactions. 1. The structured situation test: A method for studying family interaction in schizophrenia. *American Journal of Orthopsychiatry,* 1960, *30,* 445–452.

30. Thomas, C. B., & Duszynski, K. R. Closeness of parents and the family constellation in a prospective study of five disease states: Suicide, mental illness, malignant tumor, hypertension, and coronary heart disease. *Johns Hopkins Medical Journal,* 1974, *134,* 251–270.

31. Thomas, C. B., & Greenstreet, R. L. Psychobiological characteristics in youth as predictors of five disease states: Suicide, mental illness, hypertension, coronary heart disease and tumor. *Johns Hopkins Medical Journal,* 1973, *132,* 16–43.

32. Barcai, A. The reaction of the family system to rapid therapeutic change in one of its members. *American Journal of Psychotherapy,* 1977, *31,* 105–115.

BIBLIOGRAPHY

Dewitt, K. N. The effectiveness of family therapy: A review of outcome research. *Archives of General Psychiatry,* 1968, *35,* 549–561.

Langsley, D. G., Flomenhaft, K., & Machotka, P. Follow-up evaluation of family crisis therapy. *American Journal of Orthopsychiatry,* 1969, *39,* 753–759.

Langsley, D. G., Machotka, P., & Flomenhaft, K. Avoiding mental hospital admission: A follow-up study. *American Journal of Psychiatry*, 1971, *127*, 1391–1394.

Liebman, R., Minuchin, S., & Baker, L. The use of structural family therapy in the treatment of intractable asthma. *American Journal of Psychiatry*, 1974, *131*, 535–540.

McLean, J. A., & Ching, A. Y. T. Follow-up study of relationships between family situation and bronchial asthma in children. *Journal of the American Academy of Child Psychiatry*, 1973, *12*, 142–161.

Parsons, B. V., & Alexander, J. F. Short-term family intervention: A therapy outcome study. *Journal of Consulting and Clinical Psychology*, 1973, *41*, 195–201.

Richman, J. Family determinants of suicide potential. In D. B. Anderson, & L. J. McLean (Eds.), *Identifying suicide potential*. New York: Behavioral Publications, 1971, pp. 33–54.

Selvini-Palazzoli, M. The families of patients with anorexia nervosa. In E. J. Anthone, & C. Koupernik (Eds.), *The child and his family*. New York: John Wiley & Sons, 1970, pp. 319–332.

Stanton, M. D., & Todd, T. C. A critique of the Wells and Dezen review of the results of nonbehavioral family therapy. *Family Process*, 1980, *19*, 169–176.

Wells, R. A. Tempests, teapots (and research design): Rejoinder to Stanton and Todd. *Family Process*, 1980, *19*, 177–178.

4

The Nurse Therapist
and the Law

Ann Kleine-Kracht and Paul Kleine-Kracht

Within the last 100 years, nursing has been shaped and reshaped by dynamic forces both inside and outside the health care arena. The nursing profession began as a truly independent profession, moved to the area of physician assistant, passed through the period of nursing the telephone, charts, in other words, things, to finally having evolved into client advocates and independent practitioners of the art of nursing.

Throughout this entire evolution, nursing concepts have been defined and redefined. Terms such as *scope of nursing practice, delegation of authority, medical vs. nursing diagnosis, "captain of the ship," standard of care, nursing assessment and predictability,* and *nursing malpractice* have undergone change. Because of the importance that health plays in the operations of society and the acute awareness of malpractice, any and everything that alters nursing's status becomes a legal issue. Up until just recently (within 10 years), most litigation dealt with the traditional nursing role, "the handmaiden of the physician." Today, legal parameters are of primary concern as to whether the nurse is functioning in a traditional or expanded role. The future of these expanded roles will be determined, at least in part, by whether and under what conditions these are defensible by law.

The three primary parameters of legal interpretation of nursing practice are as follows:

The first parameter is nursing practice acts as enacted by the particular state legislature on the basis of legal definition. The state is seen as having the ultimate authority in matters of licensure. In 1903 North Carolina passed the first Nurse Registration Act. "This act provided that only nurses who were certified and registered by a state board could use the title *Registered Nurse* (RN). By 1923 every state had such an act" (1).

In 1938 New York passed the first exclusive Practice Act, which established a definition of the scope of nursing practice. In 1971 the last step in this evolution began with Idaho amending its Nurse Practice Act to recognize nurses' diagnostic and treatment functions. What in essence has occurred in these last 79 years is that the law that has traditionally limited the scope of nursing practice has now for the first time expanded nursing functions.

Nurse Practice Acts do not define just what constitutes malpractice or negligence (the incorrect or careless performance of a procedure). Since these acts define what is approved nursing functions, exceeding such acts is only evidence or an indicator of negligence.

> It is not, in and of itself, negligence because the action, not the mere violation of the statute, produced the injury. The plaintiff still must establish the nexus between the manner in which the act was performed and the harm which resulted (1).

Ordinarily, the failure of a nurse to follow the excepted limitation as set by statute is only pursued by the licensure agency. When, however, as a result of that action, injury has occurred, the failure to follow normal procedure would be an issue raised in any subsequent civil malpractice suit that would result.

The second parameter of nursing practice is the standards of practice as established by the American Nurses Association or by practice established by a nationally accepted organization of registered nurses. As the consumer becomes more conscious of quality in regard to health care and as the professions themselves attempt to practice defensive medicine, a recent quality control device is the use of standards or protocols. These standards or protocols outline parameters of desired practice.

Since licensure for nurses generally means achievement of minimal competency testing of all RNs regardless of basic education, the American Nurses Association and other specialist groups have established standards of care and certification as evidence of advanced competency or mastery of certain aspects of practice.

Institutions and group practices have also begun to establish practice protocols. The legal base for this has been set in some legislatures including California. *Standardized procedures* as used in this section, means the following:

> Policies and protocols developed by a health facility . . . through collaboration among administrators and health professionals including physicians and nurses (2).

Another set of protocols that have become standards of practice in many hospitals is the Patient's Bill of Rights. These standards developed and approved by the American Hospital Association have been modified and become state law in such states as Minnesota. Some hospital attorneys have suggested that once a hospital adopts the Bill of Rights as policy, the standards of the bill can be the basis for litigation just as the hospitals' bylaws and nursing procedures.

The third parameter of practice is the standards on which the courts base a determination of whether the professional has met a level of proficiency. In the medical field the test has been whether the act exhibited that degree of care ordinarily exercised by other professionals in that same field in the locality involved or in similar localities.

> To find a professional liable to a patient who has become a plaintiff in a lawsuit, the defendant's peers must testify that they would have acted differently. A nurse will be required to pay money damages to a patient when she has fallen below expected standards of performance and has injured the patient (3).

Persons who hold themselves out as professionals generally indicate by that term they possess specialized skills. *Prosser Torts* (4) states,

> Professional men in general and those who undertake any work calling for special skills are required not only to exercise reasonable care in what they do but also to possess a standard minimum of special knowledge and ability.

Malpractice, therefore, is a deviation or departure from these standard skills that a professional is deemed to possess. This would generally hold true whether the professional is a doctor, lawyer, accountant, or nurse.

From a client's point of view in order to prosecute a successful malpractice suit there are three basic requirements:

First, it must be shown that the professional has a duty to act. This can be evidenced either by basic contractual agreements, verbal agreements, institution of treatment, or by any other evidence that indicates the medical professional has accepted the responsibility of the client's care. As an example, once the nurse family therapist (NFT) accepts a person as a client, she then has a duty to provide those therapeutic services consistent with the standard of care of other NFTs in the area.

Second, it must be shown that there was a breach of duty. By this is meant that the nurse practitioner has not performed services consistent with those considered standards for nurse practitioners in the locale. So that as in the case of *Thompson* v. *Brent* (1971) LA App. (5) where a nurse was removing a cast, the resulting scar caused by the blade of the Stryker saw was found to be the result of the nurse's breach of her duty to perform the operation safely.

Third, in addition to the above, the client must show that as a proximate result of the action he was injured. Injury can include bodily, mental, emotional, or any type of trauma. When there is no resulting injury there can be no damage assessed. Injury is an intricate and necessary part of a malpractice claim, without which the parties would be dealing only in useless semantics.

Whether the professional is a nurse employed in an institution, a family therapist, nurse practitioner or clinician, the above three requirements will hold true. The question of breach of duty, however, will present the greatest problem for the family therapist and the attorney. This issue has always been the most difficult to prove and for the professional the most difficult to accept because of its subjective nature. In addition, as nurses broaden the scope of their practice and involvements, it is difficult to set guidelines beyond which there is a question of unsafe practice.

It is probably safe to assume that as a nurse accepts more responsibility she will be held to a greater scrutiny. If a nurse accepts the duties of delivering a child, it would appear to be only reasonable to expect that the procedure performed will closely meet the standards of an obstetrician. The courts have already taken some steps in this direction.

In a suit filed when a girl fainted after having given blood, it was shown that she volunteered to donate as an experiment at her university. The procedures followed were shown to be different than those normally followed when blood was taken. The court, even though the professor was not an M.D. held him liable when "The degree of care . . . fell short of that required of members of the medical profession" (6).

This instance shows the recent trend of litigation to center on the act performed, how it was performed, and the outcome as being more critical an issue than who performed the act.

There are few cases dealing with the expanded role that the nurse has assumed. Surely there will be a proliferation of such suits, whether they deal with the issue of advising that a client consult a specialist or whether they concern actual diagnosis and treatment by a nurse, all basically claiming a breach of duty. The only recent decision closely associated with this situation is *Cooper* v. *National Motor Bearing Co.,* (1955), 136 Cal. App. (7). In that case the nurse involved was an industrial nurse in charge of a company first-aid room. An injured employee was treated but the nurse failed to probe a puncture wound on the employee's forehead. Treatment continued for some months without any reference to a doctor. There was allegation that skin cancer developed, and the nurse was found guilty of malpractice.

It should not be assumed that any court will hold a practitioner to a level of competency that there is a guarantee of results. In the instance of family therapist where there is a giving of advice, there can be no guarantee that it will be followed, or if followed that there will be acceptable results. The major issue will arise where the therapist fails to recognize a condition resulting in a client harming himself or another, or fails to seek other adequate help. In any case, where the practitioner acts within the scope of the general practice of the profession in the community and in the best interest of the client, malpractice would not generally be claimed.

IMPLICATIONS FOR THE NURSE

The 1970s have been the decade of the innovative health professional. Nurses have developed a variety of work relationships with the accompanying legal implications. The nurse family therapists have been front runners in the development of new and expanded roles. The NFTs function primarily in four areas—each with its own responsibilities and legal parameters. NFTs practice as employees of an institution such as a hospital, as salaried primary care providers in a physician's office or clinic, as members of a partnership or shareholders in a medical corporation, or as private practioners. The mode of practice of NFTs "affects not just the structure of health care delivery but also the legal liability of themselves and others when a malpractice claim is made" (8). The nurse in an extended role is still considered a safe risk by insurance companies as evidenced by low premiums and relatively few suits targeted at nurses.

From 1973 to 1975 this country experienced a malpractice insurance crisis. All state legislatures were quick to respond with laws insuring professional liability insurance for providers or altering tort laws to relate to health care more closely or both. As a result of this flurry of activity coupled with the federal government's cost containment measures "recent studies indicate that the number of insurance claims and the size of jury awards have dramatically decreased" (3).

It is the opinion of several writers and shared by these authors that the decrease in litigation has been the result to a large extent of accountability and quality assurance on the part of providers—employers as well as practitioners. Considerable evidence is available that malpractice litigation is less related to "competence" than it is to the issue of alienation between provider and client. Some authorities have suggested that increased personalization of care and increased time spent with each client by the nurse in an expanded role have led to increased client satisfaction and decreased complaints.

Sadler and Bliss (9) in their paper on the physician's assistant graphically described some of the dynamics of a malpractice suit.

In our view, the utilization of a well-trained physician's assistant who performs tasks within their capacity under appropriate physician's supervision will reduce malpractice risks. We believe this for two reasons, first, affective utilization of PA's will allow the physician to concentrate on those medical procedures in judgments that only he can manage. Second, a malpractice suit often results from poor patient rapport rather than negligence, per se. When a patient is seen after a considerable wait and then only hurriedly by harrassed physician, the probability of patient dissatisfaction is magnified. Time motion studies have shown when a physician's assistant is used time periods are reduced, patients receive greater attention from various health professionals, and patients' acceptance of the PA has generally been good (9).

All nurses, especially those in expanded roles, would be well advised to know that the very attributes that make nursing unique in interacting with clients are the very attributes that diminish the risk of litigation. Areas to be especially aware of are inadequate or neglected informed consent, critical remarks made by fellow professionals, mishandling dissatisfied clients, inaccurate or inadequate record keeping, casual admissions of negligence, and mostly lack of rapport with clients and families.

In summary, nurses, due to many factors, are assuming duties and functions ordinarily solely in the realm of the physician. States have attempted to regulate and define this expanded practice with limited success. The real determinant of the boundaries of expanded nursing practice will be the nurses themselves and the competence with which they perform skills according to accepted standards.

The NFT is on the threshold of a very exciting and encouraging new world. With the public's preoccupation with health and quality providers, the qualified nurse can pursue many heretofore closed vistas. As long as the acts of the NFT can be judged within the accepted standards of care, she should be comfortable in becoming truly professional in the area of family therapy.

REFERENCES

1. Weisgerber, E. The nurse practitioner: Medicolegal considerations. *Legal Medical Annual,* 1979.
2. California Business & Professions, Code 2725.
3. Warren, D. G. Quality assurance: Insurance against malpractice. *International Nursing Review,* March–April, 1979, 2.
4. Prosser, W. L. *Torts,* St. Paul, Minn.: West Publishing Co., 1971.
5. *Thompson* vs. *Brent* (1971) La. App. 245 So. 2d 751.
6. *Butler* vs. *Louisiana State Board of Education* (1976) La. App. 331 So. 2d 192.
7. *Cooper* vs. *National Motor Bearing Co.* (1955) 136 Cal. App. 2d 229, 288 PT 581.
8. Chapman, M. W., & Recond, J. C. Defensibility of new health professionals at law: A speculative paper. *Journal of Health Politics, Policy and Law,* Spring 1979, 4.
9. Sadler, A. M. et al. *The physician's assistant—Today and tomorrow.* Cambridge, Mass.: Ballinger Press, 1975.

BIBLIOGRAPHY

American Nurses Association Division of Psychiatric Nursing. *Statement on psychiatric mental health nursing practice.* Kansas City: ANA Pub. Code PMH-3 1OM, 1976.

Kussman, R. Legal responsibilities of independent pediatric nurse practitioners. *New England Journal of Medicine,* Aug. 10, 1978, 20.

Mauksch, I. G. Critical issues of the nurse practitioner movement. *Nurse Practitioner,* November–December, 1978, 3.

Roster, J. T. Nurse practitioner and malpractice. *New England Journal of Medicine,* Nov. 16, 1978, 20.

5

The Ethics
of Family Therapy

Elsie L. Bandman and Bertram Bandman

The family may be characterized as the locus for the tasks of primary socialization of the human being in its progress from a helpless infant to an autonomous person capable of decisions and acts which profoundly affect the self and others (1). Ways of relating to others thought to be *good, right,* or *wrong* are patterned within the family setting (1). The ways in which this is accomplished (it is hoped that this would be done with a deep sense of caring) will "ultimately affect the person's identification with the society in which he (or she) lives and his (or her) commitment to its values and ethics, as contrasted with a deep-seated feeling of alienation" (1). As the human infant progresses from dependency on those who provide care through stages of growing independence, he or she is expected to express caring for others in morally sanctioned ways as a *good* parent, spouse, family member, worker, and citizen.

The central ethical issue of family life may be the extent to which its members are able to foster a milieu of caring in which each individual member is helped to achieve maximum development of capacities of caring acts, which manifest similar respect for the needs and rights of others. The process of family caring is reinforced by society. It mediates family dynamics and roles through the pressure of social norms. Although several variations of a family as a married couple of opposite sexes with children have emerged, the pressure toward legal contractual marriage and monogamy as the dominant value continues. Moreover, society sets the expectation that as each human capacity for increased understanding and self-direction emerges, the family will inculcate each child so as to act in ways that are considered to be good, right, or moral. The fiber of society depends on the expectation that everyday behavior is predicated on standards of truth-telling, promise-keeping, and respect for the life, rights, and property of others. Beyond a few such widely agreed on principles, there are wide differences of opinion concerning ethical issues of the *good* in parenting, spouse relations, and family members' participation and contribution, as examples, characteristic of a pluralistic, heterogeneous society such as the United States.

As preparation for living in that larger, diverse society of competing values, every family has the need to cope with and master unavoidable clashes of conflicting needs and wants among its members. Appeal to some principle of fairness in moral behavior defines and allocates the *good* in permitting or denying the expression of behavior. The presentation of significant ethical views and their implication for family structure, dynamics, and function and interrelationship with the therapist will be the focus of this chapter. Its objective is to provide guidance in the process of selection of *the good* among diverse and competing ethical views.

ETHICAL VIEWS THAT GUIDE FAMILY-THERAPIST INTERACTION

There are perhaps six main ethical views that guide and orient the interaction of family members and family therapists.

Utilitarianism

The first of these is the *happiness* ethic, sometimes referred to as *utilitarian* or *goal-based*, since on this view the greatest happiness of the greatest number, and consequences that bring about what is sometimes called *aggregate happiness* is striven for. The emphasis is on each individual family member satisfying an optimum number of needs, interests, and desires that are conducive to promoting the greatest happiness of the family as a whole. Each member's self-actualization through family involvement is referred to as the ethic of *flourishing*.

The happiness ethic draws its main reasoned support from such otherwise diverse philosophers as Aristotle (384–322 BC), Epicurus (341–270 BC), Jeremy Bentham (1748–1842), and John Stuart Mill (1806–1873) (2). According to Aristotle, happiness is a state of well-being that characterizes a person's disposition throughout a full life. One cannot be happy, according to Aristotle, without health, a reasonable degree of wealth, "good birth," good looks, and good children. To Aristotle, moral education consists of making use of pleasure and pain, which are the rudders that steer all behavior (3). In comparison, the emphasis Bentham gives in ethics is concern for the quality of being *sentient,* of having feelings and experiencing joy and suffering.

Deontological Ethics

A second ethical view is oriented by the emphasis on doing one's duty, ful-filling obligations (such as keeping promises), telling the truth, doing Good Samaritan acts, and refraining from taking life (one's own and the lives of others), regardless of the hardships, inconveniences, and self-sacrifice thereby imposed on oneself. The obligations based on moral principles such as self-respect and autonomy are regarded as absolute and uncompromising. These duties give rise to dignity and freedom in the face of social buffet-ings. Persons who embrace this view may be pictured as rocks of Gibraltar who are immovable no matter how tempting the shifting circumstances, needs, interests, and desires are of life. One remains firmly devoted to one's principles. Immanuel Kant (1724–1804) is perhaps the single most im-portant philosophical architect of this position, which emphasizes the morality of a person joining a moral "kingdom of ends" by acting con-sistently on one's sense of obligation in place of one's inclinations.

Agapeism

A third moral orientation is one guided by love, sometimes referred to by philosophers and theologians as *agapeistic*. This view is exemplified by the character and works of Jesus of Nazareth, who preached that all men and women are brothers and sisters, that one should love one's neighbor as much as oneself. St. Paul, in his letters to the Corinthians, taught the im-portance of hope, faith, and charity and that "the greatest of these is charity," which he regarded as love. St. Francis of Assisi found all creation worthy of love, including the singing of birds, the life of the very young and very old, the poor, the outcasts, the green vegetation, as well as all those who suffer. St. Francis is said to have kissed lepers in his exuding of the quality of love, which he showed unreservedly to all created beings and which he regarded as equally worthy of love.

There have been non-Christians such as Indian leader Mahatma Ghandi (1869–1948) who also preached and practiced a way of life oriented by peace, good will, love, and nonviolence to all fellow humans.

Egoism

A fourth point of view is that of the moral egoist: one who argues that each person who regards love of self as being of paramount importance. On this view, no one matters more than oneself. This view says "Me first." Some egoists extend this to say, "Me first and last."

This view has its traditional source in the early pre-Socratic Greek sophists, who taught against the Socratic search for absolute standards of right and wrong. The sophists taught that a person's point of view being right or wrong depends on how much power that person has. Justice was defined by one of the leading sophists, Thrasymachus, as "the interest of the stronger." In modern times, egoism is defended in economics by Adam Smith, who argues that selfishness is a basic virtue that when multiplied by all other selfish persons realizes itself in an affluent economy—"the wealth of a nation" as Smith called it. The engine of society is selfishness, the desire to amass wealth, which when believed by other selfish persons results in producing wealth. In recent times, egoism is upheld by such writers as Ayn Rand, Robert Nozick, Milton Friedman, and Arthur Jensen, who stress the importance of rewarding individual merit as a just form of desert in place of equal consideration to needs, desires, and interests of sentient beings (as does utilitarianism). To Jensen, for example, individual intelligence, not recognition of feelings, is the main criterion for judging who deserves to receive the lion's share of resources.

Existentialism

A fifth moral point of view emphasizes a person's total responsibility for one's part in interacting in psychic and physical existence with others. One exists only by taking responsibility for all of one's decisions in all aspects of one's life—physical, economic, political, sexual—about which one has a conscious reflective process at work. A famous French philosopher, René Descartes (1596–1650) held that he could prove his existence by citing the fact that he was thinking. To think is to exist, or as he put it, "I think, therefore I am." Existentialism is an extension of this fundamental point. Whatever one can think about, one is responsible for. What one does in relation to others, one thinks about and therefore is responsible, whether it is to decide to join the free French underground in World War II or to stay home and care for one's mother instead, to cite a famous example by a recent existentialist, Jean-Paul Sartre (1906–1980). By further extension, one is responsible for one's economic, marital, parental, sexual, and political roles, as well. As long as one is conscious, one is responsible for making decisions. To attempt to evade decisions or to fail to make decisions is also in effect to make decisions. As long as we are conscious, we are responsible. Insofar as we are conscious, we are, in Sartre's terms, "condemned to be free." To fail to recognize our responsibility, Sartre contends, is "bad faith" and the function of therapy is to make us authentic and responsible.

Rights

A sixth moral orientation is a *rights*-based view, one which does not justify action by reference to a calculation of aggregate happiness, nor with compliance with one's moral duty, nor on how much love and caring is manifested, nor on how much an act advances oneself, nor even on how much responsibility one takes. A rights-based view justifies social roles and acts of individuals by respecting oneself and others as persons who, as rights holders, have a sphere of autonomy and dignity. Rights are a protected domain of freedom which give a person a form of security and insurance against the desires, needs, and interests of others, and even of majorities. Rights as a form of belonging, for example, insure that a person's body is his or her own and may not be entered, touched, or interfered with without that person's permission and approval.

Although a rights-based view of ethics is not identical to those previously cited, it does, in important respects, encompass and draw from all of them. A necessary condition of rights, for example, is recognition of the needs, interests, and desires of persons emphasized by utilitarian concern with individual and aggregate happiness. Another feature of rights is respect for an individual's sphere of autonomy. The right to vote, for example, is protected institutionally by prohibiting anyone else from entering a voting booth to dictate how a person should vote. To accord a person a right (such as the right to vote) expresses public respect for a person's dignity and enshrines a person's role in the world as a member of "a kingdom of ends," a principle emphasized in the Kantian ethic. Only the rights-based view begins not with the duty we have to respect others but with a person's right to respect as the basis for other people's duties.

Rights also coincide importantly with aspects of egoism in protecting some interests, needs, and desires of an individual. A rights-oriented view counts on individuals, by and large, to claim their own rights. A rights-based view also dovetails with existentialist tenets concerning an individual's authenticity and good faith. In these ways, to acknowledge rights is to respect the boundaries of individuals and to support self-determination and autonomy.

IMPLICATIONS OF ETHICAL PERSPECTIVES FOR FAMILY AND THERAPIST RELATIONS

These ethical perspectives, which are not presented as exhaustive, have a bearing on one's role as a family member. These views also make a difference in the treatment family members accord one another. An ethical orientation that emphasizes happiness rather than duties may, for example, find parents giving fewer resources and less love to their children than a duty-based ethic, a love-based ethic, or a rights-based view. A Kantian emphasis on promise-keeping, for example, makes for a stronger relation of fidelity between spouses (4) than a utilitarian or egoist view. On the other hand, concern with rigid principles may interfere with the happiness of individual family members.

The basic element of a family, a couple in friendship seeking to provide mutual satisfaction, functions by respect for the principles and agreements that sustain the relationship. Regard for marital fidelity, implied by a Kantian ethical orientation, provides an important consideration in sustaining a two-person family. Relations marked by fidelity, trust, respect, and friendship assume further importance as new family members are added in the form of children. For in the parent-child relationship, the principles, practices, and habits adopted by the couple are an example to the children who will also learn fidelity, trust, respect, love, and kindness if they experience these qualities being practiced by their parents. The values by which parents live affect the behavior of children.

The importance of the family in the transmission of societal values and ethical views cannot be overestimated. The function of the family is to pass on to its children those values of society that the parents believe with good reason to be desirable or good (as well as those that are objectionable and forbidden) along with the *right* and *wrong* way of accomplishing these values as ends (5).

The family's choice of those values and the ethical views it supports will, in turn, depend on the parents functioning in their roles as leaders and executives of the family system. The parental selection, in turn, reflects both the socialization and the enculturation process from which they came. Religious symbols, beliefs, values, and codes may be an important part of a family's ethical orientation, which profoundly affects the relations that family members have with each other and with the nurse therapist.

The nurse therapist has at least two major tasks in working with families for therapeutic purposes. The first and most basic task is to identify his/her own ethical view(s) as the framework and foundation on which goals, strategies, and interventions are superimposed.

The second major task is for the therapist to help the family identify its ethical orientation. If enunciated as the family value belief system by the family spokesperson, usually one parent and occasionally a child, it is important to engage the family in the validation process. This may lead the therapist to the inference that the expressed value orientation may be the conviction of the whole family, part of the family, none of the family, or simply the desire of the spokesperson to be more like other families.

Another nursing task is for the therapist to note discrepancies between the family's expressed intent to adhere to principles, such as truth-telling, and actual behavioral patterns of relating that may include falsehoods and deceptions. Families need interventions in forming connections between family goals as ends and the means of ongoing interactions. Honest, open family relations based on mutual trust can only be achieved through consistent truth-telling between family members. Likewise, caring among family members as a goal can only be achieved through the nurture of each family member by every other family member and the family as a whole. This, in turn, entails sharing and caring for the welfare of all by giving up some things, if necessary, for the common good. A family vacation may be possible only if no one child goes away to camp. On the other hand, the family may decide that the vacation time and money shall be spent on children at summer camp, with parents staying at home as an economic necessity.

Fundamental questions for every family that involve ethical choices are the family's ends or goals and the means or the issue of how they shall achieve these ends. Each of the six ethical views presented offers a different response to the basic challenge of purpose and the process within the family nexus.

Utilitarian Family Ethics

The family that indicates through its statements and its interactions that it seeks to achieve "the greatest happiness for the greatest number" is asserting perhaps that most but not all of its members can be satisfied at any given time if their strategies or means work. Such a family needs help in looking at its processes from the viewpoint of each person whose view is not represented in majority decisions. Are the minority's legitimate needs or interests ignored and denied by the majority who may either be more numerous, powerful, or articulate? Examples of such practices can be found in those families in which children's desires for recreation and luxuries are gratified by sacrificing the realistic needs of the parents and/or the grandparents. Moreover, this ethical orientation may be misinterpreted so as to allow considerable *bending* or withholding of the truth on the grounds of protecting the "happiness of the greatest number." Parents may conceal all sorts of economic, emotional, or social problems from responsible children who might thereupon lend their support on the grounds of safeguarding happiness.

Deontological Family Ethics

This position may be the most difficult for any family to sustain since it involves principled behavior without exception. It also presupposes a unified family with only one ethical view without individual variation or exception. This degree of unanimity seems both difficult to achieve and undesirable if the ideal of self-actualization and autonomy as the basis for principled acts is to be realized. A further difficulty with this position is that it allows for no exceptions. Truth-telling, as in informing everyone under all conditions that he or she has incurable cancer and will soon die, may cause tragedy in a family beset with difficulties. A further difficulty in assuming a position of exceptionless principle of individual acts is that the family may be excessively rigid and inflexible regarding deviant behavior of its members, such as condemnation and rejection of a daughter who has had an abortion, perceived by the family as a violation of safeguarding the principle that all life is sacred.

Agapeistic Family Ethics

An ethical orientation guided by love is portrayed in American mass media as the ideal solution to life's difficulties. The fact that endless hours of media time are devoted to variations on this theme without notable success in resolving life's perennial problems emphasizes the difficulties of defining and applying the concept of love to family issues. For example, one parent may define love of children as unconditional acceptance of their needs and interests with immediate gratification. Another parent may define love of children as restraint of drives, impulses, and withholdings of gratification. Love can be expressed in as many ways as there are people to define it. Despite the wide variety of definitions of love and its misapplications for perverse or selfish ends, which lead to all sorts of interactional difficulties in dysfunctional families, love may be the most significant and compelling motivation that ultimately binds family members despite all differences and hardships. Love in families can be expressed as "caring for," meaning nurture of the young and helpless and/or "caring about," meaning manifest concern for the other's well-being as intense as concern for oneself. Thus, in the name of love, one finds family members rising to heights of nobility by donating a kidney for a child or sibling. On the contrary, one finds parents placing children in double binds of communication and ultimately schizophrenia, also in the name of love.

The concern of the nurse working with families who espouse a love-oriented ethics is one of continual definition of terms and analysis of patterns of interaction between family members. Discomforting and disquieting therapy over long periods of time may be endured by the parents or family who in the name of love wish to facilitate the recovery of one of its own, even though, in the name of the same concept, it created the conditions that led to depths of human despair in mental illness.

Egoistic Family Ethics

It may be difficult to imagine that families would admit to practicing ethical principles placing one's own interest above others. Yet critics make this charge of the American family in which both parents pursue a career. Young children are in the care of others at home, or away in day-care centers, or in arrangements of necessity or convenience. Parents are understandably tired. Children may receive less attention than is desirable. Millions of working American women, many of them single parents, are in this situation. For most, the alternative is either a lowered family income or what is perceived as a narrowly circumscribed life of unrewarding domestic routine.

The nurse therapist in this situation needs clear ideas regarding her own ethical position. If the nurse holds the utilitarian principle of "the greatest good for the greatest number," she may decide that the mother's added income benefits the whole family and is a right, moral action. If on the other hand the nurse translates her ethics of love into the principle that all young children need their mother's undivided attention at home, the nurse can be antitherapeutic in working with this family. The nurse might even disqualify herself on grounds of the possibility of harming a client who is already in need of help and possibly guilt-ridden as well because of violations of traditional child-rearing patterns.

Existentialist Family Ethics

An existentialist ethical view may be one of the more difficult positions for the dysfunctional family and its therapist to put into practice. It calls for each family member to assume complete responsibility for his or her own acts, that is, to take charge of one's self. The assumption is that decisions are inner-directed and the result of a self-conscious process of reflection, analysis, and uncoerced choice by each person. No one acts or speaks for another. At what point children are ready to assume choice and responsibility is not seen as a matter of age, but rather as the extent to which a family is willing to begin to differentiate each member from what Murray Bowen and others call the "undifferentiated family mass." The process of individuation and separation from the family is best accomplished as a slow, gradual process beginning early and proceeding gently in each child's life until the adult offspring establishes a family of his or her own and achieves interdependence with the family of origin.

Rights-Based Family Ethics

This view emphasizes individual choice and powers in relation to social and institutional roles of persons in a subordinate, complementary position. The language of rights has proliferated to the extent that there are now bills of rights for children, infants, women, the aged, patients, and the mentally ill, to name but a few. The issue is to insure maximum self-determination, autonomy, and respect for needs and interests. The problem is to avoid the *thinning out* of rights where rights are so widely distributed that they are no longer meaningfully attributed to any person (6).

In family therapy, the issue of rights of children and of parents becomes significant. A right-based view suggests that each person has liberties consistent with age and capacities that must be respected by all. For example, the 6-year-old child has the right to spend his or her 50 cents weekly allowance as he or she pleases. But does the same child have the right to go to bed and put out the lights when he or she wishes? Not by this view. How then are individual rights identified and justified? If, for example, the 6-year-old child shares a room with his 12-year-old brother, how are the conflicting rights for space and privacy to be settled? A rights-based ethical view emphasizes the autonomy of the individual and can be in direct conflict with family needs as a totality. The daughter's right to orthodontia may be in total conflict with the family's right to a new car to replace the undependable old one. It is not a position free of conflicting and competing rights, but it does stress maximum individual autonomy to the extent possible.

IMPLICATIONS FOR THE NURSE THERAPIST

The nurse therapist oriented by these six ethical perspectives will consider them in treating patients. The therapist, as a third party therapeutic agent, attempts to bring into play such emotions as honesty and openness, emphasized by existentialism, happiness, love, and respect for the needs and desires of others.

Since rights play an umbrellalike role in according respect to the most important needs, interests, and desires of family members, it may help to provide a brief account of the advantages and drawbacks of a rights-based view in application to family interaction.

We may compare legal and institutional rights and the rights of family members. In the family, the constellation of values such as trust, love, kindness, consideration, wisdom, hope, despair, hostility, anger, doubts, fears, tragedy, and comedy play a larger role in the array of emotions than do concepts associated with legal and institutional rights such as contracts, agreements, freedoms, duties, rules, and laws. The reason is that the relations between members is usually more permissive and more tolerated than relations in social institutions. The boundaries of displayed emotions are more flexible and dynamic, and the relationships between family members are also more ambiguous.

In buying a newspaper, for example, the relationship between buyer and vendor is more exact and specified. The transaction between them involves money exchanged from the buyer to the vendor and a newspaper given from the vendor to the buyer. The buyer does not usually ask for credit nor does the vendor tell the buyer not to bother paying.

Relations between family members, their rights and responsibilities, are not usually so specific and are more analogous to the behavior of friends at a party, where individuals are free to have a second, third, or fourth drink or portion of food and are not threatened with arrest, which would be the case if a newspaper buyer attempted too often to obtain a newspaper without paying for it.

Nevertheless, rights play an increasing role in families, partly due to the abuse of weaker members by stronger ones and due also to the relations of trust, love, and consideration giving way to mistrust, hatred, and lack of consideration in times of stress. The play of emotions in a family having fewer boundaries may reach impermissible abuses that threaten to prevent the goals the family is instituted to achieve, such as the attainment of mutual satisfaction.

Rights that normally operate in the background and that ordinarily provide a conceptual contour or threshold between the permissible and the impermissible then come into the foreground as other values such as love, trust, and kindness break down or are not in evidence.

Rights provide the boundary posts outside of which appeal for mediation and correction of behavior is made either to third party counselling or, in the case of married persons, to judicial agencies. Rights are thus invokable mainly as *rights against,* where one or more members claim that their rights have been abused by another member.

However, when family members behave with love, trust, friendship, kindness, and wisdom toward one another, they become less specific in their demands on and their complaints against one another. As love, trust, and friendship are in evidence and these values come to the foreground, rights recede to a background position.

For family members to grant rights to one another seems silly if the members of the family get along well without invoking their rights; and, yet, having rights enables family members to remind those who would violate their rights that doing so is impermissible. Rights thus provide the boundary posts for individuals in families that, while not ideally and ordinarily invoked, are nevertheless present in case they are needed, somewhat like the lock on one's door is needed so that activity can occur within one's home without thinking about who will try to enter. Or to shift the metaphor slightly, rights are an insurance policy and are there if they are needed.

How the therapist communicates in honest and open confrontation has a role in bringing love, trust, kindness, and wisdom into the foreground of family relations while helping family members forego hostility and disparagement and while pushing the boundary posts of rights further into the background, but keeping rights as an inseparable part of a person's self-perceived sovereign sphere.

CONCLUSION

The implication of these six ethical viewpoints for family members and the therapist is worthy of serious consideration both in the education of the therapist and in the treatment of family members as a necessary condition for effective and wholesome family interaction.

REFERENCES

1. Lidz, T. The life cycle: Introduction. In Silvano Arieti (Ed.), *The foundations of psychiatry* (Vol. 1), *American handbook of psychiatry* (2nd ed.). New York: Basic Books, 1974, pp. 247–248.

2. Jones, W. T. et al. (Eds.). *Approaches to ethics* (3rd ed.). New York: McGraw-Hill, 1977, pp. 47–83; 251–269, 281–294.

3. Aristotle. *Nicomachean ethics* (M. Ostwald trans.). New York: Liberal Arts Press, 1962, p. 273.

4. Wasserstrom, R. Is adultery immoral? In R. Wasserstrom (Ed.), *Today's moral problems* (2nd ed.). New York: Macmillan, 1979, pp. 288–299.

5. Lidz, T. The family: The developmental setting. In S. Arieti (Ed.), *The foundations of psychiatry* (Vol. 1), *American handbook of psychiatry* (2nd ed.). New York: Basic Books, 1974, p. 261.

6. Bandman, E. L., & Bandman, B. (Eds.). *Bioethics and human rights.* Boston: Little, Brown, & Co., 1978, pp. 3–17.

Part **II**

MODELS FOR
FAMILY THERAPY

6

Family Structure Model

Judith Maurin

Any family therapist needs a model or conceptual framework within which to view the phenomena presented by a family seeking help. With the aid of a conceptual framework, the data can be organized and understood, the "problem" can be defined, and thus interventions can be planned.

The *family structure model* conceives of the family as an open social system in transformation, characterized by an organization of hierarchical positions and recurring transaction patterns between and among these positions. This abstract model is believed to be generalizable across cultural and socioeconomic groups. The specific family organization evolving in a given cultural setting is hypothesized to be that which is most economical and effective for the particular group.

The family therapy model using the above family model is known as *structural family therapy*. It is most notably associated with the work of Salvador Minuchin, who developed and wrote of this method of family therapy while at the Philadelphia Child Guidance Clinic. Jay Haley, who was a colleague of Minuchin's in Philadelphia, also uses this model. However, his writings bear the influence of his association with the "Palo Alto Group"; therefore, he is difficult to categorize. Haley seems to represent a bridge between structural family therapy and the communication theorists. For the student trying to grasp the perspective of structural family therapy, it is recommended that one begin with Minuchin's work (1, 2) and then study Haley (3).

As discussed in Chapter 10, structural family therapy is an approach that shares the system perspective with several other schools of family therapy. The difference between these schools is one of properties emphasized, in this case, family structures (transaction patterns and subsystems) and organization. For a discussion of the basic concepts of system theory and the family as a system, the reader is referred to the above chapter.

THE FAMILY STRUCTURE MODEL

This framework approaches a person in his *social context.* It is the social context that structures the experience of the person and so contributes to the subjective experience of self. If he changes the context within which he acts and reacts, he thus changes his subjective experience. Minuchin uses Delgado's phrase, "extracerebral sources of the mind," to express the relationship between social context and the subjective experience of the person (1). Although this relationship between social context and subjective experience is assumed, they are not equally important to the model. The social context, rather than subjective experience, is stressed, analyzed, and manipulated in therapy.

A person's ecosystem includes his work place, school, neighborhood, extended family and nuclear family to name a few segments. In principle, any point within this ecosystem is available for the therapist's intervention. In practice the segment of emphasis has been the family.

Family Organization and Structure

An important feature of the family as an open social system is that of *hierarchy.* The hierarchical levels usually correspond to generational levels: grandparents, parents, children. The amount of power and status vested in the generational levels varies with different cultural groups. In some social groups, the grandparents will hold the highest heirarchical position, whereas in others, that position will be held by the parents. In some families, a person from one generational level will share in the power and status of another level. This is most clearly seen in the position of "parental child" who fulfills parental functions within his own sibling group. When considering the hierarchy of any particular family, the therapist must ask: Is the hierarchical arrangement clear, so that each knows his peer and his superior, or is it ambiguous? Are the members within each level united as a subgroup, or do coalitions consistently form across generations, so that a member at one level consistently forms a coalition against a peer with a member at another hierarchical level?

A second feature of the family system is that it differentiates and carries out its functions through *subsystems.* These subsystems may be dyads composed of persons in reciprocal role relationships, such as mother–child or husband–wife. Subsystems are also formed by generation, sex, interest, or function. Each person belongs to multiple subsystems in which he holds different levels of power and where he learns different skills. For example, the child in the mother-child subsystem usually has lower status and power than the mother, and learns to develop autonomy vis-à-vis a nuturant authority figure. This same child, as a member of a sibling subgroup, will hold power and status differentiated to some extent by age, but less pronounced than in the former subgroup. As a member of the sibling subgroup, he will learn the skills of negotiating, competing, and cooperating within a peer relationship.

Clarification of the *functions* or tasks associated with the various subgroups is not well delineated in this model. However, a general assignment of functions is suggested. Overall family functions include the support, regulation, nurturance, and socialization of its members (1). Those functions that have been specifically associated with individual subgroups include: mutual accommodation within the spouse subsystem, as each spouse must support the other's functioning in many areas; nurturing, control, and guidance functions associated with the parental subsystem; and the development of autonomy, and the ability to share, cooperate, and compete with peers associated with the sibling subgroup (6).

Each subsystem has a *boundary* defined by the rules, stating who may participate and how and expressed in interaction. A mother spending a day at the beach with her children may say to the eldest, "Now don't let Jane wander in over her waist. She doesn't swim well enough yet. And Jane, you mind Bill." By this exchange, the mother is clearly including a parental child in the parental subsystem:

M and PC (executive subsystem)
(Clear boundary) --
Other child (sibling subsystem)

Figure 6-1

At another time, she may clearly exclude all children from the parental subsystem by saying, "The next time Jane throws sand come and tell me and I will stop her." This exchange defines the subgroups as follows:

M (parental subsystem)
(Clear boundary) --
Children (sibling subsystem)

Figure 6-2

When analyzing boundaries, one considers the degree of permeability. Clear boundaries are sufficiently defined to allow subsystem members to carry out their functions without undue interference, while still allowing contact among members of different subgroups. Disengaged boundaries are overly rigid, such that in the extreme, no interaction is permitted across this boundary. Enmeshment is the polar opposite of disengagement. Enmeshment represents diffuse boundaries and thus poorly differentiated subsystems. Although the model suggests that clear boundaries best facilitate effective family functioning, Minuchin suggests one can expect to find enmeshed and disengaged subsystems in most families, and that the variation in normal limits may be associated with family developmental stages.

> The mother–children subsystem may tend toward enmeshment, while the children are small, and the father may take a disengaged position with regard to the children. Mother and younger children can be so enmeshed as to make father peripheral, while father takes a more engaged position with the older children. A parents-child subsystem can tend toward disengagement as the children grow and finally begin to separate from the family (1).

However, operations at the extremes of disengagement and enmeshment seem to be associated with pathology. The pathological implication of enmeshment has been most thoroughly explored by Minuchin and his colleagues, as that phenomena is implicated in psychosomatic families (4, 5).

Minuchin recommends mapping the subsystems, boundaries and transaction patterns that characterize a family as was done in Figures 1 and 2. Such mapping helps the observer organize the data presented by a family and visualize his assessment of family organization. (See reference 1 for the symbols and their corresponding definitions as used in his mapping system.)

The structure of this family model (subgroups, boundaries, hierarchical levels) is defined in the process of interaction. These features acquire the relative permanence implied by the word structure, because the interactions that define them are repetitive—repetitive sequences of behavior called *transaction patterns* or *family sets*. The self-perpetuating principles of the family as a system are the principles that result in the repetition of these sequences. Functional family sets are those transaction patterns that enable subgroups to carry out their functions and resolve or diminish stress for family members by accommodating the need for role changes and other conflict-resolution strategies. Dysfunctional family sets are more rigid. They repeat when stress occurs, even when a change is warranted. As such, they tend to maintain stress and block conflict resolution. The key question to ask about a specific family's sets is how much flexibility is in the patterning of this system. If dysfunctional sets are observed, which subgroups are involved and in relation to what function? What are the functional sets that can be supported and mobilized while change strategies are being directed toward the dysfunctional sets?

Organization as used in this model expresses the interrelationship among family structures and the regularity and patterning of the family's sequences of transaction. It is an assumed system characteristic of the family as a social system. Haley reports two studies aimed at validating organization as a family system characteristic (6, 7).

Finally, while the above has presented a static picture of the organization and structure of a family, it must be emphasized that the family is a social system in *transformation*. Pressures for change are generated, both internally and externally. Internal sources of change include the addition and deletion of members and the biopsychosocial changes that characterize each individual member during normal growth and development. External sources of change include such things as fluctuations in the economic well-being of the community or alterations in the community's normative expectations for the role of women. During the period of transformation, the observer can expect to find some ambiguity in the transaction patterns and thus system stress. A familiar example is the vacilation in the level of decision-making expected of the adolescent child in parent-child transactions when the adolescent child begins to move more determinedly toward the extrafamilial. Another frequently studied transformation is the change in the husband-wife subsystem when the birth of a child demands that social system accommodate the addition of mother-child, father-child, and parent-child subsystems.

The Effectively Functioning Family

From the perspective of this model, an effectively functioning family is an open social system with an organizational structure composed of differentiated subsystems and clearly delineated boundaries. It maintains links with extrafamilial systems and possesses the quality of flexibility, giving it the capacity for transformation as demanded by individual and family developmental processes. The organization of such a family will maximize the growth potential of each member.

A dysfunctional family, in contrast, exhibits a confused hierarchical arrangement and a rigidity in transaction patterns, so that demands for change are responded to by stereotyped behavior. The result is that possibilities for transformation are blocked and stress is maintained. Conceptualizing the change of such families through family therapy will be addressed in the next section.

IMPLICATIONS FOR FAMILY THERAPY

Structural family therapy is based on the above family model and three assumptions—"that context affects inner processes, that changes in context produce changes in the individual, and that the therapist's behavior is significant in change (1).

As implied by these three assumptions, structural family therapy is prospective—oriented to the present and future. If a family is in distress today, the therapist does not look to the past for an explanation. Families are influenced by past experience, but that influence will be operationalized in the distressing transaction patterns, which are today's context for that family's everyday living. Therefore, the therapist will look to this family's present organization and transaction patterns for the explanation for the distress. Second, structural family therapy is a therapy of action—the therapist must get people to *behave* differently if their family context is to change. In order to achieve a change of behavior, the therapist must become a part of the family system needing change. Minuchin expresses the prospective, action orientation of structural family therapy as follows: "The therapist joins the family with the goal of changing family organization in such a way that the family members' experiences change" (1).

The Site of Pathology

As already discussed, the site of pathology is the dysfunctional sets that sustain family stress and prevent the system transformation necessary for effective family functioning. However, a family in distress will usually define its problem as residing in or as caused by one member of the family. They will usually come to the therapist having labeled that member sick or bad. While both Minuchin and Haley look to the family organization to understand the family's problem, they disagree on the approach to the family's definition of the problem. Minuchin argues that the therapist must help the family transform the individual label offered into a diagnosis that includes the whole family (2). He may discuss other problems, explore related areas, or select another "patient," in order to broaden the focus. Haley, on the other hand, argues that the therapist's greatest leverage and first obligation is to change the problem, or symptom, as offered by the patient (3). Thus, the therapist will keep the focus on the symptom and/or problem person as defined by the client system. Both, however, will assess the family's transaction patterns and their flexibility, the family hierarchical arrangement, the delineation and permeability of boundaries, and the subsystems and their functions. The assessment will always include a search for strengths as well as dysfunctional transaction patterns. The process of assessing, diagnosing, and intervening is ongoing and inseparable in action, because diagnosis results from observing the family's response to the therapist's interventions.

For example, consider the Hicks family: Rose, Steve, and their children, Laura age 7 and Paul age 4. During the first interview, Laura is seated between Mr. and Mrs. Hicks, and Paul is on Mrs. Hicks' lap. In response to the therapist's request for a statement of the problem that brings this family for help, Rose speaks first.

ROSE: Steve isn't interested in his kids. He won't behave like a father, and they need a real father.

LAURA: Steve just comes and goes as he pleases. Mommy has to take care of us by herself.

STEVE: (responds to Laura) Shut up. You get that from your Mother.

ROSE: (Pulls Laura to herself and looking at Steve for the first time) Leave her alone. She doesn't have to get that from anyone. She lives in our house, and has learned that she can't count on you for anything.

From observation of this transaction, the therapist might tentatively hypothesize that Mrs. Hicks and the children (at least Laura) are in coalition against Mr. Hicks and that conflict between Mr. and Mrs. Hicks is detoured through the children rather than dealt with in the spouse subsystem. The boundary around the spouse subsystem has become diffuse. A cross-generational subsystem of mother and children versus father appears, and the boundary around this coalition excludes the father.

In an intervention aimed at assessing the degree of flexibility in the transaction patterns of the Hicks family, the therapist takes Laura and Paul by the hand and introduces them to the box of toys in the corner of the room. Laura is instructed to help Paul find a toy to enjoy while the therapist talks some more with Mommy and Dad. This intervention is aimed at drawing the boundary between the spouse and children subsystems and assessing the parents' ability to interact without the mediation of the children. Can they talk to one another, or will the children be drawn away from the toy box and into the interaction?

Therapeutic Tactics

While the idiosyncratic styles of any given therapist and individual family will affect the reality of what and how things happen in therapy, Minuchin has categorized tactics into two general categories—coupling tactics and change-producing tactics (2).

Coupling tactics are those interventions that facilitate the therapist's acceptance by the family and permit joining the family system in order to enhance his/her therapeutic leverage. Coupling tactics include maintenance, tracking, and mimesis. Maintenance involves supporting the family structures and obeying its rules. For example, when the therapist put Laura in charge of helping Paul find a toy to play with, she was accepting the family rules, which defined Laura as a parental child who shared responsibility for Paul. Tracking is a method whereby the therapist adapts the content of family communications, such as referring to the problem in the terms used by the family. Mimesis is adapting the family's style and/or affect, such as when the therapist accommodates to the family with a depressed mood and halting, hesitant transaction patterns by adapting a serious affect and slow patient interaction style. The aim of the coupling tactics is to adapt to the family as it presents itself, so that the therapist will be accepted by the family and permitted to join the system. The coupling tactics are to family therapy what establishing rapport is to individual therapy.

Change-producing tactics, in contrast to the coupling tactics, challenge the family's taken-for-granted style and rules. In therapy, they are aimed at changing the dysfunctional sets.

The use of space during a therapy session can be a change-producing tactic. For example, when the therapist took Laura and Paul by the hand away from Mr. and Mrs. Hicks to the toy box, she was geographically delimiting the spouse and children subsystems and the boundary normally between them. Giving directives and task assignment are also change-producing tactics richly illustrated in the writings of structural family therapists. By these tactics, the therapist instructs the family members to behave in a way that operationalizes a change in family organization. For example, the therapist might direct Mr. and Mrs. Hicks to discuss together what Steve would do if he behaved like a "real father" toward Laura. Let us imagine they decided that if he were a "real father" he would spend some time showing an interest in Laura's activities. The therapist might then introduce this behavior into the family via a task assignment to be carried out between this and the next session. The task assignment is that Steve will take Laura to her next gymnastic lesson and watch the lesson while Rose stays home and cares for Paul. In this example, the change-producing tactic is introducing "real father" behavior into the system coupled with a maintaining tactic that does not challenge the overinvolvement of Rose and Paul. Thus, an established pattern of the system is used to enable a new subsystem to interact without interference.

Finally, a potent change-producing tactic is the iatrogenic crisis induction, where the therapist forces the escalation of stress in the family, so that members are forced to deal with the conflict that has been submerged. Minuchin and his colleagues have been particularly successful in using this tactic in the treatment of psychosomatic families (8). For example, when working with families with an anorectic child, they will sit down with the family at lunch, ask the family to order lunch and direct the parents to make the anorectic child eat. All the conflict around eating is thereby reenacted and available to direct intervention in a way that merely talking about food would never accomplish. Sometimes this tactic is used during the therapy session and sometimes accomplished via a task assignment to be accomplished at home. Whenever using this tactic, however, the therapist must insure his/her availability to help the family deal with the stress so generated.

While coupling tactics and change-producing tactics have been discussed separately in practice, they occur side by side. The therapist inserts slight change-producing probes during the process of assessment, as when the therapist separated the children and Mr. and Mrs. Hicks. And, if change-producing tactics were not accompanied by some support of a familiar pattern, the change tactic would be rejected as totally foreign.

Change Maintenance

Once the therapist has succeeded in getting family members to behave differently, the same self-perpetuating system properties that maintained dysfunctional sets can be counted on to maintain the new functional sets. Thus, after achieving family organization change, the therapist can withdraw, leaving the family to maintain the family context.

CRITIQUE

The family structure model provides many concepts that prove to be sensitizing, informing, and provocative. However, these concepts need greater precision and refinement of assessment guidelines to enable greater reliability among observers. For example, how does an observer identify a subsystem boundary and reliably assess its degree of permeability? Of special need is the study of effectively functioning families across cultural and socioeconomic groups to establish the parameters of variability in family structure and organization. Minuchin's discussion of the kibbutz family (1) is a beginning. Without such knowledge family therapy from any model is burdened with an ethnocentrism. The family structure model, with its relatively neutrally labeled concepts, seems potentially well suited to this task.

Family therapists at the Philadelphia Child Guidance Clinic have certainly been successful in applying the family structure model and in teaching the structural family therapy approach. However, the action orientation of this therapeutic approach calls for a very directive, almost charismatic role on the part of the therapist. Therapists and families uncomfortable with such a style have great difficulty with this approach.

SUMMARY

This chapter has presented the concepts and assumptions central to the family structure model and discussed the application of this model in structural family therapy. The work of Salvador Minuchin and his colleagues at the Philadelphia Child Guidance Clinic have been identified as representative of family therapists who use this approach.

REFERENCES

1. Minuchin, S. *Families and family therapy*. Cambridge, Mass. Harvard University Press, 1974, pp. 55, 9, 13.
2. Minuchin, S. Structural family therapy. In S. Arieti et al. (Eds.), *American handbook of psychiatry* (2nd ed.). New York: Basic Books, 1974, pp. 178–192.
3. Haley, J. *Problem solving therapy*. San Francisco: Jossey-Bass, 1976.
4. Minuchin, S., Baker, L., Rosman, B., Liebman, R., Milman, L., & Todd, T. A conceptual model of psychosomatic illness in children: Family organization and family therapy. *Archives of General Psychiatry*, 1975, *32*, 1031–1038.
5. Minuchin, S., Rosman, B., & Baker, L. *Psychosomatic families*. Cambridge, Mass.: Harvard University Press, 1978.
6. Haley, J. Research on family patterns: An instrument measurement. *Family Process*, 1964, 3, 41–65.
7. Haley, J. Speech sequences of normal and abnormal families with two children present. *Family Process*, 1967, *6*, 81–97.
8. Minuchin, S., & Barcai, A. Therapeutically induced family crisis. In J. H. Masserman (Ed.), *Science and Psychoanalysis* (Vol. XIV). New York: Grune & Stratton, 1969, pp. 199–205.

BIBLIOGRAPHY

Aponte, H., & Hoffman, L. The open door: A structural approach to a family with an anorectic child. *Family Process*, 1973, *12*, 1–44.

Haley, J. Research on family patterns: An instrument measurement. *Family Process*, 1964, *3*, 41–65.

Haley, J. Speech sequences of normal and abnormal families with two children present. *Family Process*, 1967, *6*, 81–97.

Haley, J. *Problem solving therapy*. San Francisco: Jossey-Bass, 1976.

Minuchin, S. *Families and family therapy*. Cambridge, Mass.: Harvard University Press, 1974.

Minuchin, S. Structural family therapy. In S. Arieti (Ed.), *American handbook of psychiatry* (2nd ed.). New York: Basic Books, Inc. 1974, pp. 178–192.

Minuchin, S. The use of an ecological framework in the treatment of a child. In E. J. Anthony, & C. K. Huntington (Eds.), *The child in his family*. New York: Robert E. Keirger, 1979, pp. 41–57.

Minuchin, S., Averswald, E., King, C. H., & Rabinowitz, C. The study and treatment of families that produce multiple acting-out boys. *American Journal of Orthopsychiatry*, 1964, *34*, 125–133.

Minuchin, S., Baker, L., Rosman, B., Liebman, R., Milman, L., & Todd, T. A conceptual model of psychosomatic illness in children: Family organization and family therapy. *Archives of General Psychiatry*. 1975, *32*, 1031–1038.

Minuchin, S., & Barcai, A. Therapeutically induced family crisis. In J. H. Masserman (Ed.), *Science and psychoanalysis* (Vol. XIV). New York: Grune & Stratton, 1969, pp. 199–205.

Minuchin, S., & Montalvo, B. Techniques for working with disorganized low socio-economic families. *American Journal of Orthopsychiatry*, 1967, *37*, 880–887.

Minuchin, S., Montalvo, B., Guerney, B. G., Rosman, B. L., & Schumer, F. *Families of the slums*. New York: Basic Books, 1967.

Minuchin, S., Rosman, B., & Baker, L. *Psychosomatic families*. Cambridge, Mass.: Harvard University Press, 1978.

Rosman, B., Minuchin, S., & Liebman, R. Family lunch session: An introduction to family therapy in anorexia nervosa. *American Journal of Orthopsychiatry*, 1975, *45*, 846–853.

7

Transactional Analysis Model

Linda Dumat

Since its beginnings in 1958, transactional analysis (TA) has become an increasingly popular theoretical framework within which persons in the helping professions can view and treat dysfunctional behavior patterns. Inherent in the theory of transactional analysis is a philosophy about human beings that leads to one of the basic assumptions in TA—people are OK simply for being, and there is a clear distinction between person and behavior.

> This means that each of us, regardless of our behavioral style, has a basic core which is lovable and has the potential and desire for growth and self-actualization (1).

Transactional analysis is a theory of personality structure and human behavior, as well as an effective treatment technique to be used in facilitating change in individuals and groups. Eric Berne (1910–1970), the creator of transactional analysis was a psychoanalytically trained psychiatrist who believed that human beings with emotional difficulties could be cured, rather than being seen as "making progress."

As a *growth model,* transactional analysis focuses on the client's strengths rather than weaknesses. The continuation of dysfunctional behavior patterns is viewed as a result of the lack of options for change on the part of the client. The assumption is that the client will change if given appropriate information to accomplish the change. One of the primary goals of the TA therapist is to introduce new options in thinking, feeling, and acting that the client can use to effect change.

Transactional analysis is also a *decision model*. Dysfunctional behaviors are viewed as a manifestation of outdated decisions made in early childhood that are no longer functional. A positive premise of TA is that these old decisions can be brought into awareness and redecided in the here and now, with a resultant decrease in dysfunctional behavior.

Transactional analysis is based on a *contractual model* with the assumption that people can and will contract for changes in their lives and that they are entitled to a mutual sharing of all aspects of the treatment process.

> The therapeutic contract is simply an agreement between a person and her or his therapist which places responsibility on both parties involved. The client asks for and gives full consent and cooperation to the process of psychotherapy, and the therapist accepts the responsibility for helping to effect the desired changes and for staying within the bounds of the contract (2).

Transactional analysis, as a theory and as a treatment technique, is an appropriate treatment of pathological family systems. It provides a concise framework within which one can observe what is happening in the system. TA offers a conceptual guide for identifying dysfunctional patterns occurring in the family system.

The purpose of this chapter is to identify and briefly define certain key concepts of transactional analysis: ego states, strokes, time structuring, transactions, and games. In addition, we will demonstrate how these concepts can be applied in family treatment and how specific interventions can be made in dysfunctional marital/family systems.

KEY CONCEPTS

Ego States

Eric Berne defines an *ego state* as a coherent system of thoughts and feelings manifested by corresponding patterns of behavior (3). The concept of ego states provides a method for observing internal personality structure, the premise being that the more fully a person understands himself, the more likely he is to relate effectively with others. Each individual has three functional parts to his personality, that is, three separate ego states. These three ego states are designated as the Parent (P), Adult (A), and Child (C). When capitalized these words signify ego states, and otherwise they designate persons.

The *Parent* ego state consists of the attitudes and beliefs a person holds about life. Berne defines a Parent ego state as a "set of feelings, attitudes, and behavior patterns that resemble those of a parental figure" (4). This is the information learned and retained from authority figures in life, primarily from parents. The Parent manifests itself as either nurturing (NP) or critical (CP). An important function of the Parent ego state is to make certain decisions automatic, thereby decreasing the amount of energy required for thinking. The Parent is also used to care for and nurture ourselves and others.

The *Adult* ego state is the computer or data bank of a person's personality. The Adult processes information from external sources, as well as from the person's Parent and Child ego states. The Adult ego state is described by Berne as "an independent set of feelings, attitudes and behavior patterns that are adapted to the current reality and are not affected by Parental prejudices or archaic attitudes left over from childhood" (4). The value of the Adult ego state is that it enables the person to survive by solving problems in the here and now.

The *Child* ego state contains the urges, desires, and feelings of the person. Functionally, there are two parts of the Child ego state: the Adapted Child (AC) and the Free Child (FC) or Natural Child (NC). Berne defines the Child ego state as "a set of feelings, attitudes, and behavior patterns that are relics of the individual's childhood" (4). The Adapted Child acts under the Parental influence and modifies its expression through compliance or rebellion, while the Natural Child tends to be more free, impulsive, and self-indulgent" (4). The Child ego state is valuable in that it is the spontaneous, intuitive, creative, and feeling part of the personality. When free expression of the Child ego state is limited, options for spontaneity, awareness, and closeness are decreased.

Certain words, voice tones, facial expressions, and body language denote particular ego states and can be used to diagnose the ego state from which a person is relating. A point to remember is that no one ego state is more important than the other two. All three are essential for a human being to function effectively, and effective relating requires that the person use the ego state that will serve most functionally in any given situation.

Strokes

A *stroke* is defined as a unit of recognition of self and is a form of stimulation. Stroke exchange is one of the most meaningful activities of human beings. Each person, from birth, has a basic need or hunger for stimulation, and strokes are necessary to meet this need. Research supports the theory that infants who do not receive physical touching or stroking are severely limited in physical and emotional growth, sometimes to the point of death (5). Strokes, then, are necessary for survival. As a person grows into adulthood, the need for stroking does not decrease. Although the person learns to substitute other forms of stroking for physical stroking, the need for physical touch continues to be important throughout life.

Strokes are classified as either positive or negative and can be conditional or unconditional, verbal or nonverbal, or physical. Positive stroking promotes a sense of well-being and OKness, while negative stroking leads to negative feelings and a sense of not-OKness. Conditional stroking is based on behavior, while unconditional strokes are given simply for being. Positive conditional strokes reinforce the OKness of a behavior, while positive unconditional strokes reinforce the OKness of the person. Negative unconditional stroking attacks the integrity of the human being, usually in a psychologically destructive way. The use of conditional stroking is a powerful modifier of behavior and is used in the process of socialization to define acceptable and unacceptable behaviors. Emotionally healthy persons evolve out of an environment that provides an abundant supply of positive strokes, both conditional and unconditional. An important point to remember about strokes is that they are necessary for survival and that human beings will behave in such ways as to get the necessary quota of strokes, either positive or negative—depending on the environment experienced in early life. The more functional human being will seek positive strokes; the more dysfunctional will seek negative strokes. Dysfunctional families usually exhibit negative stroking patterns. Thus, an important intervention in dysfunctional family systems is to teach individual members new stroking patterns so that the necessary positive stroking can be accomplished.

Time Structuring

In addition to the hunger for stimulation, each person is born with a second hunger: the need for *structure*.

> Being bored for a long time hastens emotional and physical deterioration in much the same way as inadequate stroking does. To avoid the pain of boredom, people seek something to do with their time (6).

There are six basic ways to structure time, each of which is used by all human beings in varying degrees: withdrawal, rituals, pastiming activities, games, and intimacy. Since the need for strokes and time structuring is inherent in the human being, it is logical that we will structure our time to secure the strokes we need. Time structuring is the process of receiving, giving, and avoiding strokes. The categories of time structuring refer more to *how* people do things than *what* they do, and an understanding of how a person uses his time enables the person to understand why some days are better than others (7). Depending then on the kinds of strokes being sought, either positive or negative, a person will fill his time obtaining those strokes. As a person moves through the time-structuring continuum from withdrawal to intimacy, involvement of self with others becomes more intense. The more functional the person, the more likely he is to use his time giving and receiving positive strokes and relating on an intimate basis.

Transactions

Transactional analysis proper is a way of looking at what happens between two people when they communicate. Communication is conducted by means of *transactions,* that is, the exchange between two persons consisting of a stimulus and a response (8).

Transactions are considered simple when only two ego states are involved and complex when three or four ego states are involved. In any conversation the person has several options as to which ego state will determine his response and which ego state he will address in the other individual. The more functional person will exercise the option of initiating and responding from the ego state that will serve him best; for example, he will respond to a request for information from the Adult ego state rather than from the Critical Parent. In most cases, relating from the Critical Parent will invite a response from the other person's Rebellious Child. This may escalate conflict or competition and prevent the desired direction of the conversation.

The three categories of transactions are *complementary* (parallel), *crossed,* and *ulterior,* each having an accompanying rule of communication. A complementary transaction involves one ego state in each person and the communications, or vectors, are parallel (Figures 7-1 and 7-2). The accompanying rule is that communication can continue indefinitely as long as the vectors remain parallel. A crossed transaction is one in which the communications, or vectors, are parallel. The accompanying rule is that communication can continue indefinitely as long as the vectors remain parallel (Figures 7-1, 7-2). A crossed transaction is one in which the lines of communication are not parallel and the response to the stimulus is not from the expected ego state. The accompanying rule is that communication either stops or takes a different direction than originally intended when the vectors are crossed (Figure 7-3). An ulterior transaction occurs when there is a social level message (words) and a psychological level message. The accompanying rule is that the psychological level message will determine the outcome of the transaction. Ulterior transactions are frequently invitations to games (Figure 7-4).

Games

Games are sets of ulterior transactions, repetitive in nature, with a well-defined psychological payoff (3).

Games, from a TA perspective, are not played for fun and lead to bad feeling payoffs for the parties involved. They provide a way to structure time but frequently prevent intimacy with self and others. Games are played outside of Adult awareness and provide stroke exchange in an ulterior way without exposing the player to the risk-taking required for intimacy. Games are repetitive, learned behavior patterns involving a discount

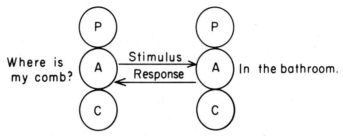

Figure 7-1 Complementary transaction, adult—adult.

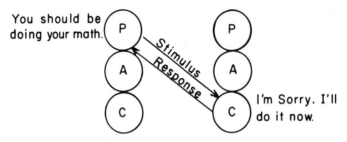

Figure 7-2 Complementary transaction, parent—child.

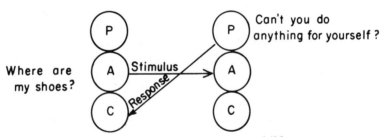

Figure 7-3 Crossed transaction, adult—adult, parent—child.

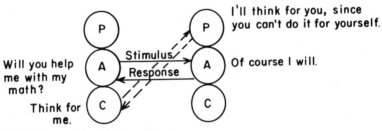

Figure 7-4 Ulterior, duplex transaction.

or "con," and most people have a selected repertoire of favorite games. People intuitively find others who play related complementary games, so it is not surprising that long-term relationships such as marital and family relationships provide an opportunity for game playing of great intensity.

Figure 7-4 demonstrates the opening transactions of a game. The reader is referred to Eric Berne's book *Games People Play* for understanding and application of game theory (9).

THERAPIST'S MODEL

> I believe that the vocabulary of TA and its concepts can be added to those of other therapies to further clarify what's happening in the lives of patients and open the way to consideration of more satisfying options (10).

Transactional analysis is an appropriate mode of therapy for use by psychotherapists from varied professional backgrounds and training. Psychiatric nurses in particular have been identified as having considerable skills and expertise in working with families.* The emphasis of treatment in a TA model is on the here and now, using what happens between family members in the session as a framework for solving problems. Use of ego states, stroking patterns, transactions, and games are observed and identified, thus forming the basis for contracting for change.

IMPLICATIONS FOR FAMILY TREATMENT

The key concepts presented in this chapter provide a framework within which specific interventions can be made with troubled marital and family systems. One of the most valuable assets of TA is the ease with which it can be taught to clients. One of the commitments of the TA therapist is to help clients facilitate their own progress by placing certain therapeutic tools at their disposal. Teaching TA concepts, an important intervention in itself, is included early in treatment and continues throughout the treatment process. The sharing of Adult information provides a method for couples and families to better understand their relationship difficulties. This sharing promotes a cooperative effort to view problems in a common framework and, therefore, decreases the emphasis on personal blames and shortcomings.

As stated earlier, the emotionally healthy person has all parts of himself at his disposal and can relate out of the ego state that will serve him best. Observation of distressed families usually reveals repetitive patterns

---

* For information about TA training programs and qualified teachers in your area, write to I.T.A.A., P.O. Box 3932, Rincon Annex, San Francisco, California 94199.

of relating out of specific ego states. There is generally little Adult-to-Adult relating, and an absence of Natural Child-to-Natural Child transactions is noted. Frequently communications are limited to Critical Parent-to-Adapted Child, Adapted Child-to-Adapted Child, and Critical Parent-to-Critical Parent transactions.

These kinds of transactions enhance conditions for conflict and competitiveness and lead to dysfunctional problem solving and family discord. In such a climate, options for sharing are limited and emotional needs are unmet. The goal of the therapist early in treatment is to demonstrate that the use of an appropriate ego state can produce a difference in the outcome of a transaction. The client can then learn to communicate in such a way that his emotional needs are satisfied.

An equally important goal of the therapist is to increase the positive stroking in the family system. As the therapist observes for stroking patterns, a lack of positive stroking will usually emerge. Steiner names five rules that ensure stroke starvation in people. These are "(1) Don't give strokes; (2) Don't ask for strokes; (3) Don't accept strokes; (4) Don't reject strokes you don't want, and (5) Don't give yourself strokes" (2). The therapist identifies how members of the family maintain stroke deprivation and then contracts for change in this area. Sessions are designed to teach family members how to ask for, give, and receive positive strokes. The therapist also "role models" by freely giving, requesting, and receiving positive strokes.

Along with the stroke theory, information is given on time structuring. Family members become aware of the relationship between how they structure time and the amount and kinds of strokes they receive. Frequently an analysis of the family's time-structuring patterns is done. With this awareness family members can then contract to spend their time differently and thus increase options for positive stroke exchange, sharing, and intimacy.

Since most distressed families are limited in their use of ego states, it follows that their transactions are frequently limited as well. Effective problem solving is often hindered because communications are locked into Critical Parent-to-Adapted Child responses, with very little Adult-to-Adult interaction. As Lester states:

> The relationship feels "out of control" as the partners struggle to meet their own and each other's needs from archaic Parent tapes and unreasonable Child demands. The result is a suppression of Free Child needs (11).

Again the TA therapist shares information and feedback about transactions and rules of communication so that family members can contract from their Adult ego states to exercise new options in relating. The use of transactional diagrams enhance the speed with which clients process this information for change.

The goal of the therapist is to teach family members to get their emotional needs met in an open, straightforward way through the use of Adult ego states. This necessitates a decrease in the number of ulterior transactions taking place between family members. As stated earlier, psychological games take place outside of Adult awareness and result in bad feelings and negative strokes. The task of the therapist is to intervene in such a way that the psychological games may be stopped. Dusay outlines four specific interventions for games: (*1*) exposing the game, (*2*) ignoring the game, (*3*) offering an alternative, and (*4*) playing the game. He further emphasizes that none of the four responses is inevitably good or bad, but that choices are to be made appropriate to the therapeutic contract (12). This author's personal experience supports *exposing the game* and *offering an alternative* as the two options most likely to promote growth in the client. Exposing the game includes identifying the game, teaching game theory, and using game diagrams; offering an alternative includes teaching new options for procuring strokes and meeting underlying emotional needs in a straightforward way. Again, the client can contract for change and is given an opportunity to practice new behaviors during the session.

SUMMARY

Transactional analysis (TA) is a popular theory concerning personality structure and human behavior and has evolved as an effective treatment technique in aiding change in dysfunctional human behavior. The primary goal of the TA therapist is to promote the client's awareness of the options for change and to demonstrate the benefits of appropriate behavior.

Treatment techniques include teaching TA methods and terminology. The concepts and vocabulary of the theory are easily learned and appeal to the lay person. It is particularly useful in family treatment in that the concepts are easily retained and understood by children. A contractual agreement is procured between the client(s) and therapist to effect positive communication in relationships. Existing behaviors are examined in a positive manner, and information regarding options for change is made available. The client takes an active part in the decision making and problem solving required to effect appropriate change. The client benefits by (*1*) acquiring an awareness of self, (*2*) recognizing his own personal needs and the needs of others, and (*3*) developing an understanding of how to satisfy those needs with positive, straightforward communication.

REFERENCES

1. Woollams, S., & Brown, M. *Transactional analysis.* Dexter, Mich.: Huron Valley Institute, 1978.

2. Steiner, C. M. *Scripts people live*. New York: Grove Press (Bantam Books), 1975. (Reprinted by permission of Grove Press, Inc., Copyright © 1974 by Claude Steiner.)

3. Berne, E. *What do you say after you say hello*. New York: Bantam Books published by Arrangement with Grove Press, Inc., 1975 (Permission granted by Random House, Inc., © 1972).

4. Berne, E. *The structure and dynamics of organizations and groups*. New York: Ballantine Books, 1973, p. 185, 184, 186 (Reprinted by permission of Harper and Row, Publishers, Inc.)

5. Spitz, R. Hospitalism: Genesis of psychiatric conditions in early childhood. *Psychoanalytic Study of the Child*, 1945, *1*, 53–74.

6. James, M., & Jongeward, D. *Born to win*. Reading, Mass.: Addison Wesley, 1975. (Reprinted by permission of Addison-Wesley Publishing Co., Reading, Mass.)

7. Elder, J. *Transactional analysis in health care*. (Reprinted by permission of Addison-Wesley Publishing Co., 1978.)

8. Woollams, S., Brown, M., & Huige, K. *Transactional analysis in brief*. Ann Arbor, Mich.: Huron Valley Institute, 1976.

9. Berne, E. *Games people play*. New York: Grove Press, 1964.

10. Horewitz, J. S. *Family therapy and transactional analysis*. New York and London: Jason Aronson, 1979.

11. Lester, G. W. TA marital therapy. *Transactional Analysis Journal*, 1980, *10*(1), p. 33.

12. Dusay, J. M. Response to games in therapy. *Transactional Analysis Bulletin* (Selected articles, Vols. 1–9), TA Press, 1976.

8

Behavioral Family Therapy Model

Susan Van Gee and Perry M. Nicassio

Behavior therapy, or behavior modification,* encompasses a wide range of therapeutic interventions that seek the systematic alteration of behaviors that are inhibiting personal adjustment. Indeed, the clinical problems that have served as targets for behavioral interventions have been as diverse as the techniques that have been employed for their remediation and have included such conditions as fears and phobias, psychotic disorders, obsessive-compulsive neuroses, insomnia, language disorders, and psychophysiological disorders to name only a few. It is the application of behavior therapy to such problems within the context of the family that constitutes behavioral family therapy.

This chapter, then, has a twofold purpose: (*1*) to describe the origins, fundamental principles, and key terms of the behavioral approach and (*2*) to discuss and illustrate the application of behavior therapy within a family therapy format.

BEHAVIOR THERAPY

The origins of behavior therapy can be traced to the experimental work of Russian scientists in the nineteenth century. Ivan Pavlov developed the classical conditioning learning paradigm that contributed significantly to

* Although distinctions occasionally have been made between behavior therapy and behavior modification, such distinctions typically have proven to be artificial or meaningless when examined on empirical grounds. Since modification is central to the process of therapy of any type, these two terms are used interchangeably in this chapter.

an understanding of both the development and treatment of anxiety-mediated disorders. John B. Watson and B. F. Skinner, American psychologists, whose research on learning and operant conditioning in the early and middle twentieth century was instrumental in developing the science of behaviorism, laid the empirical groundwork for behavior therapy as a clinical discipline. As currently conceived and practiced, however, behavior therapy extends far beyond its early experimental psychology origins and embraces a number of different theoretical influences (1).

Behavior therapy is a relatively new treatment model in the field of mental health. In large part, the impetus for the development of behavior therapy grew out of an increasing dissatisfaction with the traditional psychoanalytic mode of treatment and diagnosis, which represents an extension of the medical model of physical abnormality to the problems of psychological adjustment. Thus, a comparison of behavioral and psychodynamic treatment modalities provides a context for a more detailed discussion of behavior therapy.

Significant contrasts are apparent in the theoretical basis for each modality. Behavior therapy relies heavily on principles of operant, classical, and observational learning. It emphasizes a highly experimental data base. The psychodynamic model is nonexperimental in its orientation, emphasizing instead the phenomenology of the individual. The behavioral and psychodynamic models offer different causes for behavior problems. The behavioral approach views independent observable environmental factors as primary causes while the psychodynamic model views the causes of behavior problems as largely internal to the individual.

The contrasting theoretical bases logically lead to different approaches to diagnosis and treatment. Behavior therapy focuses directly on problem behaviors as targets of clinical intervention, while traditional psychodynamic diagnosis considers problem behaviors as symptoms of intrapsychic conflict. Differing treatment goals result from the two approaches. Behavior therapy seeks to (1) achieve experimental control over problem behavior, (2) change maladaptive behavior in the natural environment, and (3) assist patients in learning to exert independent control over maladaptive behavior. Psychodynamic treatment aims at removing internal conflict or the "disease" process responsible for the problem and assisting patients in achieving "insight" into their feelings and behaviors.

To assess progress in treatment, the behavior therapist uses systematized behavioral observation and recording procedures, directly measuring behavior during baseline, treatment, and posttreatment phases. Experimental validation of the effect of treatment is critical. The assessment of progress in psychodynamic therapy depends largely on the therapist's interpretation of the patient's experiences during treatment. The therapist relies on the patient's verbal report of such experiences to provide evidence of change. The role of the behavior therapist also differs substantively from that of the psychodynamic therapist. The behavior therapist assumes major responsibility for designing the treatment program, while the psychodynamic counterpart encourages patients to seek solutions with the therapist functioning as a catalyst or facilitator. The behavior therapist sees principles of behavior as responsible for effecting change. As a result, the interpersonal relationship between therapist and patient may facilitate, but is not central to, change in patient behaviors. In contrast, the interpersonal dynamics between the therapist and patient are the major vehicle for change in psychodynamic therapy.

With these basic points of contrast established, the special characteristics of behavior therapy can be examined. Perhaps the most salient, distinguishing characteristic of behavior therapy concerns the manner in which problems of adjustment are defined and analyzed. In behavior therapy, diagnostic considerations and therapeutic attention are directed at overt behaviors, typically defined as behavioral excesses or deficits, that are either creating adjustment problems or are otherwise limiting human functioning. In so doing, behavior therapists seek to operationally define clinical problems in terms that refer to specific behaviors that can be reliably observed, measured, and evaluated quantitatively. In a case of depression, for example, depressive behaviors would be observed and measured with subsequent therapy directed toward their remediation. Similarly, the inappropriate behaviors that schizophrenics exhibit, rather than schizophrenia as an underlying disease process, would receive the clinical attention of behaviorally oriented clinicians.

In behavior therapy, the role of learning is central to an understanding of how behavior problems may develop as well as how they may be treated. Principles of operant, classical, and observational learning are seen as both contributing to and as offering potential solutions to many clinical conditions. The principles in these learning models heavily emphasize that behavior is influenced by environmental events and that the factors that maintain behavior may be distinct from the behavior's precipitating causes.

Thus, in attempting to determine the factors that are maintaining a clinical problem, the behavior therapist focuses on the impact that environmental events have on the incidence and strength of specific observable behaviors. The behavior analysis, which provides detailed information concerning the relationship between antecedent and consequent events and the frequency of specific targeted behaviors, forms the basis for treatment interventions. Typically, treatment strategies attempt to alter environmental events using learning principles to bring about desirable behavioral changes, although recently behavior therapists have begun to attribute more instrumental importance to people themselves as their own behavior change agents. The theme of self-control is vigorously emphasized by advocates of cognitive behavior therapy who stress that cognitive processes such as perception, attention, and self-evaluation may mediate the effect of environmental events on overt behavior (2).

Another significant, distinguishing feature of behavior therapy is the emphasis on evaluation of treatment interventions. The operationalization and quantification of specific behavioral targets permits their assessment under baseline, treatment, and follow-up. Various research designs (3) may be used effectively to rule out the influence of uncontrolled factors in evaluating the impact of treatment techniques. The careful attention to assessment and systematic evaluation of treatment strategies has helped to create the emerging role of scientist-practitioner for the clinician. Systematic evaluation has also documented the validity of various therapeutic strategies and can suggest alternate procedures when the data indicate that current treatment is ineffective.

Key Terms

Baseline.   A baseline constitutes an assessment period before a treatment intervention. A baseline assessment of a behavior is an indication of the strength or frequency of the behavior under natural conditions (i.e., in the environment(s) in which the behavior occurs) before treatment is implemented. Baseline levels of targeted behaviors are used to evaluate the efficacy of subsequent treatment interventions. Example: A patient smoked an average of 51.2 cigarettes per day before receiving behavior therapy to reduce her smoking behavior.

Positive Reinforcement.   Positive reinforcement refers to a process in which the strength of a behavior is increased by the introduction of a desirable event or stimulus that follows the behavior. Example: When a schizophrenic patient exhibits nonpsychotic speech, ward staff provide social attention and praise to the patient.

Negative Reinforcement.   Negative reinforcement refers to a process in which the strength of a behavior is increased by the removal of an aversive event or stimulus that follows the behavior. Example: When an autistic child stops his self-injurious behavior, he terminates a mild electric shock to the forearm.

Reinforcement Schedule.   A reinforcement schedule defines how frequently a response is reinforced. In a *continuous* reinforcement schedule, a response is reinforced each time that it occurs. In an *intermittent* reinforcement schedule, several occurrences of the response take place before the reinforcer is delivered.

Modeling.   Learning may take place vicariously. Behaviors that are exhibited or modeled by one person may be learned and initiated by an observer if (*1*) the model is of high social status or influence, (2) the model is perceived to be similar (e.g., same sex) to the observer, and (*3*) the behavior of the model is reinforced. Example: A boy, in imitation of his father, may carry his father's briefcase to "work" while playing with his friends.

Extinction. Extinction is a process in which the withholding of all reinforcement for a response leads to a significant decline in its strength or frequency, and ultimately to its cessation. Example: In order to decrease the sick role behavior of a hospitalized patient, the nursing staff withholds all attention and care whenever such behavior is exhibited.

Punishment. Punishment refers to a process in which the strength or frequency of a response is reduced by (*1*) introducing an aversive stimulus or event immediately following the response. Example: Whenever a psychotic child exhibits self-injurious behavior, a mild, electric shock is delivered to his forearm, or (*2*) immediately deleting, or subtracting, portions of a reinforcer following the response. Example: For his aggressive behavior in the classroom, a child forfeits opportunities for free play. A variation of this latter theme occurs in time-out procedures when the person is extricated from a reinforcing environment for his or her inappropriate behavior.

Self-control. Self-control refers to the ability to exhibit a directional change in a response in the absence of any environmental contingencies or influences. The achievement of self-control should be the terminal goal of any behavior therapy program. Example: In the case of a formerly obese woman who has undergone behavior therapy in order to lose weight, self-control is exhibited when she follows her newly developed eating habits *without* rewarding herself for doing so.

Implications for Family Therapy

The behavioral therapy literature has been chiefly characterized by studies that have explored the use of learning principles in changing the behavior of problem children (4). The main thrust of such studies has been to show the profound impact that parenting behaviors may have on the problems of children. Through such procedures as the rearrangement of systems of reinforcement for appropriate behavior, the withholding of reinforcement for maladaptive behavior, and the consistent modeling by parents of classes of appropriate behaviors to children, a range of problem conditions including social aggression, hyperactivity, noncompliance, and tantrumming can be effectively controlled (5, 6).

In spite of the emphasis that has been placed on the management of the behavior problems of children within families, behavior therapy procedures have a much greater range of applicability. Indeed, behavioral techniques also can be used effectively to help remediate the problems of adults, particularly when other family members can be used as resources or behavior change agents. Thus, the spouses and other family members of alcoholics may learn to avoid patterns of interaction that may precipitate conflict leading to uncontrolled drinking and to reinforce abstinence and sobriety (7). Similarly, family members may have a direct role in reinforcing the coping behaviors of a chronically depressed spouse, parent, or sibling (8).

Many clinicians and behavioral scientists have made substantial contributions to the field of behavioral family therapy. The work of three scientists is highlighted here to illustrate areas in which behavioral family therapy has been applied successfully.

Dr. Gerald Patterson, past president of the Association for the Advancement of Behavior Therapy, has made significant contributions to both the study and management of aggressive behavior in children. Using a social learning approach, Dr. Patterson's research and clinical work has emphasized the critical role of the home and school environments in both the development and treatment of aggressive behavior problems.

Dr. Todd Risely has also done pioneering work, using principles of operant learning in the child management field. He views our society as being a detriment to the socialization of children through the stresses of moving, divorce, and lack of extended family support. His work has led several university day-care centers to provide child-rearing assistance that parents are unable to render.

Dr. Richard Stuart, also a former president of the Association for the Advancement of Behavior Therapy, has written extensively on the use of behavioral techniques in the management of marital problems and delinquent behavior. His work has highlighted the effectiveness of contingency contracting among family members in reducing marital and other types of family conflict.

Implementing a Family Therapy Program

Identifying behavioral goals and operationalizing problems in concrete, behavioral terms is vital to the success of any behavior therapy program. While establishing the direction of therapy may be quite simple, for example, in the management of the tantrumming behavior of a 3-year-old child, in other instances this task may be very difficult due to a lack of consensus on the part of the family members themselves about the nature of their problems. A series of clinical interviews with the family members individually and collectively brings behavior problems into clear focus. Indeed, several problems may be operationalized with therapeutic goals related to each.

The next step in the implementation of a behavior therapy program would be to conduct a baseline assessment of the problem behaviors in the environments in which they occur. Data would thus be provided on the incidence of the problem behaviors before treatment is initiated. During the baseline phase, particular attention also should be given to antecedent events that precipitate the behaviors as well as the consequences that follow them. It is important that baseline data be collected accurately, and if possible, unobstrusively, in order to insure that the measurement process itself does not alter the target behaviors. A variety of measurement procedures may be employed, including direct observation of the problem behaviors in the family environment, self-monitoring of the behaviors by family members, and automated recording procedures (9, 10).

After baseline data are collected and evaluated, the therapeutic plan should be constructed and implemented. The therapeutic interventions should take place in the family environments in which the problem behaviors occur and should seek to alter the environmental events that lead to and maintain such behaviors. In working with families, therapists should recognize that frequently deviant behavior patterns are reciprocally controlled by members of the family unit (11). Changes in the maladaptive behavior of one person may thus require concomitant changes in the behavior of several family members.

Typically, behavioral family therapy programs are aimed at (1) decreasing the frequency of undesirable behaviors, (2) increasing the strength of adaptive patterns of interactions, and (3) teaching new behavior patterns that have not been learned and therefore cannot be performed by family members. The breadth, as well as the specific modes of behavioral intervention would depend, of course, on the behaviors that have been measured and evaluated.

Frequently, providing positive reinforcement for adaptive behaviors that are occurring at a low frequency may not only strengthen such behaviors but may also weaken undesirable behavior if extinction procedures are concurrently implemented. For example, giving social praise and attention for cooperative behavior in an aggressive child may not only increase such behavior but may also inhibit aggressive responsiveness.

In some instances, however, undesirable behavior will not significantly decrease during extinction if previously the behavior has been intermittently reinforced. Although punishment or aversive procedures should be generally eschewed in working with families, they may be implemented when extinction is either apt to be ineffective or is likely to cause a prolongation of a behavior problem (e.g., a self-abusive behavior) that poses a threat to personal safety. In all cases, whenever extinction or punishment is used to decrease undesirable behaviors, reinforcement should be provided for incompatible, desirable responses.

Even when dealing with a focal behavior problem like the one above, clinicians should stress to other family members that they may also need to change their behavior toward the aggressive child, and that, in a sense, they all share the problem. A communal philosophy of conjoint behavioral management should pervade all behavioral family therapy efforts. Behavioral contracts are an effective means of establishing contingencies and promoting a sense of cooperation among family members in implementing a behavior therapy program. The contract specifies the relationship between behaviors to be changed and their consequences. It delineates the reinforcers desired by the members of the family for exhibiting targeted behaviors and includes sanctions for not meeting the terms of the contract and for other inappropriate behaviors.

As Kazdin notes, the behavioral or contingency contract possesses some distinct advantages (9). First, and perhaps most important, when clients are allowed to have input into the design or implementation of a behavior therapy program, their performances are usually better than if the program is imposed on them. Second, the contract makes the contingencies explicit, but at the same time it allows for the possibility of renegotiation when desired behavior change occurs. Third, the contract itself may help restructure family relationships toward successful resolution of problems.

In some cases, rearranging contingencies of reinforcement to promote targeted behavior changes may not be effective if the requisite behaviors are not performed because they have not been learned. For example, problems may exist in some families because family members have not learned to communicate or to solve problems jointly. With such families, clinicians must provide a program of structured learning experiences that are designed to teach new patterns of interaction. A variety of approaches may be applied in such instances. In one such technique, behavioral rehearsal, family members acquire experience in new forms of interaction under simulated conditions with therapist guidance. The therapist may model appropriate behaviors to be enacted by family members who then receive feedback concerning the appropriateness of their responses. The videotape can be used to evaluate interactions and to provide a measure of the progress of the therapy as well. Behavioral skills that may be applied to a number of problems may thus be acquired.

As behavioral strategies are implemented, target behaviors should continue to be assessed so that the course of therapy can be monitored. Such data are instrumental in evaluating the impact of treatment interventions and at the same time provide feedback to the therapists and clients that is helpful in making effective clinical decisions.

CRITIQUE

Despite the stereotypic view of behavior therapy as being mechanistic and impersonal, it still remains one of the most expedient, cost-effective means of treating family behavior problems. However, due to its focal thrust, it may be appropriate at times to use other types of treatment models concurrently with behavior interventions. A combination of behavioral and other types of family therapy techniques is needed, for example, to allow for exploration of interpersonal family relationships. Therefore, a therapeutic approach based on a combination of complementary techniques can often be beneficial.

Questions still remain, however, regarding the effectiveness of behavioral family therapy in many areas of clinical intervention. Although considerable evidence attests to the efficacy of behavioral techniques in parenting and child management, a lack of data exists for adequate evaluation of behavior therapy for other types of family problems. Studies are also needed that compare behavior therapy with other family therapy techniques in the same clinical areas so that the relative efficacy of behavioral procedures can be ascertained.

Questions have also risen with respect to the ethics of behavioral interventions. Since behavior therapy stresses the control of human behavior and places less emphasis than other clinical approaches on human emotion and cognitive processes, the charge occasionally has been made that behavior therapy is an unduly manipulative and perhaps even an ethically questionable treatment procedure. Indeed, behavior control and the ethics of behavior therapy and psychotherapy are extremely complex issues that have been discussed at length elsewhere (12–14). Behavior control and therapist influence, however, are factors of major importance in the practice of both behavior therapy and psychotherapy, and for many, it is primarily the explicitness with which behavior control is stated as an objective in behavior therapy that is alarming to some professionals.

Moreover, a crucial distinction must be made between the discipline of behavior therapy as a technology and the goals or ends that it serves. It may be cogently argued, for example, that as a technology behavior therapy is value-free and that ethical concerns are only relevant when discussing the manner in which it is applied (14). Behavior therapy, like other forms of therapy, may be applied coercively to meet the needs of Machiavellian controllers, or it may be implemented with the complete understanding and consent of clients to enable them to develop self-control over their personal problems and to enhance their individual freedom.

SUMMARY

Behavior therapy has experienced considerable growth and development since its relatively recent inception. Based primarily on learning principles, behavior therapy has provided an effective technology for the treatment of a wide range of clinical problems, from profound psychiatric disorders to less severe but still debilitating neurotic disturbances. It has introduced empirical rigor into the fields of clinical psychology and psychiatry with its emphasis on assessing measurable behaviors and evaluating treatment outcome. Behavior therapy, in focusing on the role of the environment in shaping human behavior, has provided an alternate model for viewing human adjustment problems that contrasts significantly with the more traditional psychodynamic perspective.

With families, behavior therapy has illustrated how maladaptive patterns of interaction may develop as well as how they may be remediated through the systematic application of operant conditioning and other types of learning principles. Behavior therapists stress the point that behaviors within the family unit typically are reciprocally controlled and that a conjoint approach involving the participation of the entire family is essential for developing more adaptive patterns of interaction.

Behavioral family therapy can be used effectively in concurrence with other types of treatment, although its efficacy in treating many family problems has yet to be demonstrated. Additional research is needed to evaluate its usefulness in solving family problems other than child management. While behavior therapy raises ethical questions concerning the control of human behavior, it must be stressed that behavior therapy itself is value-free.

REFERENCES

1. Kazdin, A. Fictions, factions, and functions of behavior therapy. *Behavior Therapy,* 1979, *10,* 629–654.

2. Meichenbaum, D. *Cognitive behavior modification: An integrative approach.* New York: Plenum, 1977.

3. Hersen, M., & Barlow, D. *Single case experimental designs.* New York: Pergamon, 1976.

4. Mash, E., Hamerlynck, L., & Handy, L. (Eds.). *Behavior modification and families.* New York: Brunner/Mazel, 1976.

5. Patterson, G. *Families: Applications of social learning to family life.* Champaign, Ill.: Research Press, 1971.

6. Patterson, G., & Gullion, M. *Living with children: New methods for parents and teachers.* Champaign, Ill.: Research Press, 1968.

7. Miller, P. *Behavioral treatment of alcoholism.* New York: Pergamon, 1976.

8. Lewinsohn, P. The behavioral study and treatment of depression. In M. Hersen et al. (Eds.), *Progress in behavior modification* (Vol. 1). New York: Academic Press, 1975, pp. 19–65.

9. Kazdin, A. *Behavior modification in applied settings.* Homewood, Ill.: Dorsey Press, 1975.

10. Christensen, A., Johnson, S., Phillips, S., & Glasgow, R. Cost effectiveness in behavioral family therapy. *Behavior Therapy,* 1980, *11,* 208–226.

11. Corson, J. Families as mutual control systems: Optimization by systematization of reinforcement. In E. Mash et al. (Eds.), *Behavior modification and families.* New York: Brunner/Mazel, 1967, pp. 317–330.

12. London, P. *The modes and morals of psychotherapy.* New York: Holt, Rinehart, & Winston, 1964.

13. London, P. *Behavior control.* New York: Harper & Row, 1969.

14. Skinner, B. F. *Beyond freedom and dignity.* New York: Knopf, 1971.

9
Family Communication Model

Beverly Young

The beginning family therapist needs to develop a basic framework to deal with the family. A communication approach is one way that can provide such a framework for working with the family.

This chapter develops a communication model using a systems perspective as a basis. Primary issues addressed include the delineation of family communication principles, levels of communication, and the interactional patterns between family members. Implications of these factors in the clinical setting are also discussed.

Haley and Watzlawick are often identified as significant contributors to the development of communication theory. Thus, the beginning family therapist attempting to use a communication approach would benefit from reviewing the work of Haley (1, 2) and Watzlawick (3, 4).

A COMMUNICATION MODEL

When one shifts to the study of the two person system, he is entering the field of *communication* and must describe the individual in terms which apply to the exchange of communicative behaviors between two or more persons (5).

This model of family therapy emphasizes recurring interaction patterns between family members in the "here and now." Watzlawick states, "Human interaction is described as a communication system" (3). Of special attention are repetitive communication patterns that appear to serve the function of handling the family distress. Watzlawick states, "the beginning point in family therapy is to start by 'scanning for patterns' within the family system" (6). Family relationships seem to have a reciprocal nature that can promote cyclical patterns of dysfunction. Family members reinforce patterns of communication within the family system.

Family Communication Principles

"An interactional system is defined as two or more communicants in the process of or at the level of defining the nature of their relationship" (3). Family systems are composed of individual human parts that communicate with other parts to develop a relationship. Further, the environment functions as a suprasystem that contributes to changes that occur within the family system.

More specifically, Watzlawick defines several properties of open systems that are useful to this approach. These include the following: (1) wholeness, (2) feedback, and (3) equifinality (3).

Wholeness. A family system can be viewed as a relationship system with each individual part having influence on all other parts. Therefore, this principle suggests that change in an individual member of the family system promotes change within the entire family system.

Feedback. Feedback is a means of putting information back into a system. All systems have inputs and outputs that cross over their boundaries, providing information to the system for its use in altering, correcting, continuing, amplifying, or changing the behavior of the system.

Equifinality. Watzlawick applies the concept of equifinality by saying that in "a circular and self-modifying system, 'results' are not determined so much by initial conditions as by the nature of the process, or the systems parameters" (3). This suggests that within the family interaction it is generally less important to be concerned with the content as it is to focus on the ongoing patterned interaction.

Levels of Communication

Communication is the actual information that is transmitted through messages sent and received between individuals. Metacommunication goes further to focus on "communicating about the communication" (5). Satir says, "Communication is like a film camera equipped with sound. It works only in the present right here, right now, between you and me" (7). For example, if a mother says to her child, "I love you," and then pushes the child away, what is likely experienced by the child is an incongruent message.

Dysfunction then may be defined as a relationship problem. Andrews suggests that "failures in communication that perpetuate a dysfunctional relationship are derived from four sources:

1. Sender's message is unclear
2. A distorted message is received
3. An inability to check out the meaning between the persons occurs
4. Combination of the above" (8)

Differentiating the Functional Versus the Dysfunctional Family

From this perspective, a functional family occurs as an open system where messages are sent and received, are clear and precise, and are congruent within the context of the situation. The functional family promotes nurturance among its family members. Individual self-worth also increases through communication among family members.

A dysfunctional family is viewed as a partially closed system where messages are sent and received in ways that are vague and/or incongruent within the context of the situation. The dysfunctional family does not fully nurture family members, and the individual's self-worth usually decreases through these patterns of family communication.

USE IN THE CLINICAL SETTING

In dealing with families from a communication approach, the therapist is often guided by "viewing family therapy not as a method but as an orientation to the arena of human problems" (1). The therapist's orientation underscores the importance of looking at processes among family members. This, then, delineates a perspective of working with people in a different light. Even if a therapist works with an individual family member as a way in intervening within a family system, there is maintained an orientation toward the processes among all family members.

As mentioned earlier, the dysfunctional family typically demonstrates dysfunctional patterns within the family system. This is the starting point in dealing with the family distress. Haley suggests that after the family members have interacted with one another, the goal for obtaining change is to determine what the family wants from therapy (2). The goal of work, then, is to deal with problems as defined by the family that the family wants to change. "The goal is not to teach the family about their malfunctioning system but to change the family sequences so that the presenting problems are resolved" (2).

Clinical Example

The J. family consists of Mr. and Mrs. J. and their daughters, S., 10 years old, and D., 6 years old. The family was referred for family therapy after S. had been seen in individual therapy at a child guidance center. The parents were being seen separately by another therapist.

At the initial interview, the two children sat between the parents. The interview began with Mrs. J. initiating the communication. The therapist asked what the family would like to get out of this session.

MRS. J.:   S. has many behavior problems at home and has been seen in individual therapy, which did not help. We simply can't control S.

(S begins shaking her head back and forth)

MRS. J.:   (points to S.) See how S. is, she constantly shakes her head. I think it is just to get attention. Won't you please stop?!

(S. stops for a few minutes)

MRS. J.:   We have tried everything to control S.'s behavior and nothing works.

MR. J.:   I agree with my wife. She has done the best she can do.

(D. remained silent and moved closer to Mrs. J. who seemed to support this move. D. was identified as having no problems).

In observing the interaction between family members, the identified problem was S.'s behavior. The interaction appeared to be one of the father being somewhat passive and the mother attempting to do the best she can for the daughter. The therapist speculated that the father was basically uninvolved and isolated without support. The mother seemed to gain support through her daughter who she repeatedly attempted "to help." S. appeared to be overly involved with her mother, thereby decreasing her ability to become autonomous.

Intervention Strategies

Haley and Watzlawick explicate several methods of intervention. These include two major modes: (1) therapeutic paradoxes and (2) reframing as a technique to promote second order change.

Paradox is defined as "a contradiction that follows correct deduction from consistent premises" (3). Thus, with a paradoxical approach, two levels of communication occur. Haley stated, "Two messages are generally communicated—'change within the framework of the message, don't change'" (2). Paradoxically, the message must be disobeyed to be obeyed.

The J. family identified S. as being the problem and their inability to get S. to follow the family rules. The identified problem within the family interview was S.'s constant head shaking, which the parents define as S.'s attention-getting mechanism. The therapist suggested the possibility that it may be better for the parents not to exercise so much conrol over S. Rather, it was suggested that it might be useful to reinforce S. being in control of herself. The therapeutic paradox employed was to have the parents encourage S.'s head shaking, which demonstrates the request of not changing, yet, also changing.

The therapist requested the parents to encourage S's head shaking. Mr. and Mrs. J. both appeared confused and looked at the therapist in disbelief. With encouragement, the parents jointly agreed to encourage S., which promoted their parental control and dissipated S.'s head shaking.

Reframing is viewed by Watzlawick as a technique for achieving second order change. "To reframe, then, means to change the conceptual and/or emotional setting or viewpoint in relation to which a situation is experienced and to place it in another frame that fits the "facts" of the same concrete situation equally well or even better, and thereby changes its entire meaning" (4).

With the J. family, for example, the therapist reframed the situation by initially agreeing with the family that S. was a problem within the family. As therapy progressed, however, the therapist's goal was to increase awareness that the family also was not quite the fit for what S. needed. To accomplish this goal, the therapist talked to S. and asked S. to suggest some changes that would assist S. in dealing with the family. In addition, family members were requested to assist in promoting change by helping S. develop ways to effect a better fit between family needs and S.'s individual needs.

The reframing promoted open communication and shifted the frame from viewing S. as the problem to viewing the family as S.'s problem. Thus, it was not possible for the family to ever see the family issue in quite the same way.

Through reframing, the family often naturally evolves in such a manner that the attention is less focused on the "problem child" and the parents begin working in improving the marital relationship.

Another example from the author's clinical work follows.

Mr. and Mrs. P.'s interview began with Mr. P. stating that his wife nagged and complained all the time. Mrs. P. disagreed and said she did not nag and that Mr. P. never paid attention to her. She stated that he paid more attention to the television than to her. As the interview continued, Mrs. P. began finding more things wrong with Mr. P., resulting in withdrawal by Mr. P.

To reframe this situation, the therapist suggested to Mr. P. that Mrs. P.'s so called "nagging" appeared to be a loving gesture. The therapist encouraged Mr. P. at this point to respond more affectionately to Mrs. P.'s loving gestures. Thus, the reframing of Mrs. P.'s nagging to a loving gesture promoted increased intimacy within the marital relationship.

CRITIQUE

A beginning look at this communication approach is designed to assist the family therapist in the development of a specific orientation to working with families. This orientation suggests a rather confrontive and provocative method of intervention. When using this approach, the therapist needs to feel comfortable initiating and directing new communication patterns among family members. This requires both practice and support for the novice.

Haley and Watzlawick offer more clinical examples to help the therapist to achieve a greater degree of comfort in the use of this mode in working with families.

Practice is particularly crucial to the effective use of such potentially powerful techniques as the therapeutic paradox and reframing. Proper timing and pacing and deciding when and how to use these techniques is crucial to their effectiveness. Incorrect timing of therapeutic paradox, for example, may result in withdrawal or termination of the therapy by the family. Similarly, overly confrontive attempts at reframing may lead to the same undesirable end. Role-playing and other practice techniques are helpful in getting the "feel" of what to do and when.

As with most approaches, the therapist needs to remember that this approach may not be indicated for working with all families. Continued and expanded research is needed to study the impact of this approach on different types of families.

SUMMARY

This chapter has provided the beginning family therapist with a specific orientation to working with families. It presented the beginning family therapist with a brief framework and general means of applying it in a clinical setting. The work of Haley and Watzlawick have been used in the explication of this approach.

Examples from the author's clinical practice were used to help define the specific techniques of the therapeutic paradox and reframing, as well as to illustrate how these techniques can be employed in family therapy.

REFERENCES

1. Haley, J. *Changing families: A family therapy reader.* New York: Grune & Stratton Company, 1971.
2. Haley, J. *Problem-solving therapy.* San Francisco: Jossey-Bass, 1976.
3. Watzlawick, P., Beavin, J. H., & Jackson, D. D. *Pragmatics of human communication.* New York: W. W. Norton, 1967.
4. Watzlawick, P., Weakland, J., & Fisch, R. *Change: Principles of problem formulation and problem resolution.* New York: W. W. Norton, 1974.
5. Haley, J. *Strategies of psychotherapy.* New York: Grune & Stratton, 1963.
6. Watzlawick, P. A structured family interview. *Family Process,* 1966, *5,* 108–116.
7. Satir, V. *Peoplemaking.* Palo Alto, Calif.: Science and Behavior Books, 1972.
8. Andrews, E. *The emotionally disturbed family.* New York: Jason Aronson, 1974.

10

Family Systems Model

Carroll Young

The twentieth century has brought increasing interest in a kind of thinking that attempts to comprehend complex organizations in their totality. The new physics of Einstein and Heisenberg, the attempts by Selye to define the human body's general reaction to stress, the technological outgrowth of the theory of cybernetics, and the efforts of environmentalists to educate the public to preserve the precarious interrelationships of nature are but a few examples of a way of looking at the world with regard to the interconnectedness of phenomena rather than their separateness. Among the caregiving professions, the most striking application of this holistic viewpoint has been the use of systems theory by family theorists and therapists in their attempt to understand and treat the human family. This chapter will discuss the uses of a holistic perspective in family therapy and provide explanations and examples of the major concepts of systems theory as it has been applied to family therapy.

SYSTEMS THEORY AS A CONCEPTUAL FRAMEWORK

The Need for a Paradigm

Man, seeking to know the universe and his place in it, is confronted by an overwhelming amount of data. In order to make sense of the universe, he

101

must assume a stance that directs his perceptions and gives priorities their relative values. In other words, he must limit his vision by assuming a point of view from which to look at the world. This viewpoint, or paradigm, may be consciously or unconsciously acquired and used. It is obvious that a paradigm is useful as a tool to the extent that it is consciously adopted and applied. The purpose of this chapter is to provide the reader with an appreciation of the holistic paradigm as a way of seeing the world in general and of systems theory as a way of applying the holistic world view to the study and treatment of the family.

A brief comparison of two world views, the mechanistic and holistic paradigms, may help the reader understand the necessity and the effects of adopting a particular stance from which to understand phenomena. The mechanistic model seeks to understand phenomena by dividing them into smaller and smaller elements and to find cause and effect relationships between the basic elements of phenomena. It employs the kind of linear cause and effect thought that led to the development of Newtonian physics and to the industrialization of the modern world. In health care, the mechanistic paradigm provided the basis for Pasteur's revolutionary contribution to the control of infectious diseases by giving him a framework within which to look for specific causes, the pathogens, leading to specific effects, the diseases. The mechanistic paradigm remains the primary mode of thought in the so-called medical model of health care.

On the other hand, the holistic paradigm seeks to understand phenomena in their wholeness and complexity. Emphasis is placed on the interrelationships of parts rather than on their individual natures, and causality is understood as being mutual and circular, a function of varied and dynamic interactions. Holistic thinking is more difficult than mechanistic thinking because of the necessity of holding the complexity of phenomena before the mind's eye, and it is more natural because it is, after all, the common sense view of the world.

The holistic paradigm does not disprove or supplant the mechanistic paradigm. Both are available to help select those data out of the multitude available to experience on which it chooses to focus. The choice of a paradigm does, however, radically alter the way in which phenomena are understood.

Theories are explanations of phenomena developed from the viewpoint of a particular paradigm. General systems theory,* a theory that uses the holistic paradigm as a conceptual framework for understanding data, is discussed in the following section.

---

* Von Bertalanffy's concepts are organized under the formal title General System Theory. Though the concepts discussed in this chapter are derived from the General System Theory of von Bertalanffy, they are less formal. We will therefore use the colloquial term, general systems theory, without capitalization.

General Systems Theory

In the course of the last 50 years, the late Ludwig von Bertalanffy and others have developed a general systems theory, a way of organizing thought according to the holistic perspective. Systems theory seeks to extend human knowledge in those areas where linear cause and effect logic proves inadequate (1). The concepts of systems theory have been refined, amplified, and fruitfully applied by various disciplines and enterprises resulting in the accumulation of a huge body of knowledge. This literature contains occasional contradictions and varies greatly in levels of intellectual difficulty and practical applicability. Because of this, and because the purpose of this chapter is limited to providing an understanding of systems theory as a conceptual framework with which to understand the family, the following explanation of the basic concepts of systems theory will avoid the use of analogies from the fields of physics and mathematics. The student interested in a more technical discussion of systems theory is referred to von Bertalanffy (1) and Hall and Fagen (2). As Steinglass suggests, systems theory is most useful when one focuses on its essence, that is, when one gives

> attention to organization, to the relationship between parts, to concentration on patterned rather than linear relationships, and to a consideration of events in the context in which they are occurring rather than an isolation of events from environmental context (3).

CHARACTERISTICS OF SYSTEMS

Some of the terms frequently encountered in applications of systems theory will be explained in this section. Most of these terms will be recognized as having been taken from the fields of biology and physics. They become increasingly abstract and less precise in descriptive properties as they are applied to living systems of increasing complexity. It is, therefore, especially important to remember that the concepts represented by these terms are abstract ideas and do not refer to facts of nature. Systems theory and the constructs within it are ways of understanding nature, not nature itself.

Structure and Organization

Von Bertalanffy defines systems as "complexes of elements standing in interaction" (1). Battista defines a system as "an abstract concept that refers to a particular relationship among things that can be actualized in a number of different ways" (4). A system, then, is any group of parts that have particular relationships and interactions with one another. A system is separated from its environment by a *boundary* that is placed in a more or less arbitrary fashion by the observer. Thus, an individual cell is recognized as separate from its environment by a bounding membrane, the human body from its environment by a boundary of skin, and groups of people such as families and institutions are recognized as separate from the environment by more abstract and arbitrary invisible boundaries. These boundaries are defined through observations of the interactions among the parts of the system and by the needs and interests of the observer.

The boundaries of a system are referred to as relatively *open* or *closed* according to their degree of permeability. It is apparent that only nonliving systems can have impermeable boundaries since the maintenance of life requires an exchange of matter and energy with the environment. In both biological and institutional systems, the extremes of complete permeability and complete impermeability lead to death. Living systems maintain selectively permeable boundaries and thus control the inflow and outflow of matter and energy.

A system is also recognized by its property of *wholeness* or *nonsummativity*. The Aristotelian adage that the whole is different from and greater than the sum of its parts refers to this property of wholeness. Battista (4) explains that the characteristic attributes of a system are as much an outgrowth of the relationships between the parts as of the attributes of the parts themselves. The parts of a system are commonly referred to as *subsystems*. There is a quality by which a system can be recognized as a whole that is a product of the interdependence and interactions of its subsystems. Therefore, a change in any one subsystem leads to changes in the others and in the complexion of the whole.

Systems are arranged in *hierarchies*.

> Any system is a part of a more encompassing system and is a synthesis of the set of component subsystems which constitute it parts (4).

Thus, another way of identifying a system is to recognize its similarity in terms of complexity with other systems of a like order. For example, molecules are systems composed of atoms that themselves are systems of a like and lower order of complexity. It should be kept in mind that, although subsystems fit into subsystems in hierarchical order like a nest of Chinese boxes, there is also considerable overlap of systems (3). For instance, the school system and family system overlap in that a family member may be viewed as being a subsystem of both.

Dynamics

We have discussed terms that describe the organizational and structural characteristics of systems. We turn now to concepts dealing with the dynamics of systems. Systems exist in a constant state of flux or change. This continual change is held within limits so that the system maintains itself in controlled balance. The term *homeostasis,* first used by Cannon to refer to self-regulating physiological systems such as thermoregulation, has been applied by systems theorists to the idea of regulation within certain limits. The term *steady state,* although differing somewhat in meaning from homeostasis, is frequently used synonymously with it. For the purposes of this chapter, homeostasis and steady state both refer to the limited range within which the behaviors of a system are allowed to fluctuate. A system responds to stress by the activation of adjustment processes through which the balanced steady state or homeostasis is restored. These adjustment processes are referred to as *feedback.*

Nurses are familiar with physiological homeostatic processes that employ feedback mechanisms to control the secretion of hormones. The drop in follicle-stimulating hormone that occurs in the female sexual cycle in response to increased estrogen and progesterone production is an example of the relationship of feedback to the maintenance of homeostasis in the female endocrine system. Feedback has been equated with information and is largely responsible for the self-regulatory and stabilizing processes of all living systems. Feedback refers to a portion of the output of a system being routed in a circular fashion to reenter the system as input that in turn affects subsequent throughput and output. The dynamics of the feedback loop are an example of what has been referred to here as circular causality. Systems incorporate many complex feedback loops that impinge on one another. For this reason it is impossible to infer causality in systems except as a result of complex interactions. The notion of feedback has been most notably used in the field of cybernetics (1).

Feedback is recognized as being of two kinds, positive and negative. *Positive feedback* occurs when the portion of output that is returned to the input channel moves the system away from, instead of toward, homeostasis. Positive feedback can move a system to a higher level of development if the homeostatic mechanisms are reestablished within limits that allow new behaviors. *Negative feedback* operates in the opposite manner, maintaining the system within its present homeostatic limits. The portion of output returned to the system as negative feedback tends to correct any deviations from the steady state.

In keeping with the decision to avoid explanations of terms by using concepts from physics and mathematics, the discussion of the next two terms will be brief. The concept of *entropy* was taken from the field of thermodynamics. It and its opposite, *negentropy,* are applicable to family dynamics only in a very general manner. Entropy refers to the *degradation* of energy in a system. In other words, as entropy increases, energy becomes less available for the work of growth and maintenance. Terms associated with entropy are error, chaos, randomness, disorder, and disorganization. On the other hand, negentropy is associated with information, accuracy, form, regularity, pattern, and organization (5). As negentropy increases, energy becomes increasingly available for organization and differentiation of the subsystems of the system. Increasing entropy thus signals the decay and eventual death of a system while negentropy signals growth as well as maintenance.

In considering the dynamics of systems we have seen that systems are capable of self-regulation, maintenance, and growth. Knowledge of a particular system is gained through the holistic perspective and observation of the field of interactions rather than through a mechanistic perspective and reductive, linear reasoning.

FAMILY SYSTEMS THEORISTS

Since the early 1950s there has been growing interest in the development of the theory of family therapy using a systems approach. Much of this work had its genesis in the observations of the families of psychiatric patients whose transactional behavior proved analogous to the characteristics of systems. The systems approach has become popular with family theorists, and a number of schools of thought have developed. Historically, the three most influential schools of thought have been that of the late Don Jackson and his colleagues of the Mental Health Institute (MHI) in Palo Alto, the school of Murray Bowen, and that of Salvador Minuchin.

The theories of Bowen, Minuchin, and Jackson all operate in the holistic paradigm, using a systems perspective, but with differing points of emphasis. The MHI group paid particular attention to communication within the family system and are known as communication theorists. They focus attention on the concepts of control, homeostasis, and feedback mechanisms (3). Bowen insists that his work was not influenced by the work of von Bertalanffy and the General System theorists and emphasizes its basis in biological principles (6). Minuchin pays careful attention to questions of structure, observing the characteristics of boundaries, subsystems, and behavior as it exits in the context of the environment. Steinglass observes that all schools of thought make use of the viewpoint provided by general systems theory and that the varying emphases reflect selected points of entry into the family system rather than basic theoretical disagreement (3). The interested reader is urged to study the works of members of the different schools of thought of family therapy in order to appreciate both the minor differences and the overriding similarities of viewpoints.

The following section will give an example of family structure and dynamics understood from a systems theory standpoint.

THE FAMILY AS A SYSTEM

A family who received the attention of various mental health professionals for a period of 3 years will be described first according to the mechanistic framework and then using a systems theory viewpoint. Mrs. Jones, who is 3 years older than her husband, holds a college degree and is employed as a teacher. Her husband, described as passive and somewhat apathetic, did not complete college. He is a salesman. The children report concern about the father's excessive drinking, but neither parent mentions alcohol as a significant factor. There are two sons, Joe, 18, and Bill, 20. Joe, whose acting out behavior first brought the Jones family to the attention of the mental health team, has been hospitalized twice on a psychiatric unit as a safeguard against impulsive behavior. The history of Joe's developmental years given by Mrs. Jones includes descriptions of his being a colicky baby and having behavior problems at school that escalated as he grew older. When Joe was discharged from the hospital the second time, his parents refused to permit his return to the family home. Two months later, Bill, the older son, who had been described as obedient, quiet, and a good student, had his first psychotic break. He has since carried the diagnosis of schizophrenia and currently lives with his parents. He is only marginally functional between psychotic episodes.

The first step in studying a family such as this from a systems perspective is to identify the family system within its *boundaries*. Who are the persons, the subsystems, of significance to the structure of the system? The boundary limiting the Jones family system may be placed where it is most helpful in establishing a workable perspective. It may include extended family members or significant persons not related by blood. In the case of the Jones family, the system boundary will be conceptualized as including parents and the two sons. The degree of permeability of the boundary is assessed. Is the Jones family capable of taking in useful information in the form of therapy? If not, what can the therapist do to increase the boundary permeability so that the therapist's interventions can effect change? Is the system so open that family members feel no sense of security and cohesion? The Jones system appears to have ejected one of its subsystems, Joe. Is Joe actually no longer a part of the system, or does he continue to influence and be influenced by the other subsystems even though he is no longer physically present?

A family therapist using a systems approach would consider the total family system as the client and would refuse to label any individual family member with a psychiatric diagnosis. The Jones family would be assessed as a system, preferably through interviews at which all four family members were present. The therapist would concentrate on transactions, nonverbal as well as verbal, among family members. The therapist would look for that quality of the Jones family that indicated its *wholeness* and that transcended the summative qualities of the individual family members.

Hierarchical structures would be observed and interactions between subsystems would be noted. Each person is a subsystem of the family. In addition, there may be child/child subsystems and, at times, child/parent subsystems that may erode the authority of the parent/parent subsystem. Mrs. Jones may maintain distance from her husband by investing energy in an inappropriately nurturing relationship with Bill. The therapist would also be alert to the effects of overlaps in systems, evidenced by involvement of members of the family system in school, work, and peer systems.

Of particular interest to the therapist using a systems approach is the concept of family *homeostasis*. A painful but steady state is preserved in the Jones family by the *negative feedback* of the children's behavior. Joe's impulsive behavior was a focus for his mother's need to control and was used by his father as justification for hopelessness and alcoholism. Although Joe's hospitalization acted as *positive feedback* that led to a major change in the system when he was expelled from the family, Bill's psychotic break brought about a return to the previous level of homeostasis. Thus conflicts between the parents that could have disrupted the system entirely were avoided because of the negative feedback of the children's pathological behavior. By focusing on the sons as identified patients, mental health professionals in the community may have reinforced their pathological behavior and thus contributed to the painfully stable organization of the Jones family. As family theorist Don Jackson pointed out:

> . . . behavior which is usually seen as symptomatic in terms of the individual can be seen as adaptive, even appropriate, in terms of the vital system within which the individual operates (7).

The Jones family is characterized by *entropy*. Energy is unavailable for the work of change and growth because it is tied up in maintaining the homeostatic state. Therapeutic interventions that help the parents make changes in their own relationship may serve to disrupt the steady state of repeated behavior patterns. If therapeutic intervention is allowed into the system as positive feedback, the Jones family may move toward a condition of *negentropy* in which energy will become available for reorganization and movement toward health.

This illustration of the application of systems concepts to family therapy has been extremely simplified. The thoughtful reader will be able to think of numerous further applications of systems concepts to the troubled Jones family. By considering the family from a systems framework, the therapist is able to identify and intervene in complex transactions and relationships that would escape the notice of the therapist who looked at the family as a simple collection of individual members.

SUMMARY

This chapter emphasizes the need for a paradigm, a world view, with which to organize the multitudinous perceptions with which the mind of man is presented. Aspects of the holistic and the mechanistic paradigms are contrasted and some of the concepts of general systems theory, a holistic paradigm, are discussed. A brief mention is made of some representative family theorists whose work exemplifies the holistic paradigm of systems theory, and a clinical example of a family system is presented from the point of view of a therapist using a systems approach in family therapy.

REFERENCES

1. von Bertalanffy, L. *General system theory: Foundations, development, applications.* New York: George Braziller, 1968.
2. Hall A. D., & Fagen, R. E. Definition of system. *General Systems,* 1956, *1,* 18–29.
3. Steinglass, P. *The conceptualization of marriage and marital therapy: Psychoanalytic, behavioral, and systems theory perspectives.* New York: Brunnel/Mazel, 1978.
4. Battista, J. R. The holistic paradigm and general system theory. *General Systems,* 1977, *22,* 65–71.
5. Miller, G. G. Living systems: Basic concepts. *Behavioral Science,* 1965, *10,* 193–237.
6. Bowen, M. Theory in the practice of psychotherapy. In R. J. Guerin (Ed.), *Family therapy: Theory and practice.* New York: Gardner Press, 1976.
7. Jackson, D. D. The individual and the larger contexts. *Family Process,* 1967, *6,* 139–147.

BIBLIOGRAPHY

von Bertalanffy, L. *Perspectives on general system theory.* New York: George Braziller, 1975.

Grey, W. Current issues in general systems theory and psychiatry. *General Systems,* 1974, *19.*

Grinker, Sr., R. R. In memory of Ludwig von Bertalanffy's contribution to psychiatry. *General Systems,* 1974, *19.*

Jackson, D. D. The study of the family. *Family Process,* 1965, *4,* 1–20.

Minuchin, S. *Families and family therapy.* Cambridge, Mass.: Harvard University Press, 1974.

Olson, H. D. Marital and family therapy: A critical overview. In A. S. Gurman, & D. G. Rice (Eds.), *Couples in conflict.* New York: Jason Aronson, 1975.

Part **III**

FAMILY CONCEPTS OPERATIONALIZED

Since the purposes of this book include providing family theories and a rational, objective means of providing family therapy, it is useful to consider the process by which nurses learn to use these theories and their concepts. Initially, the nurse recognizes a certain type of behavior or sequence of events within a family and identifies the dynamics with a known body of knowledge concerning family interactions. The nurse then perceives possible outcomes before choosing a route of intervention. The operational definition is one effective means of applying theoretical knowledge to the analysis of observed behavior in a family. An operational definition is a statement of the meaning of a concept based on a logical sequence of observations, interactions, and outcomes. Peplau states that "concepts are abstractions of events—they are built from observational data, verified by research and/or repeated usage, and when they become universal, can be called scientific terms" (1). Thus, the nurse's ability to reason, to formulate and/or use operational definitions of family therapy concepts distinguishes her from the nonprofessional who uses intuition or folk interpretations in helping a family identify and intervene in its problematic means of interacting.

FAMILY CONCEPTS AND DIMENSIONS

Barnhill attempted, through research, to conceptualize healthy family systems to facilitate unifying the various theories of "health and pathology in family functioning" (2). He then identified "eight dimensions of family mental health and pathology" (2). After reviewing the eight dimensions, he isolated four basic family themes: role structuring, identity processes, information processing, and change. Through further study he was able to assign the health/pathology aspects of each of the dimensions under the four basic themes.

In studying the health/pathology aspects of each of the family dimensions, a therapist can more easily analyze how the family is functioning. When a pathological dimension is identified, the therapist can look at its contrasting healthy dimension and develop goals for the family which, when attained, would negate the pathology.

In Part III the eight dimensions are used as chapter headings. In each chapter, family concepts related to those dimensions are operationalized and a clinical example of each of the identified concepts is presented along with problems encountered, principles of intervention, and, finally, the identification of short- and long-term goals needed when dealing with families demonstrating the type of function/dysfunction identified in that concept.

REFERENCES

1. Peplau, H. *Interpersonal relations in nursing.* New York: G. P. Putnam and Sons, 1952.
2. Barnhill, L. E. Healthy family systems. *The family coordinator,* January 1979, pp. 94–100.

11

Role Structuring Theme: Role Reciprocity

Role reciprocity refers to mutually agreed upon behavior patterns or sequences in which an individual complements the role of a role partner. These behavioral exchanges are usually defined implicitly but can also be explicit. *Unclear roles or role conflict,* in contrast, refers to a lack of clearly agreed upon behavioral complementarity between family members. The result is unclear and confusing role behavior or persistent conflict among the poorly defined role-oriented behaviors (1).

Scapegoating and family projection are two concepts exemplifying role conflict. In this chapter each of these will be analyzed.

Section 1. Scapegoating

Ruth Belew

NOMINAL DEFINITION

Scapegoating is a conscious or unconscious process resulting from unresolved tension between family members whereby an appropriate member is assigned an object role by the collusion of the other members to draw off the tension.

OPERATIONAL DEFINITION

1. Unresolved conflicts produce tension in family members.
2. The tension cannot be satisfactorily contained by other mechanisms of defense.
3. The solidarity of the family is threatened.
4. The tension persists with such intensity that it demands some discharge.
5. An appropriate family member is chosen to symbolize the conflicts and draw off the tension.
   a. The expendability of that member is established.
   b. Blame is assigned to that member.
6. Family members collude to use the chosen member.
7. The chosen member is inducted into the object role.
   a. That member internalizes the role and accepts it.
   b. The role is reinforced and maintained by the family.
8. Other family members are free to perform their roles effectively.
9. The solidarity of the family is achieved.
10. Family tension decreases.

Clinical Example

Annie B. was brought to the mental health center at the age of 3. The complaint was given as "she is wetting the bed at night after she has been toilet trained for over a year." She had been referred by the pediatrician who said it was not a physical problem.

Annie is the youngest of five children. Mrs. B. had stayed home with the children until this year. Now she has a part-time job outside the home. The four older children attend school and Annie goes to a day-care center.

Mr. and Mrs. B. stated that something had to be done about the child's bedwetting because it was disrupting the family and the marriage. Thus, the problem was presented as being the child's problem and blame has been placed on the child for problems in the family.

Mrs. B. does not know how to handle the bedwetting behavior so she ignores it. Mr. B. spanks the child in an attempt to punish her. Mrs. B. becomes angry with Mr. B. because she feels that he is being too harsh on the child. Mr. B. says that Mrs. B. is denying that there is a problem. Mr. B. admits that he is angry with his wife; but he also feels guilty that she now has to work outside the home. Mrs. B. complains that her husband spends very little time at home with her, but she accepted this saying that he was under financial pressure and had to work long hours. At the same time, Mrs. B. admits to doubts about her husband's fidelity to her.

The focus of the family tension is in the marital relationship. Mr. and

Mrs. B. are fearful of each other's behavior. They cannot communicate their fears and needs to each other. The child internalizes the tension and develops pathological behavior.

In assessing the family, it was learned that Annie was not planned and not wanted. She is the most appropriate family member to become the scapegoat, the unwanted, helpless, expendable child. The conflicts of the parents are symbolized in her, and she is blamed for the family problems. This role is reinforced by the inconsistency of the parents in dealing with the bedwetting behavior. The parents cannot agree on how the bedwetting is to be handled. The fact that the child developed the symptomatic behavior added some stability to the family system. Tension was decreased within the family. It was much easier for the parents to complain of a child's problem behavior than to face the instability of their marriage.

Problems Encountered in Clinical Practice

1. There may be resistance to focus on the real sources of conflict and tension and reasons for using the scapegoating process.
2. The scapegoating process maintains family solidarity and it may be threatening to the family to disrupt the process.
3. The scapegoat may be a child who lacks the social skills to deal with those who scapegoat him.
4. The presence of a therapist may increase the family's tension.
5. There may be an attempt to use the therapist as a scapegoat, or to shift the scapegoat role among family members.

Principles of Intervention

1. In assessing the implications of the use of scapegoating within the family, the following must be considered:
   a. What is the real source of conflict and tension?
   b. Who is the scapegoat?
   c. Which family members are in collusion to use the scapegoat? Why?
2. The therapist needs to do more than examine the process and provide a solution to the immediate problem. She/he needs to provide new ways of coping that can be applied to other areas of the family's life.
3. Since the underlying feelings in scapegoating may be anger or aggression, the therapist must be prepared to deal with these feelings and help family members find appropriate outlets.
4. Since scapegoating is a dynamic process involving the whole family, the treatment must be to the whole family. This involves helping family members become aware of their part in the process.

Immediate Goals (Therapist)

1. Establish a therapeutic relationship with the whole family and with each individual family member.
2. Assess the implications of the use of scapegoating in the family.
3. Make observations of communication patterns and of the way family members relate to one another.
4. Foster recognition of sources of conflict and tension.
5. Foster ventilation of feelings.
6. Explore ways the family has used to cope with conflict and tension.
7. Explore positive ways family members can deal with conflict and tension.

Outcome Goals (Family)

1. Family members employ healthy ways of resolving tension and dealing with conflict.
2. Family members have clear perceptions of each other.
3. Family members maintain appropriate roles within the family system.
4. Family members use clear, congruent communication.
5. The family exhibits increased solidarity.

Section 2. Family Projection System

Marion Fitzsimmons Briel

NOMINAL DEFINITION

The family projection process is a mechanism used by the family to decrease stress within the family system. The process involves the covert identification of a family member as the source of stress; the projection of problems to that person; an acceptance in the family member of this role, and a concerted effort by the entire family to reinforce the projection. The result is a decrease in family stress at the cost of a maladaptive individual.

OPERATIONAL DEFINITION

1. Stress is experienced within the family system.
2. Homeostasis of the system is threatened.

3. An individual is identified as the cause and source of the stress.
4. Family problems are projected onto the individual.
5. The individual introjects this projection.
6. Stress within the system decreases.
7. The projection is reinforced.

Clinical Example

NURSE: Mrs. B., we are interested in working with your family.

MRS. B.:   There's no need to work with the whole family, just take care of my daughter.

NURSE: Mrs. B., we believe that when one member of a family is having problems, the entire family is involved and needs to look at what's going on.

MRS. B.:   That's ridiculous. My family is fine. It is just Shiela. If we can cure her we'll be fine. She's been a problem ever since she was little. You have to agree that there's something wrong with her. Don't you?

Problems Encountered in Clinical Practice

1. The therapist is often pressured by family members to confirm the labeling of the *problem* individual and diagnose him as *sick*.
2. The family members who reinforce the projection process are unable to assume partial responsibility for family problems. In their immaturity, they want to place total blame on a particular individual.
3. A refusal of the labeled individual to perpetuate the process by denying his role or introjection of the projection, throws the system into a high state of stress.
4. A total collapse of the labeled individual may also result in increased stress within the family system.

Principles of Intervention

1. Do not join in the labeling of the identified patient.
2. Individual psychotherapy for the identified patient only reinforces this projection process. Use a family systems approach.
3. Focus on parental problems that have caused anxiety (get a good family history).

4. Encourage individual identification for their individual responsibility in family problems. Do not allow total self-blame or total other blame.
5. Foster maturity and encourage differentiation of all family members.

Immediate Goals (Therapist)

1. Gain family consent to participation in family therapy sessions while discouraging hospitalization of identified patient.
2. Explain systems theory and concepts in relation to mental illness and identified patients.
3. Have family members agree that they may possibly be responsible for part of the stress within the family system.
4. Have each family member explore his own role in family relationships and problems, identifying the mechanisms he uses to reduce stress in the family.
5. Move the family toward positive alternative ways of problem solving, using appropriate exercises.

Outcome Goals (Family)

1. Increased autonomy and self-responsibility for each family member.
2. Increased mutual assertiveness among family members.
3. Ability of each member to modify his/her role to meet other family members' needs.
4. Increased consensual/democratic leadership within the family.
5. Increased ability of each family member to negotiate differences.

REFERENCES

1. Barnhill, L. E. Healthy family systems. *The family coordinator, 28,* 94–100. Copyrighted 1979 by the National Council on Family Relations. Reprinted by permission.

BIBLIOGRAPHY

Ackerman, N. *Treating the troubled family.* New York: Basic Books, 1966.

Bell, J. *Family therapy.* New York: Jason Aronson, 1975.

Bell, N., & Vogel, E. (Eds.). *A modern introduction to the family.* New York: The Free Press, 1968.

Bermann, E. *Scapegoat.* Ann Arbor: University of Michigan Press, 1973.

Boszormenyi-Nagy, I., & Framo, J. (Eds.). *Intensive family therapy.* New York: Harper & Row, 1965.

Bowen, M. Family psychotherapy with schizophrenia. In I. Boszormenyi-Nagy, & J. Framo, (Eds.), *Intensive psychotherapy.* New York: Harper & Row, 1965, pp. 213–243.

Bowen, M. Theory in the practice of psychotherapy. In P. Guerin, (Ed.), *Family therapy.* New York: Gardner Press, 1976, pp. 42–91.

Bowen, M. *Family therapy in clinical practice.* New York: Jason Aronson, 1978, pp. 472–486.

Glossary of psychiatric terminology. In A. Freedman et al. (Eds.), *Modern synopsis of comprehensive textbooks of psychiatry II* (2nd ed.). Baltimore: Williams and Wilkins, 1976, pp. 1322–1323.

Smoyak, S. (Ed.). *The psychiatric nurse as a family therapist.* New York: John Wiley & Sons, 1975.

Theodorson, G., & Theodorson, A. *A modern dictionary of sociology.* New York: Thomas Y. Crowell, 1969.

12

Role Structuring Theme: Clear Generational Boundaries

Clear generational boundaries refers to certain specific types of role reciprocity among family members; that is, to specific differences between marital, parent-child, and sibling relationships. Members of each generation are allied more closely with their own than across generations, with the parents serving as the executive control function. *Diffuse or breached generational boundaries* refer to a lack of clarity in the generational boundaries. Diffuse refers to vague or unclear alliances which blur the differences between generations. Breached generational boundaries refers to an alliance between members of two different generations against a member of the peer generation, e.g., a parent and child against the other parent (1).

Coalition and family schism, two concept examples of breached generational boundaries, are discussed in this chapter.

Section 1. Family Coalition

Ruth Belew

NOMINAL DEFINITION

A coalition is a freely chosen union between two or more individuals or groups for the purpose of working or acting together. There are two parts to a coalition: ally to ally and allies versus a third party. Coalitions can be expected when power and its use are observed. There is more power in coalition than an individual could have alone.

OPERATIONAL DEFINITION

1. A family of at least three members exists.
2. The relationships within the family are negotiated and defined through social interaction.
3. The behavior of one member within the family affects the behavior of other members.
4. Each of the other members is unable to control the behavior of the first member.
5. Two members unite against the first member.
6. The power of the united members can control the first member.
7. The system stabilizes.

Clinical Example

Jim and Mary Santucci and their 7-year-old son, Tony, recently approached the family therapy clinic for counseling. Mrs. Santucci had initiated the appointment. She was very concerned about her relationship with Tony, who would no longer "listen to her" and who was becoming a behavior problem at school. Mary also mentioned that she had begun having migraine headaches in recent months. Jim did not think there was anything wrong with the family but came because Mary insisted.

In taking the family history the therapist found that, since Tony's birth until 5 months ago, Mary had stayed home to care for the family and the home. Five months ago she accepted a position as a bookkeeper in a trucking firm. Jim appreciated the added income and approved of her decision. He offered to help with the household chores on Saturday morning even though he felt it was not a man's work. Tony said he didn't like staying at the neighbor's until his mother came home, but he did like his father doing things with him that he didn't do before.

Mary related that her "migraines" had started about 4 months ago. As the therapist listened she learned that the headaches started one Saturday morning. Two days before that Saturday, Tony had asked her if he could join a junior league baseball team that met on Saturday mornings. His mother negated the idea because neither she nor Jim were free to accompany him to the practice sessions. Tony then approached his father with the request. Jim encouraged Tony's desire to play baseball, and together they approached Mary with all the advantages of participating in the junior league. Finally Mary relented even though she knew that, in doing so, Jim would be spending Saturday mornings at the junior league park instead of helping her with the housework.

Problems Encountered in Clinical Practice

1. In a power struggle, the problem of control for the therapist centers in the attempts by family members to bring him/her into coalitions with them.
2. The family therapist is dealing with more than one person at a time. The therapist's influence on one member may have repercussions on his relationships with others.
3. The anxiety aroused by the therapist's mention of an intention of coalition on the part of any member can jeopardize the therapy.
4. Coalition patterns may have already been formed in the family, and there may be resistance to change.

Principles of Intervention

1. The therapist must consider the question: Where will I fit into the coalition pattern?
2. Coalition attempts must be acknowledged as messages that need to be clarified if inclusion of family members is to be accomplished.
3. By not responding on the family's terms when there is an identified patient, the therapist requires the family to handle the situation in other ways.
4. The family therapist gains control of the relationship with the family by laying down ground rules for the sessions with the family.

Immediate Goals (Therapist)

1. Form a therapeutic coalition with the whole family.
2. Make a beginning assessment of the family problems.
3. Include each family member in the family therapy sessions.
4. Get family members to sit down together and talk about their relationships with each other to observe their usual behavior and patterns.
5. Assess the implications of coalitions that have already formed.
6. Establish ground rules that will guide treatment.
7. Interrupt unhealthy coalition patterns.

Outcome Goals (Family)

1. Family members are supportive of each other.
2. Each family member feels safe and securely included in the family.
3. Family members respect each other's autonomy and do not get into power struggles.
4. Family members trust each other and are able to negotiate their relationships.

Section 2. Family Schism

Susan Thomas

NOMINAL DEFINITION

Family schism is a pathological type of familial relationship characterized by parental rivalry that results in the family being chronically severed into opposing parties. This division between the parents creates a developmental environment that inhibits proper parenting and the establishment of clear sexual identity by the children (2, 3).

OPERATIONAL DEFINITION

1. Both partners enter into the marital relationship while still caught up in their own personality difficulties (2).
2. The personality difficulty of each person involved is greatly worsened by entry into the marital relationship.
3. In many instances, the marital partners' loyalties continue to be linked to their original families to the exclusion of the formation of emotional ties to their own nuclear family.
4. There is chronic failure on the part of the spouses to establish interrelating roles with each other or with their children (4).
5. The family is split due to the constant conflict and disagreement between the spouses (5).
6. The spouses do not emotionally support each other. They show no mutual understanding, trust, or cooperation (6).

7. There is an inability to provide the children with adequate role models (5).

8. Rivalry between spouses for the children's loyalties is severe. One spouse will devalue the worth of the other spouse to solicit support and affection from the children (7).

9. Children from such families are placed in a double bind. To choose to like and side with one parent incurs the wrath and rejection of the other parent (8).

10. Due to the familial system the children are forced into making a decision as to which parent they are going to support, thus alienating the child from the other parent. This may result in faulty role identification by the child and improper maintenance of generational boundaries between parents and children (4).

11. The child will feel guilt due to his/her rejection of one parent.

12. The child will not receive proper socialization to his/her culture due to the failure of the family as a social institution.

Clinical Example

The Kendalls were an upper middle-class family consisting of the parents who were in their early fifties and two teenage children—17-year-old Karen who was a senior in high school and her 16-year-old brother Mark. The marriage of 25 years had been very stormy from the first and seemed to worsen with the birth of the two children. As the children entered their teens the family problems intensified. Mr. Kendall had been an only child born to a wealthy family. He married his wife at the age of 24 and had never seriously dated before his marriage. Mr. Kendall was an overly aggressive man and did not make friends easily. Mr. Kendall met his wife, Peggy, while she was working as a clerk in a department store. She was lonely, away from her family, and without friends. She moved to a larger city to "get away from home" and to see what she could make of her life. She met Mr. Kendall in the store and they were married a year later.

When the children were born, Mr. Kendall blamed his wife for the pregnancies. As far as he was concerned, it was her fault that they had two unwanted children. The Kendalls even separated for a while and Mrs. Kendall took the two children and lived with her sister for a year after her son's birth. This arrangement adversely affected the relationship between Mrs. Kendall and her sister, and she moved back in with Mr. Kendall. Following Mrs. Kendall's return the marriage became very hostile and was centered around the children.

Mrs. Kendall was overly severe and rigid in rearing her daughter. She was less restrictive in rearing her son. She remained responsible for rearing the children throughout their marriage. Mr. Kendall offered no emotional support. The Kendalls established a pattern of his constantly depreciating his wife to the children and of her responding by telling the children how worthless he was as a human being and as a father.

As Karen grew older, Mr. Kendall tried to persuade her to be on his side. He bought her special things and granted her special privileges. He was always cynical and made biting comments about his wife to his daughter. When Karen reached her teens, her mother became more intrusive and suspicious of her. Her mother frequently insisted that she tell her everything that she did when she went out with friends. This forceful intrusion into her daughter's life drove Karen to side with her father on all issues. When she reached adolescence, Karen came to view her father as perfect and came to distrust her mother as much as her father did.

Mark was reared differently than his sister. His mother did not overly restrict him and screen his friends. Because he was a boy his mother was not as concerned about his getting into trouble. He was aware that much of the family's difficulty was his mother's fault; but at the same time, he had few illusions about his father. Mark tended to side with his mother and would try to protect her when his mother and father exchanged physical blows.

Problems Encountered in Clinical Practice

1. The spouses frequently deny having any personality problems and place all the blame on the other spouse. There is a vicious circle of placing blame by one spouse onto the other (2).
2. The constant devaluing of each other may make it difficult for the therapist to establish rapport with either parent (5).
3. Mutual mistrust of motivations of the spouses hinders therapeutic communication and intervention (2).
4. Frequently, one or both partners are still dependent on their families of origin and turn there for advice and support.
5. Frequently, the spouses are simply incompatible. Even through therapy the marriage fails to achieve complementarity of purpose or role reciprocity.

Principles of Intervention

1. Parental coalition is necessary for children to develop a clear sexual identity. Children need to see parents supporting each other and cooperation between the father and mother. A child needs a significant other of the same sex with which to identify. It is also important for the child to have a significant other of the opposite sex who is seen as a worthwhile and lovable human being (3).

2. Maintenance of generational boundaries between parents and children is necessary for the child's normal adjustment. The child needs to know that he cannot take the place of a parent (4).

3. The parents need a clear understanding of their own sex roles and need to remain consistent in these roles so that the children will not become confused (5, 6).

4. The parents need to teach the child the instrumental techniques of the culture.

5. Rational verbal and nonverbal communication needs to be modeled by the parents so that the children will learn to communicate more effectively (2, 6).

Immediate Goals (Therapist)

1. Establish rapport with the family.
2. Observe and note the quality of interpersonal relationships among family members; for example, who sits next to whom, who talks to whom, which members support each other?
3. Make an assessment of the areas of conflict in the family system and the usual methods that the family uses for coping with conflict.
4. Give these observations to the family members.
5. Help the family recognize sources of conflict.
6. Assist the family in identifying need for change.
7. Assist the family members in identifying priorities for change.
8. Include the family in planning strategies for change.
9. Assist the family in problem solving.

Outcome Goals (Family)

1. Acceptance and understanding by all family members that a parental coalition is necessary for adaptive family functioning.
2. Parents' recognition that children need to identify with appropriate, functional role models for development of a clear sexual identity.
3. Maintenance of clear generational boundaries in the family system.
4. Parents consistently role-model appropriate sex-linked traits.
5. Proper socialization of the children by the parents.
6. Rational verbal and nonverbal communication role-modeled consistently for the child by the parents.
7. Emotional loyalties tied to nuclear family rather than family of origin.
8. Prevention of future communication breakdown between the parents and other family members.

REFERENCES

1. Barnhill, L. E. Healthy family systems. *The Family Coordinator, 28,* 94–100, Copyrighted 1979 by the National Council on Family Relations. Reprinted by permission.
2. Lidz, T., Cornelison, A., Fleck, S. & Terry, D. Schism and skew in the families of schizophrenics. In N. Bell (Ed.), *A modern introduction to family.* New York: The Free Press, 1960, pp. 650–661.
3. Freedman, A., Kaplan, H., & Sadock, B. (Eds.). *Modern synopsis of comprehensive psychiatry II.* Baltimore: Williams and Wilkins, 1976, p. 187.
4. Lidz, T., & Fleck, S. Schizophrenia, human integration, and the role of the family. In D. Jackson (Ed.), *The etiology of schizophrenia.* New York: Basic Books, 1960.
5. Kneisel, C., & Wilson, H. (Eds.). *Psychiatric nursing.* Menlo Park, Calif.: Addison-Wesley, 1979.
6. Fleck, S. Family dynamics and origin of schizophrenia. In R. J. Morris (Ed.), *Perspectives in abnormal behavior.* New York: Pergamon Press, 1974.
7. Weiner, I. *Clinical methods in psychology.* New York: John Wiley & Sons, 1974, p. 479.
8. Arieti, S. *Interpretation of schizophrenia.* New York: Basic Books, 1979.

BIBLIOGRAPHY

Caplow, T. *Two against one—Coalitions in triads.* Englewood Cliffs, N.J.: Prentice-Hall, 1968.

Haley, J. *Strategies of psychotherapy.* New York: Grune & Stratton, 1963.

Sluzki, C. The coalitionary process in initiating family therapy. *Family Process,* 1975, *14,* 67–77.

The living webster encyclopedic dictionary of the english language. Chicago: The English Language Institute of America, 1977, p. 192.

Theodorson, G., & Theodorson, A. *A modern dictionary of sociology.* New York: Thomas Y. Crowell, 1969, p. 54.

13

Identity Process Theme: Individuation

Individuation refers to independence of thought, feeling, and judgement of individual family members. It includes a firm sense of autonomy, personal responsibility, identity and boundaries of the self. *Enmeshment,* in contrast, refers to poorly delineated boundaries of self, to an identity dependent on others, to symbiosis, and to shared ego fusion (1).

Enmeshment, emotional fusion, symbiosis, and undifferentiated ego mass are all terms referring to insufficient individuation. The conceptual orientations of the different major theorists account for the differences in terms, although, to a large extent, all the terms refer to the same phenomenon. Bowen (2), for instance, coming from a psychoanalytic background, focuses on ego function within the family system. For him, the term *undifferentiated family ego mass* is central. Minuchin (3), on the other hand, focuses on the social structure of the family. He talks about rules of social participation and uses the term *enmeshment* to describe insufficient individuation. These two approaches are described here as illustrations of the several ways of conceptualizing the dynamics of differentiation of self.

Section 1. Undifferentiated Family Ego Mass

Florence Roberts

NOMINAL DEFINITION

Undifferentiated family ego mass is basically a fusion of individual identities within a family resulting in confusion as to who *owns* whose feelngs, thoughts, and behaviors.

OPERATIONAL DEFINITION

1. As a child grows and develops, he/she fails to separate from parents and remains strongly emotionally attached.
2. Such children lack a sense of their own identity and are unable to differ from their parents.
3. When inevitable differences in their relationships occur, the child (now an adult) either denies the differences and becomes very dependent or breaks off the relationship entirely.
4. Because the relationship problem is not resolved by these tactics, however, it is likely to be reenacted in other close relationships.
5. People tend to marry others who are at approximately the same level of individuation; thus, a woman with low individuation would tend to marry a man with low individuation.
6. Because of the needs present in unresolved problems of differentiation, marriage partners with low individuation fuse emotionally with each other, both attempting to recreate the dependent relationship they had with their parents. This, then, is the undifferentiated marital ego mass.
7. The marriage tends to develop a pattern in which one person consistently "gives in" to avoid conflict and, in this way, loses self to the other person, who gains ego strength through the shared ego mass.
8. Sometimes the person who consistently "gives in" develops some chronic condition, such as illness or alcoholism, that stabilizes the marriage so long as the sick person does not recover.
9. Children (or at least one child) of the marriage will tend to attain a lower level of individuation than either of the parents, thus escalating the problem across generations.

Clinical Example

Sarah Johnson had been very dependent on her mother. As a young child she was very fearful and had a phobic reaction to school. She was afraid to go to school—actually afraid to be away from her mother. Her mother "babied" her and allowed her to stay home frequently. At the age of 16, Sarah met George and was attracted to him because of his "macho" ways. She ran away to marry George when she was 17. George prided himself on his unwillingness to "be told what to do" by authority figures. They had a daughter within a year and were reported to Protective Services for neglect and abuse of the child in her early months.

At the time of intake into therapy, Sarah commented that the baby simply would not be quiet. She seemed to see the infant as criticizing her and felt that the child needed to be "straightened out." George complained that his wife was too "dumb to make decisions" and that she was so lazy that the house was always a mess and meals were poorly prepared. He complained that Sarah spent hours on the phone every day talking to her mother and crying "at every least thing." He bragged that he had been on his own since he was 14 and that he had never spoken to his parents again after leaving their home following a beating.

It seems evident in this family that George had assumed the position of family leader while Sarah had given her ego strength to him in assuming the helpless posture. The fact that she spent long periods crying and talking on the phone with her mother lends further credence to the notion that she had not individuated from her. George's lack of individuation is surmised to be low also because of his abrupt departure from home, his lack of further contact with his parents, and his further acting out of that conflict by refusing to accept advice from any authority figure. The neglect and abuse of the infant is probably due to a large extent to Sarah's confusion of the infant with the dominating mother and her consequent failure to perceive the infant as a separate individual.

Problems Encountered in Clinical Practice

1. The lower the level of individuation of the marital pair, the less chance for successful intervention.
2. Family members from the generation before the one seeking help may sabotage efforts because of their own investment in maintaining dependency relationships with the clients.
3. Spouses who are in the dominant position may sabotage the weaker person's efforts to individuate because of a need to be dominant.
4. Families with lower levels of individuation may drop out of therapy before major problems are resolved because immediate interventions bring about temporary relief from the stress.

Principles of Intervention

1. Identify the adult family member with the highest level of individuation and concentrate efforts on helping that person individuate further and establish identity separate from the undifferentiated family ego mass.
2. Relate to the parents that a child's problems are really a reflection of their problems and refuse to concentrate efforts on working with the child.
3. As therapist, maintain an emotional distance from the couple and insist that they think and talk about issues in a rational way rather than being heavily involved in shared feelings.

4. Emphasize the responsibility each person has for his/her own actions, thoughts, and feelings.

Immediate Goals (Therapist)

1. Produce the most rapid change in the family system possible.
2. Assist the strongest (most individuated) spouse to individuate further from the undifferentiated family ego mass.
3. Avoid establishing a relationship with the identified patient.
4. Help the marital couple talk with each other rather than reacting to each other emotionally.
5. Generally assist the over-functioning member of the marital couple to decrease his/her functioning for the dependent one.

Outcome Goals (Family)

1. Both marital partners gain a sense of identity that is separate from the other.
2. The marital partners feel safe in being separate persons.
3. The children move away from the parental ego mass and thus increase their individuation.
4. The family members become so skilled in analyzing and correcting family dynamics that they can identify and correct their relationship problems without outside help.

Section 2. Enmeshment

Florence Roberts

NOMINAL DEFINITION

Enmeshment is essentially the failure of a family to draw clear boundaries between individuals or subsystems within the family.

OPERATIONAL DEFINITION

1. When individuals marry, they develop certain roles and responsibilities that become routine and comfortable for them.

2. If they do not keep a sense of individual autonomy, however, one partner or both may attempt to live through the other one or to control the other one.

3. A sense of belonging evolves but it requires a loss of autonomy from at least one partner.

4. When children are born, they become a part of the emotional fusion of the family and are controlled inappropriately by their parents or are looked to for nurturance of the parents.

5. Cognitive and problem-solving skills may fail to develop among the children.

6. The parental subsystem and the sibling subsystem fail to differentiate, and some children in the family may assume functions that are actually parental functions, just as one parent may function in a childlike manner.

7. One parent may be excluded from a parent-child subsystem.

8. Any stress in the system or stress experienced by one individual tends to be magnified and may precipitate a crisis.

Clinical Example

John and Linda sought counseling 2 months after their marriage because of extreme conflict. Because of unusual circumstances, they were living in cities 100 miles apart and were spending only weekends together. John traveled in his job and arrived home on Friday evenings. Linda left work on Fridays and traveled the 100 miles to the city where John lived. John complained that Linda spent most of the weekend trying to "change him." A particularly sore point was that she did not approve of the way he dressed and "made" him change into something she thought was suitable before she would go out with him. For her part, she complained that she never had any time to relax, that he was always "at her" to do things with him. She felt trapped and smothered. Further exploration revealed that John arrived home before Linda and spent a frantic 2 or 3 hours cleaning up the house to "get ready" for her visit. He had a long agenda of chores to be done every weekend because that was the only time he was home, and he was very particular about how the house looked. He resented her unwillingness to help him with these chores. Linda was much less particular about housekeeping. Being tired after working all week, she would have preferred a leisurely weekend with some fun time in the evenings, but she felt guilty about not helping with the housework.

After consideration, it seemed that, partly due to living in different towns, they had not spent enough time together to establish norms in their relationship. Both were perhaps trying too hard to live up to imagined expectations of the other, and both were trying too hard to gain an appearance of unity. For instance, Linda thought that her "suggestions" about John's clothing were part of her "duty" as a good wife and that failure to make such comments would indicate that she really didn't care. John, on the other hand felt "left out" when Linda tried to do handwork or reading on Saturdays. He saw sharing chores as a kind of togetherness symbolizing solidarity. Neither partner was asking for what he or she wanted directly, using "I" statements, but both were attempting to impose their standards (she about his clothing and he about the housework) by demanding compliance from the other. In addition, both were exhausted when they arrived "home" on Fridays, and there was no recovery time before the togetherness of the weekend began.

The first step in resolving the issues was an agreement for John to have Friday evening alone in his city to recover from his out of town traveling. Linda, likewise, would go to her apartment after work on Friday and rest, driving to John's city Saturday morning. They began to take responsibility for their own needs and agreed to "let go" of the attempts to control each other in the problem areas. Linda agreed not to comment on John's clothing unless he asked specifically for her opinion, and he agreed not to require her to meet his housekeeping standards. They were hopeful that they would be able to settle in one city in the near future, but they agreed not to force that issue until both partners felt comfortable with the move. For Linda, the move meant leaving the security of a job and friends; for John it meant finding a place to live that was larger and more suitable for a couple.

Problems Encountered in Clinical Practice

1. It often is difficult to identify the appropriate boundaries, especially in this time of changing relationships within the family.
2. Since anxiety is high around control issues, it may be difficult to help the family disengage sufficiently to try new boundaries.
3. Secondary gains, such as power experienced by a parental child, may interfere with moving into appropriate roles.
4. Conflict between persons who would appropriately form a subsystem (for example, parents) may encourage the enmeshment of inappropriate persons (for example, mother and child).
5. Appropriateness of boundaries change as children mature. Patterns that are very functional for an infant may become dysfunctional when the child is a preschooler; thus, frequent readjustment is necessary.

Principles of Intervention

1. Identify and negotiate individual boundaries that allow for age-appropriate interdependence and autonomy for all family members.

2. Separate parental and sibling subsystems.
3. Establish the authority of the parental subsystem while protecting the rights of the children to appropriate freedom for growth and development.
4. Establish the need for the sibling subsystem to function as a "social laboratory" without undue parental interference.
5. Avoid all blaming and labeling.
6. Emphasize the transactional nature of family interaction.
7. Help the family form appropriate openness of the family with extrafamilial systems. Allow helpful extrafamilial transactions and discourage destructive extrafamilial transactions.
8. Assist the family in recognizing developmental changes that require different boundary rules.

Immediate Goals (Therapist)

1. Identify with the family the subsystems that exist.
2. Introduce the concept of boundaries.
3. Separate the parental subsystem from the sibling subsystem and the parent-child subsystem. Give the parents support both for closing some of the boundaries around the parent subsystem and for strengthening the marital relationship.
4. Stress the transactional nature of family interaction.

Outcome Goals (Family)

1. The family is able to structure functional boundaries for individuals and subsystems within the family.
2. The family structures functional boundaries between themselves and the external system.
3. The family members recognize when new rules of interaction need to be negotiated and have the skill to accomplish that negotiation without outside assistance.

REFERENCES

1. Barnhill, L. E. Healthy family systems. *The Family Coordinator, 28,* 94–100. Copyrighted 1979 by the National Council on Family Relations. Reprinted by permission.

2. Bowen, M. *Family therapy in clinical practice*. New York: Jason Aronson, 1978.

3. Minuchin, S. *Families and family therapy*. Cambridge, Mass.: Harvard University Press, 1974.

BIBLIOGRAPHY

Foley, V. D. *An introduction to family therapy*. New York: Grune & Stratton, 1974.

Goldenberg, I., & Goldenberg, H. *Family therapy: An overview*. Monterey, Calif.: Brooks/Cole, 1980.

Miller, J. R., & Janosik, E. H. *Family-focused care*. New York: McGraw-Hill, 1980.

14

Identity Process Theme: Mutuality

Mutuality refers to a sense of emotional closeness, joining, or intimacy which, however, is only possible between individuals with clearly defined identities. *Isolation,* in contrast, refers to alienation or disengagement from others. . . . Isolation can occur either with enmeshment (identities are so fused that they are not separate enough to "become close"), or with isolated withdrawal from family relationships. The first two dimensions are closely linked as identity processes (1).

Disengagement and *skew* are concepts exemplifying isolation and are discussed in this chapter.

Section 1. Disengagement

George A. Lee

NOMINAL DEFINITION

Disengagement is a state that exists when persons, groups, nations, or machine parts are not connected to one another for the purpose of dynamic interaction. Among people this is accompanied by apathy or lack of emotion and delayed or absent response to persons around them. In the context of the family, disengagement results in a rigid boundary that prevents various family members from being aware of and responding to normal stimuli of family life. Disengagement is negative or pathological because it leads to inadequate communication and to blighted patterns of primary socialization.

OPERATIONAL DEFINITION

1. A child has a need for bonding with parents.
2. Parents provide the infant with visual, touch, and vocal stimulation as well as disciplinary direction.
3. The child responds with emotions of pleasure (smiling, gurgling, laughing) to various attentions of parents. By disciplinary direction he maximizes this pleasure and minimizes discomfort.
4. As the child is cycled through steps one, two, and three repeatedly, social habit develops within the context of primary socialization.
5. The child comes to expect steps one, two, and three to happen as a matter of course.
6. On occasion, parents separate themselves from the process of giving the child stimulation and direction (step two).
7. This separation breaks a pattern of expectation for the child (step five).
8. Separated by his usual pattern, the child responds with:
    1. emotions of displeasure or rage.
    2. independent actions of his own.
    3. apathy and/or nonresponsiveness.
9. Emotions of displeasure and independent action result in the child receiving parental punishment (for example, spanking).
10. The child learns to minimize pain of parental punishment by becoming apathetic and nonresponsive.
11. In some families the parental separation involving the mother, father, or siblings becomes habitual.
12. When habitual filial and/or sibling separation occurs, the child will develop an habitual response pattern of apathy, atomism, and absence of or delayed responsiveness in his primary field of contact.

Clinical Example

James and Jean Johnson and their son Billy met with the therapist for the first time at Jean's request. James and Billy had little to say as the therapist started taking the family history.

In discussing how life had been during their first years of marriage, Jean described James as having been a warm, attentive husband who had taken much pride in her and their home. He had worked hard to keep the house and car in good repair. The lawn and shrubs had been his special pride—the prettiest in the neighborhood.

When Billy was born, there was no prouder father or more attentive husband. James had often found excuses for her to drop by the office where he worked to "show them off." When Billy started first grade, James had taken the day off from work to make sure everything went all right for Billy. In turn, Billy had idolized his father.

About a year ago James became upset when he didn't get a promotion he had expected. He started spending longer hours at the office, sometimes until 7:30 or 8:00 in the evening. More recently he had begun stopping off at a club for a few drinks, often getting home after Billy had gone to bed. Since James spends his Saturdays at the office and his Sundays at the club, neither Jean nor Billy see him very much.

Jean indicated she has tried to talk with him but he tells her that he's busy and just to do the best she can. When the car needs repair she has to take it to the garage. She has also finally taken over the house repairs.

Billy used to cry himself to sleep when his father wasn't home in the evenings. Now he has become more sullen and quiet at home. His grades have been slipping, and his teacher called Jean to school because of Billy's acting-out behavior. He has become very aggressive and even threw rocks at his classmates at recess. He was sent to the principal's office, and counseling was suggested for him. When Jean discussed this with James, he just shrugged his shoulders and replied that "boys will be boys." When Jean pressed the issue, he told her to do whatever she wanted.

Problems Encountered in Clinical Practice

1. Because of limited cognitive perception, parents who are disengaged may not recognize the inherent difficulties their children face in family and extrafamilial context. From an emotional point of view, they may hotly deny difficulties disclosed by the nurse therapist, stating that, after all, *they* are the parents and they did not see anything wrong.

2. The adults in the situation avoid all but minimal contact with the children. Since the children are not stimulated by their parents to communicate the knowledge of their past, present, and future, the nurse therapist will have a difficult time working through this barrier of apathy.

3. Many of the disengaged families are products of poverty and slum living. Nurse therapists are often themselves products of lower middle to upper middle social class background and have families of origin that have cared deeply for their welfare. Such nurse therapists may have difficulty relating to and projecting themselves into the *spirit* of disengagement.

The nurse therapist may insist, for example, that the parent "control" his child.

4. Problems of counterdependence often arise in disengaged family settings as one or more of the siblings acts out his hostility toward the system. In some instances the sibling may become a parental child. In such cases the nurse therapist will have to work with both the child and the parent to encourage normal child dependent roles.

Principles of Intervention

1. A thorough knowledge of extrafamilial support patterns is needed for the nurse therapist to open up communication channels. Significant others must be used to bring as much reality to bear on the situation as possible. The nurse therapist has to discover which specific friend or agency might be most able to further the potential for change and begin to move the family toward engagement.

2. The nurse therapist must barter strength concomitantly to all family members to promote normal patterns of dependence. If the mother gains without balance in the sibling position, counterdependence may be increased. If the siblings gain without the parents, the hopelessness of the total family pattern is increased.

3. Intervention requires the familial acceptance of change-oriented role modeling by the nurse therapist. Simply to tell the mother that she is paying no attention to her children ignores the basic premise that the mother is disengaged. If the mother can come to accept concern of the nurse therapist for the children and other family members, a step toward bonding has been taken.

4. Bargaining becomes a useful tool in working with disengaged families after they take first steps toward accepting the roles of other family members. Disengagement initially minimizes stimulation to the point that bargaining will not succeed. As the nurse therapist assists in shifting emotional moods toward engagement, bargaining can become the basis of more open communication.

Immediate Goals (Therapist)

1. Establish trust between oneself and the disengaged family as the initial therapeutic step.

2. Join and accommodate the family in order to continue the therapeutic process.

3. Execute communication exercises between family members to draw members into closer interaction.

4. Explore existing affective modes of interaction among family members.
5. Assess extrafamilial patterns of support for the family.

Outcome Goals (Family)

1. Increased family ties of nurturance and support.
2. Use of extrafamilial significant others to sensitize family members to matters of mutual concern for the family.
3. Increased ability of each family member to honor agreements and commitments.

Section 2. Family Skew

Susan Thomas

NOMINAL DEFINITION

Skewed families are those in which there is a distorted family milieu due to the severe emotional instability of one parent. The marriage, however, appears satisfactory because the dependent spouse passively gives in to the psychopathology of the more domineering partner (2).

OPERATIONAL DEFINITION

1. A dependent person marries a spouse who appears to be a protecting parental figure.
2. The dominant partner suffers from severe psychopathology.
3. The dysfunctional communication patterns exhibited by the dominant partner create a distorted developmental milieu (3).
4. The dominant partner is unable to realize that other family members perceive things differently than he/she does. The dominant partner sees his spouse's and children's lives only in relation to his own.
5. The dependent spouse attempts to make peace in the family in order to maintain the marriage (4, 5).
6. The dependent spouse's acceptance and masking of potential sources of conflict creates a distorted development milieu.

7. On the surface the marriage appears to be happy and stable to both partners; however, in such arrangements parental obligations suffer and a faulty marital coalition is formed (2, 5).

8. These parents provide faulty role models of identification for their children. The familial environment is strange and unreal, but the children are forced into fitting into this strange environment (6).

9. Sometimes there is a violation of generational boundaries and a close relationship is formed between the dominant parental figure and the child (7).

10. The dominant parental figure opposes any movement toward autonomy on the part of the child (5).

11. As the child grows older, he is not allowed the freedom to assert himself and establish his own identity. This can result in psychopathology for the child (4, 8).

Clinical Example

The Mitchell family is dominated by Mrs. Mitchell. The Mitchells consider their marriage to be satisfactory and with few arguments. Mr. Mitchell says that he generally goes along with his wife's decisions because they have been married long enough for him to know that it is hopeless for him to try and change her. When together, Mrs. Mitchell dominates the conversation and even answers questions that were obviously intended for Mr. Mitchell.

Mrs. Mitchell is extremely ambitious for her 18-year-old son whom she has pushed into going to college next year. The son wanted to stay out of school for a year or so and find a job. This plan did not meet Mrs. Mitchell's expectations of a career in law for him. Mr. Mitchell is very quiet and unassertive about his son's future, as he is about most decisions which concern the son. He takes the stance that he is sure that Mrs. Mitchell knows what is best for their son.

When her son was small, Mrs. Mitchell was overly concerned with his well-being and safety. She even feared exposing him to other children lest he would develop an illness from them and possibly die. Throughout school and adolescence she never stopped worrying about him. When he entered junior high school, she was fearful that young delinquents would influence her son in vile and corrupt ways. She did not permit him to have many friends.

Problems Encountered in Clinical Practice

1. The dominant, dysfunctional partner suffers from severe psychopathology that must be treated and identified before family therapy or along with family therapy (3, 5).

2. The dominant, dysfunctional partner is impervious to the needs of other family members (7).

3. The dominant partner is usually extremely intrusive into the child's life (2, 4).

4. The dependent partner provides a very poor role model for the child. This person is usually a weak and ineffectual human being who is not able to counter the dominant partner's ways (2, 5).

5. The dominant partner is usually overprotective of the child and has a difficult time differentiating her/his own needs, anxieties, and feelings from those of the child (5, 7).

6. The dominant partner attempts to keep the child very dependent throughout his life and fights the child's progression to autonomy (2, 7).

7. In many instances, the dominant partner conveys to the child that she/he is not to grow up to be like the dependent partner. This sometimes fosters inappropriate sex role identification.

8. Since the dominant parent suffers from distorted perception of events, and facts are being changed to suit the perceptions of the dominant parent, the family environment provides training in irrationality for the child (5).

9. Due to lack of honest communication, the marriage appears satisfactory. The dependent partner has such fear of not being attached to the dominant partner that he/she goes to great lengths to see that the marriage survives (9).

Principles of Intervention

In planning intervention strategy the therapist must be aware that:

1. A strong parental coalition fosters proper growth and development of the children. Children need to see parents being cooperative and supportive of one another (2, 4).

2. Maintenance of generational boundaries between parents and children is necessary for the child's normal development. The child needs to know that he/she cannot take the place of a parent (8).

3. The parents need a clear understanding and acceptance of their own sexual identity to provide good role models for their children.

4. The parents need to assume the responsibility for proper socialization of the child to the culture (7).

Immediate Goals (Therapist)

1. Establish a therapeutic relationship and build trust with the family members.

2. Assist the family members to recognize, define, and limit the problem.
3. Assist the family in identifying a need for change.
4. Analyze and evaluate the problem.
5. Collect data concerning the family problem and take a psychosocial history of the family.
6. Encourage participation by all family members in the formulation and selection of a desired solution to the problem.
7. Assist the family in implementing the chosen solution to the problem.
8. Evaluate the success of the chosen solution.

Outcome Goals (Family)

1. An adaptive, functional family system exists with a clear parental coalition.
2. Children are provided with appropriate role models for identification in order to foster development of a clear sexual identity.
3. Strong generational boundaries are maintained between parents and children.
4. Proper socialization of the children by the parents is promoted.
5. Parents and children interact in rational patterns.
6. An increased independence and a healthier self-concept of the dependent parent is evident.
7. Each child is progressing toward development of autonomy.
8. Honest communication exists between family members.
9. Emotional illness of the dominant parent is controlled so that the dominant spouse can participate effectively in the family system.

REFERENCES

1. Barnhill, L. E. Healthy family systems. *The Family Coordinator, 28,* 94–100. Copyrighted 1979 by the National Council on Family Relations. Reprinted by permission.
2. Lidz, T. *The origin and treatment of schizophrenia disorders.* New York: Basic Books, 1973.
3. Kneisel, C., & Wilson, H. (Eds.), *Psychiatric nursing.* Menlo Park, Calif.: Addison-Wesley, 1979.
4. Arieti, S. *Interpretation of Schizophrenia.* New York: Basic Books, 1979.
5. Fleck, S. Family dynamic and origin of schizophrenia. In R. J. Morris (Ed.), *A modern introduction to family.* New York: The Free Press, 1960.

6. Lidz, T., & Fleck, S. Schizophrenia, human integration, and the role of the family. In D. Jackson (Ed)., *The etiology of schizophrenia.* New York: Basic Books, 1960.

7. Freedman, A., Kaplan, H., & Sadock, B. (Eds.). *Modern synopsis of comprehensive psychiatry II.* Baltimore: Williams and Wilkins, 1976.

8. Weiner, I. *Clinical methods in psychology.* New York: John Wiley & Sons, 1974.

9. Lidz, T., Cornelison, A., Fleck, S., & Terry, D. Schism and skew in the families of schizophrenics. In N. Bell (Ed.), *A modern introduction to family.* New York: The Free Press, 1960.

BIBLIOGRAPHY

Hinterhoff, C. *Disengagement,* London: Atlantic Books, 1959.

Minuchin, S. *Families and Family Therapy,* Cambridge, Massachusetts: Harvard University Press, 1974.

———. *Families of the Slums,* New York: Basic Books, 1967.

———. *McGraw-Hill Encyclopedia of Science and Technology,* New York: McGraw-Hill, 1977.

———. *Websters' Third New International Dictionary of the English Language,* unabridged, Philip Gove, Ed., Springfield, Massachusetts, 1968.

15

Information Processing Theme: Perception

Clear perception refers to undistorted awareness of self and others. As a shared phenomenon, it refers to clear joint perceptions and consensual validation of shared events (e.g., conflict, affection). In contrast, lack of clear perception refers to confusing or vague perceptions, or perceptions distorted for another (1).

Two concepts demonstrating distorted perceptions are *sham* and *family myth*.

Section 1. Sham

Carroll Young

NOMINAL DEFINITION

Sham is the concealment of the actual feelings, thoughts, and behaviors evoked by a relationship and replacement of these actual feelings, thoughts, and behaviors with bogus reactions. Sham is a learned defensive technique most frequently operating at an unconscious level. It is a function of the vulnerability of the relationship to disruption.

OPERATIONAL DEFINITION

1. A relationship between two or more persons is felt to be necessary by the persons involved.

2. The persons involved in the relationship perceive that the relationship is vulnerable to disruption because of felt antagonisms, disinterest, or dissimilarities between the persons involved.

3. Because the relationship is felt to be both necessary and subject to disruption, the factors inclining the relationship toward disruption are concealed.

4. The concealed factors are covered over by bogus but nonthreatening factors.

5. Depending on the degree of closeness of the relationship, sham may be seen as aiding or destroying healthy social interactions.
   a. Sham in close relationships leads to dysfunction.
   b. Sham in distant relationships aids interaction.

6. The family members continue to feel the relationship is necessary.

Clinical Example

A family group consists of a husband, a wife, and two sons (ages 14 and 16 years). Both parents are college graduates; the father has a graduate degree in a high status profession. The father spends long hours at his office and on weekends devotes his time to tennis, golf, and social activities. The mother, who is not employed, spends considerable energy on volunteer work and social activities. The parents do not communicate on other than a superficial level except for occasional outbursts of sarcasm. The family lives in a well-kept house in an affluent neighborhood. The children attend a private school. The family is both respected and powerful in the community.

The oldest son has begun spending a great deal of time away from home. Teachers have informed the mother that his grades are slipping. When the mother passes this information on to the father he replies that "boys will be boys" and buys his son a four-wheel drive vehicle for his birthday. The younger son, who has always been quiet and compliant, experiences a psychotic break while on vacation with friends. The mother denies that the child's behavior has changed in any way and remains aloof and uninvolved during interviews with the nurse therapist. The father finds it inconvenient to talk with the therapist because of work commitments.

Because their primary value is placed on conformity to the mores of an affluent suburban life-style, this family goes through the motions of respectable life, wearing a mask of bland conformity. The older son's behavior may be seen as an unconscious attempt to jolt his parents' masks of imperturbability, while the younger son's psychotic break may be interpreted as a more serious reaction to the dishonesty that is a way of life for this family.

Problems Encountered in Clinical Practice

1. The sham practiced by the family may deceive or intimidate the therapist so that an incorrect assessment is made.
2. The threat of losing the protection of the sham may be so great that the family will not remain in therapy.
3. Family members may institute severe injunctions or sanctions against an individual family member who reveals the sham practiced by the family, thus threatening that member's continued disclosure.
4. Family members tend to protect themselves and one another from perceiving information that may reveal the sham.

Principles of Intervention

1. The family system should be considered the client, rather than one or more individual family members.
2. The practice of sham should be recognized as a defensive mechanism that family members feel is necessary for preservation of their identities.
3. Resistance to therapy should be anticipated and should not be interpreted as consciously obstructive behavior.
4. Instances in which family members protect themselves and other members from the therapeutic exploration of the family should be used to illustrate the existence of the problem of sham.

Immediate Goals (Therapist)

1. Establish a trusting relationship within which family members may begin to feel that truthful disclosure is safe.
2. Assess the process by which the practice of sham was learned.
   a. Obtain a history of the families of origin.
   b. Obtain a history of the courtship and early marriage of the marital pair.
   c. Assess the influence of other significant persons and institutions on the family value system.
3. Assess individual feelings of vulnerability that lead to the practice of sham.
4. Explore and teach alternate ways of coping with vulnerability and fear such as helping family members express their feelings and needs directly to one another.
5. Foster and support conscious awareness of sham practices.

Outcome Goals (Family)

1. Family members will develop trust in one another so they will be able to express their true feelings and thoughts.
2. The practice of "white" sham or tact will be accepted but will be practiced in conscious awareness and by choice.
3. Family members will recognize that maintenance of the status quo is a matter of choice and that all family members have a degree of responsibility for family processes.
4. The family will feel less vulnerable in the outside community.

Section 2. Family Myth

Ruth Belew

NOMINAL DEFINITION

Family myth is a false or distorted belief system that binds the family together, a belief system concerning the family role images shared by the whole family.

OPERATIONAL DEFINITION

1. Family members evolve a system of beliefs about themselves as a family. These beliefs concern family role images, and the whole family accepts the role images of individual members.
2. The beliefs underlie the interactions of the family:
   a. There is an assigned role for each member in a particular pattern of interaction.
   b. The role images are either distortions or only a part of the observable behavior.
3. The beliefs go unchallenged from within the family. The role images remain intact and are reinforced and maintained.
4. The beliefs bind the family members together.

Clinical Example

In the collusive marital system of George and Martha in the film *Who's Afraid of Virginia Woolf,* a son is incorporated in a family myth. A son who never existed in reality is born into the imaginations of George and Martha. Both George and Martha accept the image of the son. Their beliefs about this son underlie the interactions between them. This role distortion is an attempt to deal with the conflict in the marriage. Both George and Martha accept the belief about their son as an indisputable fact, and both participate in the belief system. The role image of the son is reinforced and maintained. The son confirms the image of their marriage and the role images of each other in the marriage. The myth of the son keeps George and Martha together as husband and wife.

Problems Encountered in Clinical Practice

1. The therapist may become part of the family's myth if their beliefs about him/her fit into such a role image.
2. The family may view the problem as being one member's problem, or they may have an "identified patient."
3. Family members may try to get the therapist to collude with them in support of the beliefs they hold about each other.
4. The family therapist needs to do more than explode the family myth. The therapist needs to be sensitive to the family's need for the myth and should help the family members change their belief system and their way of relating to each other.

Principles of Intervention (2)

1. When the family comes for treatment, they may be trying to reestablish a threatened family myth. This gives the therapist clues to the nature of the myth, to what requires immediate attention, and to where change can begin.
2. The intervention into the family myth requires a balance between an understanding of the family's defensive needs and a capacity for not colluding in the myth.
3. A direct challenge to the family myth may lead to family resistance to change or to termination with the therapist.
4. Family myths may be hiding more disturbing conflicts. The therapist must help the family face these conflicts and find constructive resolutions.

5. In this family, it is the family system that needs to be changed. The therapist must help the family realize this and then deal with the feelings connected with this realization.

Immediate Goals (Therapist)

1. Establish a therapeutic alliance with the whole family.
2. Make a beginning assessment of the family's defenses, of the nature of the family myth, and of the family's problems.
3. Assess the implications of the family myth.
4. Make observations of the family members' perceptions of each other and of their expectations for each other.
5. Involve each family member in the family sessions to see how each family member has colluded in the family myth.
6. Confront the family myth and begin to work on changing the family system.

Outcome Goals (Family)

1. Family members have clear perceptions of each other and of their family roles.
2. Healthy defense mechanisms are established.
3. Clear messages are sent and received among family members.
4. A healthy family system of beliefs exists.
5. Family solidarity is maintained.

REFERENCES

1. Barnhill, L. E. Health family systems. *The Family Coordinator, 28,* 94–100. Copyrighted 1979 by the National Council on Family Relations. Reprinted by permission.
2. Byng-Hall, J. Family myths used as defence in conjoint family therapy. *British Journal of Medical Psychology,* 1973, *46,* 239–250.

BIBLIOGRAPHY

Cavendish, R. *Man, myth, and magic.* New York: Marshall Cavendish Corporation, 1970.

Evans, B. *Dictionary of mythology*. Lincoln, Neb.: Centennial Press, 1970.

Ferreira, A. J. Family myth and homeostasis. *Archives of General Psychiatry*, November 1963, *9*, 457–63.

Glick, I. D., & Kessler, D. R. *Marital and family therapy*. New York: Grune & Stratton, 1974.

Henry, J. *Pathways to madness*. New York: Random House, 1971.

Lederer, W. L., & Lederer, D. D. *The mirages of marriage*. New York: W. W. Norton, 1968.

Murray, H. A. *Myth and mythmaking*. Boston: Beacon Press, 1960.

16

Information Processing
Theme: Communication

Clear communication refers to a clear and successful exchange of information between family members. It includes the necessity of "checking out" communication in order to clarify meaning, intention, etc. In contrast, lack of clear communication refers to vague or confusing exchanges of information, paradoxical communication (when one part of a message invalidates another part), or prohibitions against "checking out" meaning (1).

Two concepts demonstrating the *communications* processing theme are *double bind* and *paradox*.

Section 1. Double Bind

Carol Seeger

___

NOMINAL DEFINITION

A double bind is an outcome from an interaction that is generated through a structured sequence of events and uses multilevel, conflicting injunctions. It results in a behavioral change in the recipient, the person to whom the double bind is directed. It carries a negative connotation since it disallows alternate responses on the part of the recipient that are based on internal perceptions. A person effects a double bind through communication processes.

OPERATIONAL DEFINITION

1. A complementary relationship exists between at least two people, described by its own cohesion, communication, leadership, roles, and goals.
2. All identified persons in the relationship are highly invested in maintaining and continuing it.
3. Person A in the relationship is in an overtly advantageous power position.
4. Person B, the recipient of a double bind, is in an overtly less advantageous power position.
5. B manifests a behavior that is uncomfortable or threatening to A.
6. To begin altering the situation, A delivers a directive to B that is related to B's behavior. A also assigns a punishment to that directive if it is not completed.
7. A delivers a second, more abstract directive to B that directly contradicts the first. This second command generally, but not exclusively, appears through nonverbal behavior. Once again, A assigns a punishment for failure to meet the second command.
8. Throughout the entire interaction, A enforces that only the first directive has been issued.
9. B is prevented from escaping the field of interaction.
10. B experiences internal confusion in attempting to choose the message with which to comply.
11. B chooses and responds to one message and redefines the significance of the information obtained from the remaining directive. Therefore, internal confusion diminishes.
12. B's behavior is altered. A feels less threatened. The double bind is complete.
13. In repetitive instances of the double bind, B will learn to respond consistently at one level to the dual commands.
14. Eventually, not every element of the double bind structure will be required for B to behave as though in a double bind.

Clinical Example

Eighteen-year-old Judy L. and her mother were discussing Judy's choices of college. Judy announced that she planned to attend an ideal college that was 500 miles away from home instead of the local college selected by her parents. Judy's mother quickly agreed that her daughter should make her own decision on where to attend college. Mrs. L. added that Judy should not be flighty or fickle about her decision. If that were the case, her parents would not interpret her indecision as adult behavior.

Mrs. L.'s facial expression was one of shocked dismay when Judy made her announcement. She attempted to regain her composure, but felt her face flush at the thought of Judy rejecting the parental decision that she commute to the local college. The mother checked her reaction while rifling through the pages of the local college's catalogue. Mrs. L. made several predictions about Judy's future referring to her loss of familial support and the extreme financial burden that she would have to assume.

Judy shifted her position in her chair while listening to her mother. She had a strong sense of being disobedient about choosing the distant college. Judy attempted to intercede in her own behalf by saying, "But, Mom, I'll always be your girl." Mrs. L. interrupted, "Of course, you're my daughter!" Judy said that she needed more time to consider her decision and picked up the application for the local college. Judy felt that she instinctively had done something right since her mother got up and gave her a hug.

Subsequent circumstances between mother and daughter concluded with Judy claiming she was considering her application to the local college. Several weeks later, Judy announced at the dinner table that she planned to attend the local college.

Problems in Clinical Practice

1. The family nurse therapist needs to recognize that a family member may be reacting to a segment of a double bind which indicates that it has become a learned reaction.
2. If the double bind has become a multigenerational pattern of communication, all participants may not be present in treatment.
3. The family may demonstrate resistance in working through the implications inherent in the double bind, especially if these are associated with strong emotions such as rage.
4. The remaining family members who are not immediately involved in the double bind phenomena may not be cognitively aware of the phenomena.
5. Many people experience double binds without developing recognized psychopathology. Therefore, the significance of the double bind phenomena must be assessed for each family.
6. The family nurse therapist needs the objectivity to ensure that the family will not become a recipient of a double bind due to the treatment process.
7. The family nurse therapist must recognize that the family member who may currently be a recipient of a double bind can later generate a double bind in a subsequent interaction.

8. The family nurse therapist must be cognizant of the double-bind mechanism and avoid being incorporated into that manner of communicating with the family.

Principles of Intervention

1. Recognize the communication patterns used within a family and identify the participants of the double bind.
2. Identify how the generator of a double bind expresses a directive in an interaction. Look for incongruence between verbal, paraverbal, and nonverbal cues.
3. Observe the manner in which the recipient of the double bind acknowledges and responds to the directive in that interaction. Identify the recipient's usual level of response, whether it is at the level of the overt directive, or at a more abstract level, or at an irrelevant, bizarre level.
4. Note any attendant anxiety in the recipient of the double bind and intervene accordingly.
5. Note the response of the generator of the double bind to the recipient. Note any disqualification if the recipient had responded at a more abstract level than the overt directive.
6. Seek clarification through the family members of all directives issued by the generator of the double bind within that interaction that includes messages by verbal, nonverbal, or paraverbal means. Make these directives explicit.
7. Break the double bind by proposing an alternative response at a level more abstract than the overt directive.
8. Explore the possibilities that the recipient of a double bind may have in order to break the double bind outside of the therapy session.
9. Teach the family members to be sensitive to nonverbal and paraverbal cues. Assist the family members in skills that will aid in accurate interpretation of these cues.
10. Provide a model of effective communication skills for the family in terms of both listening to and sending messages.
11. Observe how the double-binding communication contributes to the cohesion within the family and the rigidity of the family's boundaries.

Immediate Goals (Therapist)

1. Establish rapport with the family.
2. Explain the purpose of the family-oriented approach.

3. Demonstrate professional competence in dealing with the family system and its subsystems and provide a role model for all family members.

4. Obtain an identification of the problem(s) that brought the family into treatment.

5. Contract for progressively building goals that will resolve the problem(s). Explain how these smaller goals are related to the larger ones.

6. Make an assessment of the family system's strengths and weaknesses both as a whole and through smaller subsystems.

7. Maintain control over the therapeutic process.

8. Make an assessment of the structural framework of the family.

9. Make an assessment of the communication processes that are used by the family.

Outcome Goals (Family)

1. Family members continue to improve their listening skills. Such skills include the ability to paraphrase a message, the search for clarification among other members, and the capability to accurately report on the affective component of a message as well as the content.

2. Family members state their needs clearly to other members.

3. Family members send congruent messages to one another.

4. Family members use metacommunication effectively and constructively.

5. Family members value the elements of a communication: the speaker, the message, and the recipient.

6. Family members continue to develop greater individual differentiation and more appropriate levels of intrafamilial trust.

7. Family members become more adaptable to change through teaching and support of the system.

8. Family members become more assertive in their interactions and increase their negotiating skills.

9. Family members dispel or modify detrimental myths about rules of their family.

10. The family adopts a more adaptive power configuration among the members.

11. Family members have more spontaneous expressions of affect and thoughtful messages.

Section 2. Paradox

Carol Seeger

NOMINAL DEFINITION

A *paradox* is a type of interaction between two or more people that makes use of the contrast between contradictory messages at two levels of abstraction in order to alter a person's behavior. A paradox tends to be either benevolent or neutral for the person who receives the paradoxical communication.

OPERATIONAL DEFINITION

1. There are two or more people in a complementary relationship.
2. The context of the relationship is variable in terms of its duration, familial ties, etc.
3. Person A, who presents the paradox, is in a more overtly advantageous position, especially in terms of objectivity.
4. Person B, who receives the paradox, is in an overtly less advantageous position, by virtue of feeling compelled to modify a particular behavior. More than one person can be involved in receiving a paradox.
5. B maintains the option of discontinuing the relationship with A.
6. B manifests a behavior that is unsatisfactory for B and/or his/her significant environment, within the given context that he/she uses the behavior.
7. A offers the directive that B not change the unsatisfactory behavior and discusses the reasons why that directive has been given.
8. B experiences relief for not having to change that behavior.
9. A offers a second, more abstract directive that contradicts the first. It increases the possibility for B to resolve the problematic behavior in lieu of having different context in which to categorize the behavior.
10. B must identify the difference between the two messages and achieve an adequate resolution between them.
11. B alters the problematic behavior. The paradox is completed.
12. In some cases, the relationship may dissolve after the paradox since the resolution of the particular behavior had been the entire purpose of the relationship. In other relationships, there may be a series of paradoxes that are offered before the relationship culminates.

Clinical Example

A family nurse therapist saw Mr. and Mrs. Jones after they had discontinued two prior unsuccessful therapeutic relationships. Having reviewed data from the previous therapists, the therapist concluded that conventional interventions did not help the couple resolve their problem.

Mrs. Jones had convinced her husband to attend therapy in an attempt to resolve their marital discord. Mrs. Jones claimed that their major problem was that Mr. Jones consistently threw his dirty clothes on the bedroom floor. Since Mr. Jones was extremely particular as to the way the laundry was cleaned, if he did not like the way an item of clothing appeared, that was tossed to the floor as well. Mrs. Jones worked full time at a job she enjoyed; she viewed her husband's habit as time consuming as well as annoying. The habit was the subject of numerous quarrels each week.

Mr. Jones claimed that his wife was overreacting to a minor matter. He pointed out that he was a good provider and that his wife could not appreciate his needs because she was so involved with her job. The couple began to argue once again over the laundry.

The therapist decided to introduce a paradox. She defended Mr. Jones' right to throw his clothes on the floor without Mrs. Jones' interference, since this was his method of asserting his prerogative as the man in the household and as a way of expressing his desire to have the laundry done to his satisfaction. He was not to put his clothes into the laundry hamper, and if Mrs. Jones were to find dirty clothes in the hamper, she should toss them onto the bedroom floor. Mrs. Jones was requested to respect her husband's means of self-expression. Mrs. Jones was freed from excessive laundry detail since the therapist stated that Mrs. Jones should only launder clothes in the hamper because she was so busy with her job and other housework. She was to spend her extra time investigating alternative plans for a weekend trip for the couple to take out of town. The therapist gave two stipulations: (1) that they go at least 100 miles out of town and (2) the plans must be an activity that neither had done before. Mr. Jones was to monitor Mrs. Jones' progress on the planning. He was to make the final decision from his wife's alternatives. The couple agreed to follow the instructions.

The remainder of the session was devoted to a discussion on different marriages. The therapist pointed out that any marriage involved certain obstacles that would be distressing to the individuals or the couple. The therapist reflected on a number of situations that centered on couples making allowances for one another's personality, making mutually satisfactory compromises, and accommodating one another's needs. The therapist concluded with the observation that things seemed to get done much more efficiently with less strife under those circumstances. A return appointment was scheduled.

At the next meeting, the couple reported success with the paradox.

Mrs. Jones stated that she was pleased with her husband's choice among the alternatives for the trip. Mr. Jones stated that he looked forward each evening to discovering what alternative his wife had found and investigated. After several days, when Mr. Jones needed clean clothes for their trip, the couple had mutually agreed that Mrs. Jones would do the laundry as best she could and Mr. Jones would place his clothes in the hamper. The couple had redefined their primary problem as one of ineffective communication.

Problems in Clinical Practice

1. The family nurse therapist must assess whether other, more straightforward interventions for a family would be successful.
2. The person who is the focus for the paradox generally may be resistant or ambivalent about changing a behavior that has been assessed as a key element for progress toward problem resolution.
3. The paradox must be very specific to that family system.
4. The paradox that has been devised may require cooperation with another family member. The family nurse therapist must assess the likelihood of that family member's compliance.
5. The family member who is the focus for the paradox must follow through on the directive given by the family nurse therapist.
6. When other interventions have not worked, the family may have a sense of not having made progress. That feeling must be addressed appropriately by the family nurse therapist.

Principles of Intervention

1. The therapist offers conventional interventions for resolving a problem. If a member consistently succeeds in avoiding a major therapeutic element, a paradox is considered.
2. The person is encouraged not to change a behavior for the very reasons he gives for maintaining it. The therapist enlarges on the context of the behavior and its meaning for the family.
3. The removal of overt pressure for the family member to change should enable that member to relax to a greater extent.
4. The therapist offers alternative contexts and alternative behaviors that are compatible and more adaptive than those that are used by the family member.
5. The family member is given a chance to practice the problematic behavior without restrictions over a specific time period.
6. During the practice period, the family member will become inundated by the repetition of the behavior and specific response set, if other family

members are given corresponding directives in how to respond to the behavior.

7. The family member who is the focus of the paradox will become aware of the extreme nature of the behavior and/or will come to recognize that the behavior conflicts with more significant interpersonal or intrafamilial intents.

8. The family member who is the focus of the paradox is now in a position of making a choice between keeping the behavior or accepting another, such as suggested by the therapist.

Immediate Goals (Therapist)

1. Establish rapport with the family.
2. Explain the purpose of the family-oriented approach.
3. Demonstrate professional competence in dealing with the family and its subsystems to provide a role model for all family members.
4. Obtain an identification of the problem(s) that brought the family into treatment.
5. Make an assessment of the family system's strengths and weaknesses both as a whole and through smaller subsystems.
6. Maintain control over the therapeutic process.
7. Assess the particular behavior that stymies problem resolution for the family.
8. Discover the contextual meaning of the problematic behavior.
9. Devise an appropriate paradox.
10. Enlarge upon the problematic behavior and its context in order to explicitly present that into the family's awareness and to explain its pertinence.
11. Present the initial directive to the member who is the focus of the paradox and the remaining family members.
12. Offer alternative contexts with corresponding behaviors that are compatible with the intent of the family member who is the focus of the paradox.
13. Give the family an opportunity to live for a limited time with the directive operational.

Outcome Goals (Family)

1. Family members value the messages sent, the speaker, and the recipient in their communications with one another.

2. Family members accept and offer appropriate feedback about others' behavior and its implications for the family and its subsystems.

3. Family members communicate at more abstract levels in order to clarify the purpose of their behavior.

4. Family members become more assertive as to their needs.

5. Family members strive for appropriate levels of differentiation.

6. Family members adapt to unfamiliar ideas or situations through problem solving and through behavioral or interactional changes.

7. Family members improve their bargaining skills in order to reach decisions that are considerate of all members' needs.

8. Family members develop and maintain structural relationships that are appropriate to their status and human development.

REFERENCES

1. Barnhill, L. E. Healthy Family Systems. *The Family Coordinator, 28,* 94–100. Copyrighted 1979 by the National Council on Family Relations. Reprinted by permission.

BIBLIOGRAPHY

Bateson, G., Jackson, D., Haley, J., & Weakland, J. A note on the double bind—1962. In D. Jackson (Ed.), *Communication, family and marriage* (Vol. 1). Palo Alto, Calif.: Science and Behavior Books, 1968, p. 55.

Bateson, G., Jackson, D., Haley, J., & Weakland, J. Toward a theory of schizophrenia. In D. Jackson (Ed.), *Communication, family and marriage* (Vol. 1). Palo Alto, Calif.: Science and Behavior Books, 1958.

Watzlawick, P., Bearin, J. H., & Jackson, D. D. *Pragmatics of human communication.* New York: W. W. Norton, 1967.

17

Change Theme: Flexibility

Flexibility refers to the capacity to be adjustable and resilient in response to varied conditions and to the process of change. *Rigidity,* in contrast, refers to lack of flexibility, to inappropriate and unsuccessful responsiveness to varying circumstances that is stereotyped and repetitive (1).

Family adaptability and family rigidity are the change concepts discussed in this chapter.

Section 1. Family Adaptability

Anita Turner Kinslow

NOMINAL DEFINITION

Family adaptability is the ability of a family unit to maintain optimal, socioculturally appropriate balance between morphostasis (stability) and morphogenesis (change) as each member within the family unit strives for individuation for himself as well as viability for the family unit; this balance is achieved by changes in the family's power structure, role relationships, relationship rules, and feedback (both positive and negative). In times of stress the family may require greater morphogenesis while still maintaining some degree of morphostasis; but in order to keep the family viable, a static state cannot occur at either extreme on an adaptability dimension, that is, morphostasis or morphogenesis.

OPERATIONAL DEFINITION OF FLEXIBLE/STRUCTURED ADAPTABILITY

1. Family member desires maximum personal satisfaction within family homeostasis.
2. Family member experiences situational or developmental stress.
3. Family equalitarian or democratic controls exist.
4. Controls produce good negotiations and good problem solving.
5. Family shares roles and changes rules that are usually enforced.
6. Family reduces stress and maintains a balance between both morphogenesis (change) and morphostasis (stability).
7. Family member achieves personal satisfaction, and family unit maintains homeostasis.

OPERATIONAL DEFINITION OF CHAOTIC ADAPTABILITY

1. Family member desires maximum personal satisfaction within family homeostasis.
2. Family member experiences situational or developmental stress.
3. Family has no leadership and very lenient controls.
4. Lenient controls produce endless negotiations and poor problem solving.
5. Family roles and rules shift dramatically and rules are enforced only arbitrarily.
6. Family spends extended period of time in morphogenesis (change).
7. Stress is not reduced.
8. Family system does not allow for adaptation (a dysfunctional family).

OPERATIONAL DEFINITION OF RIGID ADAPTABILITY

1. Family member desires maximum personal satisfaction within family homeostasis.
2. Family member experiences situational or developmental stress.

3. Family is authoritative and autocratic controls exist.
4. Controls produce limited negotiations and poor problem solving.
5. Rigid family roles and rigid family rules exist, and rules are strictly enforced.
6. Family spends extended period of time in morphostasis (stability).
7. Stress is not reduced.
8. Family system does not allow for adaptation (a dysfunctional family).

Clinical Example of Flexible/Structured Adaptability

The Baker family consists of a father, a mother, and one daughter. The controls within the family have always been decided democratically with the father showing some authoritarian leadership regarding certain issues. As the daughter is now a teenager, these controls have become a difficulty in problem-solving sessions where the teenager's activities are discussed. Basically, their family negotiations are good. Leadership roles are shared by the mother and father to an extent, and all three clearly understand the rules of the family. Rules are negotiated, and a few have been changed as the daughter has approached adolescence. The teenager is now pushing for more independence from parents, which is being resisted by both parents, but this change is openly discussed.

Clinical Example of Chaotic Adaptability

The Johnson family has two teenage boys who live with their mother; their father died 6 years ago. The mother is very passive and always has been very lenient in disciplining the boys. She is now unable to talk with them regarding her desire for them to attend school, and the school principal has recently informed her that both boys display unacceptable conduct at school, have destroyed school property, and will be unable to return to the present school system. The family's problem-solving skills are poor; neither of the boys has been expected to follow rules and refuses to discuss the topic with his passive mother. They are referred to a therapist by the school counselor.

Clinical Example of Rigid Adaptability

The Smith family consists of father, mother, and two young daughters who are beginning to become interested in dating. The father is the "boss" of the family, and the mother has never been able to negotiate with her husband. Both girls have always been taught that children are to be seen and not heard, and both know the father will not allow them to date until they are 18 years old. Like all rules, this one will be strictly enforced by the father. Roles are rigid within the family as the father is the "breadwinner" and the mother is the "housekeeper." One daughter, age 16, has practically withdrawn from the family, remains in her room except to do the required chores, and displays a sad, forlorn look on her face. She is brought to the mental health center by the mother for possible treatment.

Problems Encountered in Clinical Practice

1. If a therapist is too eager to either impose structure for the chaotic family or to decrease structure for the rigid family, he/she may be perceived as too threatening.
2. All members may not agree regarding the need for modifications within the family system and may block the therapeutic process.
3. Some areas may pose a threat to the therapist's own adaptability, and he/she may not allow the family to openly negotiate.

Principles of Intervention

1. In assessing the adaptability of a family, the following concepts should be evaluated: the style of assertiveness; the family power structure including leadership, type of discipline, and negotiation pattern; family roles; family rules; and the feedback given by family members (positive and/or negative).
2. The therapist should allow the family to assume the responsibility for modifying its own power structure, roles, and/or rules, thus making the family more functional.
3. Plan for gradual changes within the family in order to avoid total resistance or a dramatic shift to the opposite extreme from present pattern of adaptability.

Immediate Goals (Therapist)

1. Establish a therapeutic relationship with the family.
2. Assess the degree of adaptability with the family unit.
3. Assess the implications due to *position* on the adapatability continuum, especially the extremes.
4. Explore methods of modifying a pattern of adapting so that a more functional family unit can be achieved.
5. Foster recognition of the family as a system.

6. Emphasize bargaining as a way to ensure that each family member will have a voice in the decisions made.

Outcome Goals (Family)

1. Family members are able to modify their roles to meet the changing needs of the family.
2. Family members understand the family's pattern of adaptability and, if their methods are inadequate, are willing to explore other ways of dealing with situational and developmental stresses.
3. Family members, through more effective negotiations, prevent regression into inadequate patterns of adaptability.
4. Family members become increasingly able to negotiate successfully differences and reach decisions acceptable to all members of the family.

Section 2. Family Rigidity

Francesca Farrar

NOMINAL DEFINITION

Family rigidity exists when the family system is resistant to change. A rigid family is a closed type family heavily committed to maintaining homeostasis through successive developmental phases by adhesion to a rigid structure. Stability is sustained by tradition. Exploration of alternatives is closed because of the family system's resistance to change. Responsiveness to varying circumstances is stereotyped and repetitive and does not provide for growth and individuation in the family because of the inflexible family structure.

A family very low on adaptability is rigid. The family denies the need for (or reality of) change. There is authoritarian leadership with overly strict discipline. Negotiations are limited; therefore, problems are left unresolved to threaten again and again, thus activating the system's avoidance circuits.

Family roles are fixed and stereotyped. Rules are strictly enforced, including many explicit rules. The system feedback contains primarily negative loops and few positive loops.

Events take place with little or no variation from rigid, regular daily schedules. Time dimension is oriented toward past or future in order to preserve the ideals of the past and to strive for better things in the future.

OPERATIONAL DEFINITION

1. Knowledge, beliefs, and customs are handed down from one generation to the next and become so strongly rooted as to be as inviolable as law.
2. Knowledge, beliefs, and customs are incorporated into the family system to maintain homeostasis.
3. Many explicit rules are established and strictly enforced by an autocratic leader.
4. Rigid, stereotyped roles evolve.
5. Family is subjected to stress from a situation that threatens the stability of the family.
   a. Internal pressure from developmental phases in family members and subsystems.
   b. External pressure from interpersonal socializing processes.
6. Family experiences difficulty in accommodating the changed circumstance.
7. Family denies the need for (or reality of) change.
8. Family responds by adhering to previous structural schemas to reduce stress and maintain homeostasis.
   a. Negotiations are limited.
   b. Problem solving is poor.
   c. Exploration to alternatives is closed.
9. Response to the situation is inflexible, stereotyped, and repetitive despite the context of the circumstance.
10. Stress is reduced.
11. Although the family structure limits growth and autonomy of the family, homeostasis is maintained through the successive developmental phases and the socializing processes by the rigid family structure.

Clinical Example

An example of a rigid family is explicable in the popular play *Fiddler on the Roof* by Joseph Stein, Jerry Block, and Sheldon Harnick. *Fiddler on the Roof* is the saga of the little village of Anateoka in Russia within which Tevye and his family functions. The story involves the process of adaptation caused by social change in which injustice is practiced by a ruling majority (Russian) against a weak minority (Jewish). A series of events lead to the collapse of the town and the Jewish families are evicted from the village.

The rigid family structure is illustrated by Tevye and his family. Tevye, an autocratic leader, incorporates tradition into the family system to maintain homeostasis. All things are done according to tradition—how to eat, how to sleep, how to wear clothes, etc. Everyone knows who he is with tradition, and without it life would be shaky.

The family is subjected to stress when the daughter, Chava, falls in love with Freyaka, a Russian. Chava and Freyaka's love threatens the stability of the family when Chava tells her father that they want to be married. Without negotiations, Tevye angrily forbids the marriage because of tradition and religious reasons. Chava leaves home the next morning and marries Freyaka.

The family experiences difficulty in accommodating the changed circumstance. Although Chava begs Tevye to accept her marriage, he says no because of tradition (you can't turn your back on faith and people). The response is inflexible and stubbornly maintained. Tevya declares that Chava is dead to the family. The family's adherence to their belief system restores stability in the rigid family structure but at the expense of disowning the daughter. This poor adaptability encourages family stasis, thus limiting growth and autonomy.

Problems Encountered in Clinical Practice

1. Control is by authoritarian leadership.
2. Discipline is autocratic and overly strict.
3. Negotiations are limited.
4. There is poor problem solving.
5. Roles are rigid and stereotyped.
6. There are many explicit rules that are strictly enforced.
7. Feedback loops are primarily negative with few positive loops.
8. Stability is maintained by tradition.
9. Exploration of alternatives is closed.
10. A strong religious or ethical value is used as a rationale for avoiding conflict.
11. There is resistance to and denial of change.
12. Poor adaptability encourages family stasis, limiting growth and autonomy.
13. The therapist may have difficulty understanding the family's adherence to beliefs and customs.
14. Change will be a slow process.

Principles of Intervention

1. Gain experimental knowledge of the family system.
2. Respect family hierarchies and values.

3. Maintain authority and mobility of a leader.
4. Explore with family members their views of reality and offer alternatives that promise hope.
5. Support family subsystems.
6. Support process of change.
7. Challenge and undermine patterns that are stereotyped and that limit family members' experience.

Immediate Goals (Therapist)

1. Assess family structure as a system.
2. Assess clinical indicators of rigidity.
3. Assess family's strengths and liabilities.
4. Maintain areas of strength and use models to support change.
5. Focus on the area closest to family's definition of the problem; work on weak areas could promote change in others.
6. Assist the family in the identification of a need for change.
7. Plan strategies for change; include family members in the plan.
8. Focus on increasing flexibility and allowance for individual growth.
9. Develop problem-solving techniques.

Outcome Goals (Family)

1. Family moves gradually toward flexibility.
2. Change facilitation.
   a. Family breaks family maladaptive interaction patterns.
   b. Family implements new adaptive patterns.
3. Family members continue to increase their ability to generate new ideas and change patterns as new situations arise.
4. Family members are able to explore alternatives to change-threatening issues.
5. Family members demonstrate an increased mutual assertiveness and also an acceptance of each other's ideas.
6. Growth and autonomy in the family are encouraged.
7. A balance of positive and negative feedback loops is developed within the family.

REFERENCES

1. Barnhill, L. E. Healthy family systems. *The Family Coordinator, 28,* 95–96. Copyrighted 1979 by the National Council on Family Relations. Reprinted by permission.

BIBLIOGRAPHY

Barnhill, L. E. Healthy family systems. *Family Process,* 1979, *28,* 94–100.

Beavers, R. W. *Psychotherapy and Growth—A Family Systems Perspective.* New York: Brunner/Mazel, 1977.

Burr, W. R. et al. (Eds.). *Contemporary Theories About the Family.* New York: The Free Press, 1979.

Lederer, W. J., & Jackson, D. D. *The mirages of marriage.* New York: W. W. Norton, 1968.

Olson, D. H. et al. Circumplex model of marital and family systems: I. Cohesion and adaptability dimensions, family types, and clinical applications. *Family Process, 18,* 1979 3–28.

Russell, C. S. Circumplex model of marital and family systems: III. Empirical evaluation with families. *Family Process,* 1979, *18,* 29–45.

Satir, V., Stachowiak, J., & Taschman, H. A. *Help families to change.* New York: Jason Aronson, 1975.

Sprenkle, D. H., & Olson, D. H. L. Circumplex model of marital systems: An empirical study of clinic and non-clinic couples. *Journal of Marriage and Family Counseling,* 1978, *4,* 59–74.

18

Change Theme: Stability

Stability refers to consistency, responsibility, and security in family interactions. *Disorganization,* in contrast, refers to a lack of stability, or consistency, in family relations. It includes a lack of predictability and clear responsibility (1).

Morphogenesis and morphostasis are two concepts studied in this chapter that are related to stability.

Section 1. Morphogenesis

Susan Thomas

NOMINAL DEFINITION

Morphogenesis is a process whereby systems undergo successive transformations in response to internal and external changes in the system. It is a self-directed process that departs from old established rules and norms. This process enables a system to change and adapt and, therefore, survive and remain viable.

OPERATIONAL DEFINITION

1. There is a communication of incongruent information into the system that conflicts with the system's values and goals.
2. A comparison and evaluation is made of incongruent information to internal standards of the system.
3. Subsequent effector operation to widen the gulf between the system's status and the internal standards of the system.
4. Transformation occurs in basic structure, organization, and values in response to changes in the internal or external environment of the system.
5. The morphogenic process is complete when the system has changed, grown, adapted, or found new solutions.

Clinical Example

K.T.: Mom, Jim and I have decided to share an apartment next semester at school.

M.T.: You know that your father and I won't pay your expenses if you and Jim decide to live together. Living together without being married is a sin.

K.T.: I knew that you wouldn't see it my way or let me live my own life.

M.T.: I can't believe that you are even thinking of doing such a thing.

K.T.: Well, you know that I need financial help from you and Daddy, and I still want Jim and I to be welcome here and treated as part of the family.

M.T.: You want everything your way. You want your father and me to keep paying your expenses and welcome you with open arms even though you are going against everything that we have taught you. It will not work that way.

K.T.: I am sorry that you feel that way about it, because Jim and I have talked about it a lot, and this is what we want to do even if it means my finding a job and supporting myself and not coming here anymore.

(Later, after the mother and father have had a chance to discuss the situation)

M.T.: Karen, your father and I were talking and we think that we were overly hard on you and Jim. You are our daughter and we love you. We want you to finish school and come home to see us. Times have changed and young people are living together more now without being married than when we were young. As long as you keep your grades up, we will continue to support you.

Problems Encountered in Clinical Practice

1. Family systems differ greatly in their need for homeostasis. The nurse must make an individual assessment of each system's level of stability. What may be adaptive for one family system may not do at all for the next.
2. When family systems are having difficulty maintaining the necessary degree of homeostasis, the anxiety level of individual family members becomes high, and the nurse must realize the issue at hand may be more difficult to resolve when the family system is faced with the prospect of disintegration.
3. If family stability is a highly desired quality in the family system, then the nurse should be watchful that the change-resistant or change-minimizing processes are not called forth to overcompensate in order to prevent changes in structure or goals. Maintaining stability at great expense to the family is one form of system dysfunction.
4. Individual members in a family system may not be in agreement that a basic change is necessary or what change should be made and by whom. When one member indicates that something needs to change, the other may attempt to diminish and modify the need for change.
5. Minimal input of new experiences or knowledge into the system creates a condition where the system is locked in at old levels of functioning.
6. Change may not be viewed as positive by some family members.
7. Change-resistant factors can be restrictive of a system or of an individual reaching his/her full potential. Family members may inhibit their own growth because they do not want to go against the norm.
8. Individual members in a family system may be changing and growing at a faster pace than the system as a whole can keep up with.

Principles of Intervention

1. A certain amount of stability is a necessary condition for the survival of a family system.
2. The family is an open system that is in part made up of individual members and is a part of a larger system such as the community, school, etc.
3. Boundaries of family systems need to be flexible for successful adaptation of the family system to its constantly changing environment.
4. The healthy, adaptive family maintains an appropriate balance between stability-promoting processes and change-promoting processes.
5. Ground rules of a healthy, adaptive family system need to be consensually validated as important by all members.

6. The adaptive family system is required to endure successive transformation in basic structure in order to survive and remain viable.

7. The family system increases in complexity and flexibility as it increases in viability.

8. A system can only be as good as the wealth of the information and experiences put into it.

Immediate Goals (Therapist)

1. Establish a therapeutic relationship.

2. Assess the degree of stability of the family system, and determine if the family is faced with the prospect of immediate disintegration.

3. Assess where the family system fails on the morphostatic-morphogenic continuum.

4. Assess the family system's usual methods for handling conflict.

5. Explore alternative methods of dealing with conflict and stress.

6. Assess how decisions are made in the family and if all members are included in the decision-making process.

7. Foster recognition of sources of conflict within the family system.

8. Help the family to identify a method for change.

9. Include the family in planning strategies for change.

10. Assist family members in problem solving.

Outcome Goals (Family)

1. Family members accept and understand that flexibility is necessary if the family system is to be healthy. Increasing flexibility will encourage family members to become more creative in their thinking and more accepting of new ideas. When confronted with a new idea or situation, family members will have increased ability to change patterns of behavior and/or interaction style.

2. Style of family leadership is more democratic/consensual rather than authoritarian or laissez-faire.

3. Prevent future stagnation or disintegration of the family system through development of healthier methods of dealing with conflict. This includes family members becoming more mutually assertive rather than passive or aggressive and an increase in the family members' ability to negotiate differences. Limiting negotiation or being involved in endless negotiation is detrimental to the family system.

4. Family members are involved in consensual validation of family rules as an ongoing process. Consensual validation of rules should be accompa-

nied by modification of rules to meet the changing needs of family members.

5. Family members understand that family roles change many times throughout the lifespan of the family system and that modification of family roles must occur to meet the changing needs of family members.
6. A constant flow of constructive, positive (morphogenic) and negative (morphostatic) feedback is maintained between family members. Family members receive and use feedback from each other and their environments.

Section 2. Morphostasis

Susan Thomas

NOMINAL DEFINITION

Morphostasis is the process whereby systems are primarily concerned with maintaining homeostasis or the status quo of the system in response to receiving information that is incongruent with the values and standards of the system. It is the process that brings the system's behaviors back in line with the internal standards already established by the system. Morphostasis is the stabilizing process of the system.

OPERATIONAL DEFINITION

1. There is input of incongruent information into the system that conflicts with the system's values and goals.
2. A comparison and evaluation is made of incongruent information to internal standards of the system.
3. Deviant counteracting operations are triggered by the input of incongruent information.
4. Subsequent effector operations act to bring the system's behavior back into line with the internal standards of the system.
5. The morphostatic process is complete when homeostasis and stability are apparent in the system again.

Clinical Example

J.T.: Dad, you know my draft number is right at the top of the list, and I will probably be drafted.

P.T.: Yes, son, I was in World War II and fought to defend this country. A lot of my buddies did not make it back. I hope you get a chance to serve your country, too.

J.T.: That's what I wanted to talk to you about; I am not sure that I can go to war and fight.

P.T.: If you are called, son, you will go and do your duty. I know you. You wouldn't let the family or yourself down. No man enjoys killing another, but you will do it if you are called.

J.T.: The country can't have everyone trying to get out of their responsibilities to the country. I still don't like the thought of going, but then no one does. If I am called I will go just like you did, Dad, when you were called.

Problems Encountered in Clinical Practice

1. Family systems differ greatly in their need for homeostasis. The nurse must make an individual assessment of each system's level of stability. What may be adaptive for one family system may not do at all for the next.

2. When family systems are having difficulty maintaining the necessary degree of homeostasis, the anxiety level of individual family members becomes high, and the nurse must realize the issue at hand may be more difficult to resolve when the family system is faced with the prospect of disintegration.

3. If family stability is a highly desired quality in the family system, then the nurse should be watchful that the change-resistant or change-minimizing processes are not called forth to overcompensate in order to prevent changes in structure or goals. Maintaining stability at great expense to the family is one form of system dysfunction.

4. Individuals in a family system may not be in agreement that a basic change should be made and by whom. When one member indicates that something needs to change, the other may attempt to diminish and modify the need for change.

5. Minimal input of new experiences or knowledge into the system creates a condition where the system is locked in at old levels of functioning.

6. Change may not be viewed as positive by some family members.

7. Change-resistant factors can be restrictive of a system or individual reach-

ing his/her full potential. Family members may inhibit their own growth because they do not want to go against the norm.

8. Individual members in a family system may be changing and growing at a faster pace than the system as a whole can keep up with.

Principles of Intervention

1. A certain amount of stability is a necessary condition for the survival of a family system.
2. The family is an open system that is in part made up of individual members and is a part of a larger system such as the community, school, etc.
3. Boundaries of family systems need to be flexible for successful adaptation of the family system to its constantly changing environment.
4. The healthy, adaptive family maintains an appropriate balance between stability-promoting processes and change-promoting processes.
5. Ground rules of a healthy, adaptive family system need to be consensually validated as important by all members.
6. The adaptive family system is required to endure successive transformation in basic structure in order to survive and remain viable.
7. The family system increases in complexity and flexibility as it increases in viability.
8. A system can only be as good as the wealth of the information and experiences put into it.

Immediate Goals (Therapist)

1. Establish a therapeutic relationship.
2. Assess the degree of stability of the family system, and determine if the family is faced with the prospect of immediate disintegration.
3. Assess where the family system fails on the morphostatic-morphogenic continuum.
4. Assess the family system's usual methods for handling conflict.
5. Explore alternative methods of dealing with conflict and stress.
6. Assess how decisions are made in the family and if all members are included in the decision-making process.
7. Foster recognition of sources of conflict within the family system.
8. Help the family to identify methods for change.
9. Include the family in planning strategies for change.
10. Assist family members in problem solving.

Outcome Goals (Family)

1. Family members accept and understand that a certain amount of stability is necessary if the family system is to be healthy. Family members need a certain degree of reassurance of what to expect from their family system.
2. Style of family leadership is more democratic/consensual rather than authoritarian or laissez-faire.
3. Exploration is made of ways for the system to maintain a healthy balance between change-promoting (morphogenic) processes and change-resistant processes (morphostatic). This includes the development of healthier ways of dealing with conflict, such as family members becoming more mutually assertive rather than passive or aggressive and an increased ability to negotiate differences. Limiting negotiation or being involved in endless negotiation is detrimental to the family system.
4. Family members exhibit increased understanding that family rules are a necessary part of the family system because they provide consistency and stability. Family members need to be aware that some rules are more easily modifiable than others. Family members need to decide on which rules need to be changed and to which ones they will adhere.
5. Family members show an increased understanding that family roles provide consistency and stability to the family system, and some roles change much more frequently than others.
6. A constant flow of constructive, positive (morphogenic) and negative (morphostatic) feedback is maintained between family members. Family members receive and use feedback from each other and their environment.

REFERENCE

1. Barnhill, L. E. Health family systems. *The Family Coordinator, 28,* 94–100. Copyrighted 1979 by the National Council on Family Relations. Reprinted by permission.

BIBLIOGRAPHY

Maruyama, M. "The Second Cybernetics: Deviation—Amplifying Mutual Causal Processes" in Buckley, W. [ed.] *Modern Systems for the Behavioral Scientist.* Chicago: Aldine Publishing Company, 1968.

Olson, D., Sprenkle, H., Douglas, H., & Russell, C. "Circumplex Model of Marital and Family Systems: I Cohesion and Adaptability Dimensions, Family Types, and Clinical Applications," *Family process, 18,* 3–28, 1979.

Speer, D. "Family Systems: Morphostasis and Morphogenesis, or "Is Homeostasis Enough?" *Family process, 9,* 259–277, 1970.

Wertheim, E. "The Science and Typology of Family Systems II. Further Theoretical and Practical Considerations," *Family process, 14,* 285–308, 1975.

Part **IV.**

FAMILY CONCEPTS: COMPARISON AND CONTRAST

19

Family Projection System and Scapegoating

Margaret McAvoy Trimpey

This chapter will explore two concepts used in family therapy: Murray Bowen's family projection system and Norman Bell and Ezra Vogel's interpretation of the scapegoating process. It will include a discussion of each concept as defined by its author, identification of points of comparison and contrast, and implications for clinical practice.

FAMILY PROJECTION SYSTEM

The family projection system, described by Bowen, a psychiatrist, is part of an overall theory of how family systems operate that is multigenerational in scope. Over a 20-year period, his theory has been refined by the use of research into schizophrenic families, by the multigenerational investigation of his own family, and by the practice and teaching of family therapy.

Other concepts in Bowen's theory must be defined to understand the projection system. After deciding that all behavior patterns found in disturbed families also occur with less intensity in functional families, he developed a theoretical continuum covering all levels of human functioning called the differentiation of self scale. Bowen (1) describes people who function at the highest level as inner directed, totally responsible for their behavior, having a sense of identity, and as being realistically aware of their dependency on others. At the other end of the scale, the less differentiated person holds others responsible for personal happiness and a sense of self. This person has difficulty with emotional closeness and tends to become fused, or emotionally stuck together, with the other person in a relationship. At the same time the person has a sense of losing his/her own sense of identity. The more intense the fusion, the more extreme the attempts a person makes to pull away. The results of such attempts may include emotional and/or physical distance, the development of conflict between the two, impaired communication, and physical or emotional illness.

The undifferentiated ego mass is the feeling of "we-ness" in the nuclear family, in which it appears that "on one level each family member is an individual, but at a deeper level the central family is one" (2). This feeling operates even when individuals within the family move away or maintain minimal contact with one another.

Triangling, another important concept of Bowen's, occurs when tension develops between two people in a relationship and they bring in a third person or issue to relieve the anxiety and achieve some distance between them.

Bowen (1) found that when conflict and tension mount between a poorly differentiated couple (who have each sought a spouse at the same level of differentiation), the family system must absorb a large amount of anxiety and immaturity. To do so, the family ego mass may focus on certain members. A common example is the triangle that occurs when the husband attempts to distance himself from the couple's fusion through such maneuvers as underinvolvement with his wife and children, passivity, or overinvolvement with his job. The wife, in her role as mother, responds by drawing in a particular child and becoming overinvolved in the child's life. The couple can then project their basic conflict and immaturity onto the child who accepts the loser position but gradually learns to achieve some relief by attaining the distant position in the triangle by playing the parents against one another.

A particular child may be the recipient of projection when the parents are recreating unresolved problems within their own families of origin through the child who most closely fits the pattern of that conflict. For example, projection may involve a child of a particular sex or sibling position or the child may be simply the first available safe place to release tension. The choice may also be influenced by the mother's level of anxiety at the child's conception or birth or the parent's positive or negative attraction to it, such as the reaction that may accompany the birth of a long-awaited son or a child born with a deformity.

Bowen (1) believes families project varying degrees of "maturity or immaturity over multiple generations," producing both children who are more differentiated than their parents and children who are less differentiated. Depending on the stress levels within the family, some children could "collapse into dysfunction, such as schizophrenia, at any effort to survive outside the family."

SCAPEGOATING

The second concept, scapegoating, occurs in antiquity as a method of effecting "a total clearance of all the ills that have been infesting a people by loading them on a 'material medium' who draws the evil away from the group" (3).

In recent years the term has been used by several authors to describe a particular family phenomenon. Ackerman (4) explored the prejudicial meanings families attach to qualities of difference in their members. Boszormenyi-Nagy (5) described how one person cannot exert a social sanction alone; besides the victim there needs to be a third person who will validate the identity of the scapegoat as bad. Bermann (6) described how scapegoating results when other protective mechanisms fail.

Bell and Vogel (3) have taken a sociological view of the family as a social system and have attempted to focus on both the relationship between the family and the external world with which it interacts and the relationship between the family and the individuals within it. In that context, scapegoating maintains equilibrium in the family by the projection of hostilities on the child that are too dangerous for the husband and wife to confront openly or directly. They contend that, although the scapegoating process is functional within the family, it is harmful to both the child's emotional stability and the child's ability to function outside the family.

In an intensive study of disturbed and healthy families of differing cultural backgrounds, the authors found scapegoating did not occur in healthy families. Where it did occur, a couple had selected each other because of a sense of shared conflicts and feelings of mutual understanding. Yet both partners moved to opposing positions when anxiety increased concerning the relationship and the other person's behavior. To survive, the couple developed an equilibrium involving minimized emotional conflict and limited expression of intense or negative feelings between them.

As tension and anxiety continued to build, the equilibrium became unstable and a release sought by the choice of a child as the target of hostility since a child is dependent, powerless, and malleable. Since it is "important that those family members performing essential, irreplaceable functions for the family not be scapegoated" (3), it is less costly to the family to select a child.

The child is somehow related to the conflict; he may be the one who personifies a conflict of values between the parents, the one most like the source of the parents' unresolved childhood difficulties, the child with characteristics most like one parent, or a deformed child who serves as a symbolic representation of family failure.

The parents must also induce the child to accept the scapegoat role through a fragile balance between reward and punishment. Punishment allows a safe avenue for parental hostilities. Then, by undermining the punishment by delay or through indifference to the child's symptoms, or by providing secondary gratification through attention and release from responsibilities, the parents covertly encourage the behavior.

The child slowly internalizes the scapegoat role and absorbs the hostility until it builds and he/she, in turn, releases tension by punishing the parents. When this counteraggression raises family anxiety to an intolerable level, or when the child moves from the home into the school or community and is identified as disturbed, the family may seek help.

COMPARISON AND CONTRAST

After looking at the concepts of family projection system and scapegoating separately, it is possible to draw some comparisons between them. The authors are describing essentially the same phenomenon that begins with the choice of a spouse and the development of the marriage relationship, the effects of anxiety and tension on the relationship, and the selection of a child as a safe outlet for the emotions that the two cannot express to one another. Each author, likewise, agrees that although family stability is maintained, it is at great cost to the child.

Each author recognizes that the child develops retaliatory maneuvers against the parents, and if these maneuvers increase family tensions sufficiently, the parents may seek professional help for the child.

There are several differences between Bowen's and Bell and Vogel's concepts. For example, Bowen's theory defines a range of relationship patterns occurring in all family systems and disavows terms like normal, sick, and well, while Bell and Vogel clearly separate disturbed from well families. Also Bell and Vogel describe the methods used to induce the child into the role, but Bowen omits that aspect. Bowen believes that family projection occurs in every family to some extent, while Bell and Vogel restrict scapegoating to dysfunctional families. Bowen's ideas are more general, theoretical, and therapy oriented than are Bell and Vogel's who are reporting research results and exploring a specific concept.

Although Bowen limits his basic theory to family and multigenerational patterns, Bell and Vogel also consider cultural, ethnic, and community impact on the family. Bowen (2) has begun to expand his theory to include man's involvement in the larger society by exploring the idea that the same concepts and patterns that he has identified in the family are replicated in society.

IMPLICATIONS FOR THERAPY

Despite the differences between Bowen and Bell and Vogel, the major implication for therapy is that both concepts give support to the idea that the identified patient is part of a system of interacting members and not a "helpless victim of a disease or malevolent force outside his control" (2). In both concepts, basic unresolved problems exist in the relationship between the parents and between them and their own parents and siblings. Yet the child will be identified as the problem and the parents' expectation will be that therapy will take place only with the child.

Convincing the parents to participate in the therapeutic process is essential. To assist the child, the therapist must treat the family and focus on the tension in the parents' relationship. But it must be kept in mind that the intense anxiety in and about the marital relationship led to the scapegoating/projection process originally. The therapist needs to dissipate some of the overall anxiety so the couple could tolerate dealing with their relationship. Bowen achieves this by acting as a consultant whose role is to teach the parents to become experts in how the system operates in their nuclear and extended families and how they can change their own functioning within those systems. Bowen also lowers anxiety by directing discussion through him, which decreases the emotionality of direct communication between the parents, yet forces one to listen to the other.

In addition, the therapist must be aware that because of anxiety in the parents' relationship and because the family maintains stability by projecting onto a scapegoat, resistance to change is to be expected. The therapist must recognize that the family most likely sees the consequences of the child's problems as easier to live with than the potential disaster that could be brought about by exploring parental conflicts. It is possible, however, that such resistance might be balanced by the family's inability to tolerate the child's counteraggressive behavior.

Even while working on the basic family conflicts, the therapist must find some way to counter the child's internalization of the scapegoat role. As Bell and Vogel indicate, simply removing the external pressures from the child will not solve the problem.

In looking at both concepts, it is evident that much work and research has been done by Bowen to develop a theory of family therapy and by Bell and Vogel to understand the mechanisms operating on the family from without and within. Although approached from different perspectives, scapegoating can be viewed as a dysfunctional family projection system that can occur in families whose members function at the lower levels of the differentiation-of-self continuum. In these dysfunctional families, the child is subjected to more emotional damage than children in families whose members are more differentiated. These families can use other methods of relieving tension in the family in addition to or instead of projecting their tensions onto a child.

REFERENCES

1. Bowen, M. *Family therapy in clinical practice.* New York: Jason Aronson, 1978.
2. Bowen, M. The family as a unit of study and treatment. *American Journal of Orthopsychiatry,* January 1971, *31,* 45–60.
3. Bell, N. W., & Vogel, E. F. *A modern introduction to the family.* New York: The Free Press, 1968.
4. Ackerman, N. W. *Treating the troubled family.* New York: Basic Books, 1966.
5. Boszormenyi-Nagy, I. A theory of relationships: Experience and transition. In I. Boszormenyi-Nagy, & J. Framo (Eds.), *Intensive Family Therapy.* New York: Harper & Row, 1965.
6. Bermann, E. *Scapegoat: The impact of death-fear on an american family.* Ann Arbor: University of Michigan Press, 1973.

20

Family Morphostasis and Family Rigidity

Francesca Farrar

Negative feedback provides the family system with behavior that attempts to maintain homeostasis. Too little change in the family system can lead to morphostasis and rigidity. Family morphostasis and family rigidity are both concepts in which the family system is resistant to change. Placed on an adaptability dimension, at one extreme would be morphogenesis (change) and flexibility (growth enhancing) and on the opposite extreme would be morphostasis (stability) and rigidity (stasis). The purpose of this chapter is to explore these two change concepts, morphostasis and rigidity. The chapter will include a review of the literature, a description of the concepts, points of comparison and contrast, reformulation of the concepts, and clinical implication for family counseling.

MORPHOSTASIS: A REVIEW

In a review of the literature, it was found that Magoroh Maruyama coined morphogenesis (positive feedback) and morphostasis (negative feedback) in place of multilateral mutual simultaneous causal relationship. Morphostasis is equilibrium maintaining and is defined as the process to maintain the structuredness of a structure (1). Maruyama calls the phenomena of negative feedback *the first cybernetics* (2). Morphostasis means that the system must maintain constancy in the face of environmental vagaries, which is done through the error-activating process known as negative feedback (3). Negative feedback results in family stasis.

Equilibrium is a term that applies to a closed mechanical system. Cannon coined the term *homeostasis* for biological systems to avoid the static connotations of equilibrium. In dealing with the higher level of the sociocultural system, Buckley coined the terms *morphostasis, structure maintaining,* and *morphogenesis,* changing the feature of the unstable system (4). Morphostasis refers to "those processes in complex system-environment exchanges that tend to preserve or maintain a system's given form, organization or state" (4). Morphostasis is negative feedback.

Several family therapists viewed families as primarily morphostatic. These therapists include Haley, Lederer, Jackson, Bateson, Lennard, Bernstein, Riskin, and Satir (3). The term homeostasis was used in place of family morphostasis. Don Jackson coined the term *family homeostasis* and described the family as a closed information system that was self-regulating (3). Haley elaborated on family homeostasis by the development of the first law of relationships:

> When an organism indicates a change in relation to another, the other
> will act upon the first so as to diminish and modify that change (5).

This Law suggests that family systems function primarily to maintain the status quo. Bateson, Weakland, and Satir speak of the family as a feedback-governed, error-activated system characterized by constant action and counteracting reaction oriented to regain balance.

Wertheim proposes that there are two levels of morphostasis: consensual morphostasis and forced morphostasis. Consensual morphostasis has intrafamily distribution of power in which there is genuine stability of the family system, consensually validated by its members. It contributes to the development of positive family group and individual identity. In contrast, forced morphostasis derives from intrafamily power imbalance that contributes "to intra-family and individual alienation and to disturbed or deviant functioning of the system as a whole and of one or more of its sub-systems" (6).

The principal characteristics of the morphostatic system are the maintaining of the energy level within controlled limits and the structure of behavior of the system within preestablished limits. The system is oriented primarily to self-regulation (5).

Olson views morphostasis and morphogenesis as extremes on the adaptability dimension. Olson further divides the adaptability dimension into four levels of adaptability: chaotic, flexible, structured, and rigid (7). The most viable family systems are those that maintain a balance between flexible and structured.

After analysis of the review of the literature on morphostasis, nominal definition was synthesized. Family morphostasis is a process to maintain the system's given form, organization, or state against ever present tendencies to reduce it, which is done through negative feedback. The structure of the family system is maintained within preestablished limits and is oriented to self-regulation. A family moderately low on adaptability is morphostatic. The family has a relatively high level of organization. The boundaries are semipermeable surrounded by a constant but changing external environment. The family is resistant to change.

Control in the family is democratic with a stable leader. Discipline has predictable consequences. The family has structured negotiations with good problem-solving skills. There is some role sharing within the family (7).

Family rules are usually enforced with few rule changes. There are more explicit than implicit rules. The system feedback contains more negative than positive loops (7).

Clinical development of morphostasis begins after receiving error or mismatch information resulting from a comparison of data about behavior with internal standards or criteria. The subsequent effector operations act to reduce the discrepancy between the system's or member's status and the original goal or standard values (5). Speer gives a good example involving family morphostasis, which is as follows:

> An example involving the family might be the reaction of parents with strong negative feelings about associating with minority group members to their grade school daughter's friendship with a minority child (5).

The interchange might contain intense personal acceptance messages as to force the young person to accept his parents' view in order to insure their acceptance and support. The negative feedback is homeostasis maintaining and a change-resistant set of operations (5).

RIGIDITY: A REVIEW

A review of the literature on the second change concept, rigidity, suggests that it is a family that maintains old static forms of adaptive stability. Family rigidity is a low extreme for family role adaptation that lowers receptivity to new social learning, and it reduces the range of exploration of new alternatives (8).

The rigid triad family structure occurs when "the boundary between the parental subsystem and the child becomes diffuse, and the boundary around the parents-child triad, which should be a diffuse, becomes inappropriately rigid" (9). A family with rigid structure is a closed type family (10).

Minuchin describes rigid families as being committed to maintaining the status quo. In periods when change and growth are necessary, they experience great difficulty. The family insists on retaining the accustomed methods of interaction. They deny any need for change in the family. The rigidity in the family makes their thresholds for conflict very low and usually a strong religious or ethical code is used as a rationale for avoiding conflict. Problems are left unresolved (9).

The McMaster model of family functioning describes family rigidity as a style of behavior control in situations where "the rule involves a very constricted and narrow standard that allows little latitude or room for negotiation and change despite the context of situations" (11).

Ackerman, Haley, Lederer, Jackson, Minuchin, Whitaker, Felder, Warkentin, and Wynne agree that family rigidity refers to a "lack of flexibility, to inappropriate and unsuccessful responsiveness to varying circumstances that is stereotyped and repetitive" (12).

A nominal definition was formed after synthesis of the literature review of family rigidity. A rigid family is a closed type family that is committed to maintaining homeostasis (through successful developmental phases) by adhesion to a rigid structure. Stability is sustained by tradition. Exploration of alternatives is closed. Responsiveness to varying circumstances are stereotyped and repetitive, which does not provide for growth and individuation for the family system.

A family very low on adaptability is rigid. The family denies the need for (or reality of) change. There is authoritarian leadership with overly strict discipline. Negotiations are limited; therefore, problems are left unresolved to threaten again and again, thus activating the system's avoidance circuits. Family roles are fixed and stereotyped. The rules are strictly enforced including many explicit rules. The system feedback contains primarily negative loops and few positive loops. Events take place with little or no variation from rigid daily schedules.

Clinical development of rigidity may occur in periods when change and growth are necessary. The family system experiences great difficulty. For example, when a child in an effectively functioning family reaches adolescence, his family can change its rules and transactional patterns in ways that allow for increased age-appropriate autonomy while still preserving family continuity. But the rigid family insists on retaining the accustomed methods of traditional interaction. They deny the need for change. Usually a strong religious or ethical code is used as a rationale for avoiding conflict.

COMPARISON–CONTRAST

Analysis of the two change concepts included comparison and contrast of morphostasis and rigidity. The two concepts are similar in that:

1. Both primarily function to maintain stability in the family system.
2. The family is resistant to change.
3. Systems feedback contains primarily negative loops.
4. The family's adaptability is low.
5. There is a high level of organization.
6. There is a stable leader.
7. There are few rule changes.
8. There are many explicit rules.
9. The rules are usually enforced.

Differences between the two concepts exist as follows:

1. Family control is by authoritarian leadership in rigidity, whereas control is democratic with a stable leader in morphostasis.
2. Discipline is autocratic and overly strict in rigidity compared to discipline being democratic with predictable consequences in morphostasis.
3. Negotiations are limited with poor problem-solving skills in family rigidity contrasted to good problem-solving skills with structured negotiations in family morphostasis.
4. There are stereotyped roles in rigidity contrary to some role sharing in morphostasis.
5. Rules are more strictly enforced in rigidity.
6. More negative feedback in rigidity than morphostasis.
7. Boundaries are rigid and closed in rigidity compared to boundaries being semipermeable in morphostasis.
8. Adaptability is very low in rigidity, whereas adaptability is low in morphostasis because the family system operates within a larger set of limits.
9. Family rigidity is more dysfunctional than family morphostasis.

Reformulation of the concepts would be that morphostasis and morphogenesis are extremes on the adaptability dimension. Family morphostasis is divided into two levels of adaptability; moderately low, which is called structured, and low, which is called rigidity.

CLINICAL IMPLICATIONS

The major implication for counseling is that both concepts are resistant to change because they function primarily to maintain stability in the family system. The therapist should focus on the adaptability dimension by assessing "the ability of a marital/family system to change its power structure, role relationship, and relationship rules in response to situational and developmental stress" (7).

There are four phases of family therapy:

1. Formation of the therapeutic system.
2. Diagnostic assessment of family functioning on the dimension of adaptability.
3. Sharing of diagnostic assessment with the family and defining the problem.
4. Formulation of treatment goals.

The therapist facilitates the formation of the therapeutic system by joining the family and by assuming the system's leadership. He joins the family by "recognizing and supporting family strength: respecting family hierarchies and values, supporting family subsystems, and confirming individual members of their sense of self" (13).

The therapist has to join the field of stabilized family interaction in order to observe them. He must gain experiential knowledge of the controlling power that the system exerts.

The therapist should next do a diagnostic assessment of family functioning on the dimension of adaptability. He/she appraises variables such as family power structure, negotiation styles, role relationships, feedback system, boundaries, and style of communication.

The therapist then shares the diagnostic assessment with the family and involves them actively in the decision regarding the specific goals of treatment (7). The family is assisted in identification of the problem and of the need for change. A rigid family will require more guidance because problem solving is poor.

Formulation of treatment goals should be based on areas of weakness and focus on the area closest to the family's definition of the problem. The therapist should plan strategies for change involving family members. The desired goal is to maintain a balance between the central level of morphostasis and morphogenesis, which is a balance between structured and flexible. In family rigidity, the therapist aims to gradually move the family from the "adaptability" level of rigidity to the level of structured and then to a balance between structured and flexible.

In an ideal adaptive family system, there is a free-flowing balance between morphostasis and morphogenesis. The treatment goals are directed to achieve the following:

1. Mutually assertive style of communication.
2. Equalitarian leadership.
3. Successful negotiation.

4. Positive and negative feedback loops.
5. Role sharing and role making.
6. Few implicit rules and more explicit rules (7).
7. Transaction with the environment by adaptive processes.
8. Family system with complex open boundaries.

SUMMARY

Family morphostasis and family rigidity are both concepts for coping with change. Morphostasis, stability promoting, and morphogenesis, change promoting, are extremes on the adaptability dimension. Family morphostasis is divided into two levels of adaptability: moderately low, which is called structured, and low, which is called rigidity. The major problem for counseling is that both concepts are resistant to change because they both function primarily to maintain stability in the family system.

The therapist must challenge and undermine patterns that are self-regulating. The family members must be supported through the processes of change. It is important to execute therapeutic maneuvers of high intensity in order to make any impact on its homeostasis.

REFERENCES

1. Maruyama, M. Morphogenesis and morphostasis. *Methods*, 1960, *48*, pp. 256, 164.
2. Maruyama, M. The second cybernetics: Deviation-amplifying mutual causal processes. *American Scientist*, 1963, *51*, 164–179.
3. Hoffman, L. Deviation-amplifying processes in natural groups. In J. Haley (Ed.), *Changing families*. New York: Grune & Stratton, 1971, pp. 11, 287, 290.
4. Buckley, W. *Sociology and modern systems theory*. Englewood Cliffs, N.J.: Prentice-Hall, 1967, pp. 15, 58.
5. Speer, D. Family systems: Morphostasis and morphogenesis, or is homeostasis enough? *Family Process*, 1970, *9*, 259–278.
6. Wertheim, E. Family unit therapy and the science and typology of family systems. *Family Process*, 1973, *12*, 361–376.
7. Olson, D., Sprenkle, D., & Russell, C. Circumplex model of marital and family systems: 1. Cohesion and adaptability dimensions, family types, and clinical applications. *Family Process*, 1979, *18*, 3–27.
8. Ackerman, N. *Treating the troubled family*. New York: Basic Books, 1966, p. 90.
9. Minuchin, S. *Families and family therapy*. Cambridge, Mass.: Harvard University Press, 1974, pp. 32, 94.

10. White, S. Family theory according to the cambridge model. *Journal of Marriage and Family Counseling*, 1978, *4*, 91–100.

11. Epstein, N., Bishop, D., & Levin, S. The McMaster model of family functioning. *Journal of Marriage and Family Counseling*, 1978, *4*, 19–29.

12. Barnhill, L. Healthy family systems. *The Family Coordinator*, 1979, *28*, 94–100.

13. Minuchin, S. *Psychosomatic families*. Cambridge, Mass.: Harvard University Press, 1978, p. 95.

21

Pseudo-Mutuality and Placating

Debra Gooden Woosley

The purpose of this chapter is to compare and contrast the concept of pseudo-mutuality as developed by Lyman Wynne and the concept of placating as developed by Virginia Satir.

Lyman Wynne began a study in 1954 to develop a psychodynamic interpretation of schizophrenia that takes into account the social organization of the family as a whole. He formulated a series of concepts applicable to various phases of schizophrenic processes. The concept of pseudo-mutuality was a major formulation among them.

Wynne assumed that movement into a relationship with other human beings is a basic need of human existence. He also postulated that every human being strives consciously and unconsciously, in a lifelong process, to develop a sense of personal identity. The sense of identity consists of "those self-representations, explicit and implicit, that give continuity to experience despite the flux of inner and outer stimuli" (1). In dealing with the problems of relation and identity, three main solutions result. According to Wynne, these three resultant forms are *mutuality, nonmutuality,* and *pseudo-mutuality.* Only pseudo-mutuality will be dealt with in this chapter.

DEVELOPMENT OF CONCEPTS

Pseudo-mutuality refers to a quality of relatedness with several ingredients. Each person brings into the relationship a primary investment in maintaining a sense of relation. The past experience of each person and the current circumstances of the relationship lead to an effort to maintain the feeling that each person's behavior and expectations mesh with the behavior and expectations of the other persons in the relationship.

All interpersonal relations that persist are structured in terms of some kind of fitting together. However, in describing pseudo-mutuality, Wynne emphasizes a "predominant absorption in fitting together at the expense of the differentiation of the identities of the persons in the relation" (1).

With growth and situational changes, altered expectations come into any relation. In pseudo-mutuality, the subjective tension aroused by divergence of expectations, including the open affirmation of a sense of personal identity, is experienced as disrupting that particular transaction and possibly demolishing the entire relation.

In pseudo-mutuality, emotional investment is directed more toward maintaining the sense of reciprocal fulfillment of expectations than toward accurately perceiving changing expectations. Thus, the new expectations are left unexplored, and the old expectations and roles continue to serve as the structure for the relation. In short, "the pseudo-mutual relation involves a characteristic dilemma: divergence is perceived as leading to disruption of the relation and therefore must be avoided; but if divergence is avoided, growth of the relation is impossible" (1).

After many years of observing interactions among people, Virginia Satir became aware of certain universal patterns in the way people communicate. Whenever there was stress, she observed four dysfunctional ways and one functional way people had of handling it. These dysfunctional patterns occurred only when a person was reacting to stress and at the same time felt his self-esteem was involved. The dysfunctional pattern of communication that will be dealt with in this paper is placating.

As Satir studied these four patterns of comunication, she began to see that the self-esteem is destroyed more easily when the person has not really developed a solid, appreciative sense of his own self-worth. Not having developed his own self-worth, the person uses another's actions and reactions to define himself. Little by little the person's self-worth is lowered until a threat of rejection is sensed. The person begins to feel and react to the threat, but because he does not want to reveal weakness, he attempts to conceal it. Placating is one way he conceals his weakness.

The placator agrees to everything verbally. He goes along with the wishes of others, often feeling he is just there to make others happy. His body is seen as helpless, and he feels worthless, often experiencing feelings of being a nothing.

The placator is always trying to please and apologize, never disagreeing, no matter what. The placator communicates with *"double-level messages."* The person's voice is saying one thing, and the rest of him is saying something else. Virginia Satir provides us with the following schema of a double message:

Verbal communication	words
Body/sound communication	facial expression
	body position
	muscle tension
	breathing tempo
	voice tone

The placator usually holds the following views that elicit double-level messages:

(1) he has low self-esteem and feels he is bad because he feels that way, (2) he feels fearful about hurting the other's feelings, (3) he fears rupture of the relationship, and (4) he does not want to impose (2).

In order for the placator to develop and thrive, there must also be a blamer present. The blamer is "a fault-finder, a dictator, a boss" (3). He acts as the superior being over the placator and seems to be saying, "If it weren't for you, everything would be all right." Like the placator, the blamer also has poor self-concept. The blamer gets someone to obey him, and he in turn feels he counts for something. Both the placator and the blamer are searching for their identity and relationship within the family. Due to a breakdown in communication, dysfunctional patterns are set up and, if continued, become a vicious cycle. Each communication pattern emphasizes the other; however, both must be present for the other to exist.

The two concepts, placating and pseudo-mutuality, have been defined and their development presented. The following is a comparison and contrast of the two concepts.

COMPARISON AND CONTRAST

According to Wynne, pseudo-mutuality develops as the result of the individual striving to develop a sense of identity. Satir states that placating develops from a sense of poor self-worth. Referring to Erik Erikson's stage of adolescence, identity versus identity diffusion, it is the writer's inference that both theorists are relating to the teenage years when the person is forming his self-worth (identity). Thus, the development of pseudo-mutuality and placating is the result of not forming a good self-concept and develops at relatively the same time in the life span of the person.

The relationship that exists between the placator and another person, like the relationship that exists between the person who uses pseudo-mutuality and another person, is one that can neither be given up nor allowed to develop. They are both highly invested and often intensely charged emotionally, but at the same time they constrict growth and impoverish any sort of interpersonal experience. Without mutual perceptions and recognition of the identity or self-worth of each person appropriate to the current life situation, the continuing relationship increasingly becomes subjectively empty, barren, and stifling.

Positive aspects of the relationship cannot be explored and expanded. In pseudo-mutuality and in placating, the full impact of alienation and loneliness is avoided, but a sense of relation that is unsupported by the perception of reality becomes a hollow and empty experience.

In pseudo-mutuality, emotional investment is directed more toward maintaining the sense of reciprocal fulfillment of expectations. New expectations are left unexplored. Placating is basically the same in that the person feels, "I am no good; you are better than I am," and thus he does not think he deserves a reciprocal fulfillment, unless that fulfillment is being a part of the relation. The emotional investment is directed toward hiding weaknesses that have developed as the result of a poor self-concept.

The two concepts, pseudo-mutuality and placating, developed and grew in basically the same ways. While researching the literature, the writer found the two concepts to be so much alike in development and theory that it was difficult to provide a contrast between the two. Pseudo-mutuality can be seen as the process among two or more people and placating can be a part of this process, especially on the part of one or more people in the relationship above. If a person who placates becomes involved with someone who does not blame or will not contribute to pseudo-mutuality, a new relationship will form. Also in this case the terms pseudo-mutuality and placating are synonymous because placating may be going on in the absence of pseudo-mutuality. As a result of the new relationship several things might occur with A (placator) and B (nonblamer):

1. A might stop placating; therefore, the relationship becomes mutual.
2. A might withdraw from the relationship with B.
3. B might start blaming A and the relationship then becomes pseudo-mutual.
4. B might withdraw from the relationship with A.

IMPLICATIONS FOR FAMILY THERAPY

Since pseudo-mutuality and placating are very similar, they will be dealt with as one in the implications for the therapist. In the normal family, role structure affects the personality development of the people and is reworked or modified in accordance with the changing needs and expectations of the family members toward each other. However, when pseudo-mutuality and placating occur, expressions of the changing or emerging needs of family members are not reflected in changes in the role structure of the family.

In predysfunctional families, the predominant picture is a fixed organization of a limited number of engulfing roles. While the roles existing in the overall family social organization tend to remain fixed, the particular people who enact these roles may vary. Thus, there may be considerable competition about who takes the position of the most dependent and helpless family member.

Family pseudo-mutuality and placating show certain characteristics that can be observed by the therapist. These observations include:

> (1) a persistent sameness of the role structure of the family, despite physical and situational alterations in the life circumstances of the family members, and despite changes in what is going on and being experienced in family life; (2) an insistence on the desirability and appropriateness of this role structure; (3) evidence of intense concern over possible divergence or independence from this role structure; (4) an absence of spontaneity, novelty, humor, and zest in participation together (1).

Rapport and trust must be established between the therapist and family to form a working relationship. This is necessary in any therapist/client relationship but essential when working with pseudo-mutuality or placating in family relations.

The therapist can assist the dysfunctional family by helping all members strive to form separate personal identities. Each person should be assisted toward understanding his feelings in order to help him achieve a more mature level of functioning. Members of these families suffer from a sense of being unable to reach one another on a feeling level. Each person strives for relatedness, but feels that the others block his efforts, preventing intimacy or affection.

The therapist needs to have a thorough understanding of each member's self-concept and assist him in strengthening it. The member's self-concept can be enhanced through consistent positive feedback and acceptance from the therapist. The therapist also serves as a role model for the members who are allowing one person to assume the role of the placator.

When placating occurs in therapy, it should be discussed with the family in relation to emotions about the event. The therapist needs to assist the family in becoming aware of their feelings. This can be done through confrontation to include open-ended sentences and direct questioning.

SUMMARY

Similarities have been drawn between pseudo-mutuality and placating as developed by Lyman Wynne and Virginia Satir. Stifling structures that constrict autonomy consist of ambiguity, meaningless, and emptiness. Individuality poses a great threat. During therapy sessions, effort is directed at recognition of patterns and intervention. After there is agreement that members feel a discomfort, strategies can be directed at making former covert mechanisms an overt process. The therapist's main goal should be the strengthening of each family member's self-concept, and an understanding of pseudo-mutuality and placating can assist in this process.

REFERENCES

1. Wynne, L. C., Rycoff, I. M., Day, J., & Hirsch, S. I. Pseudo-mutuality in family relationships of schizophrenia. *Psychiatry*, 1958, *21*, pp. 205–220.
2. Satir, V. *Peoplemaking*. Palo Alto, Calif.: Science and Behavior Books, 1972.
3. Satir, V. *Conjoint Family Therapy*. Palo Alto, Calif.: Science and Behavior Books, 1976.

BIBLIOGRAPHY

Bandler, R., Grindler, J., & Satir, V. *Changing with families*. Palo Alto, Calif.: Science and Behavior Books, 1976.

Smoyak, S. *The psychiatric nurse as a family therapist*. New York: John Wiley & Sons, 1975.

22

Labeling and Scapegoating

Gloria Russell

This chapter discusses the theoretical definitions of labeling and scapegoating. A comparison and contrast is made between these terms along with clinical implications for family therapy. Although both terms sometimes carry synonymous interpretations, each term can stand on its own merits. Labeling, as a learned reaction, generally occurs before scapegoating. Scapegoating becomes a control mechanism with the advent of human interaction.

LABELING

Labeling goes beyond the time of Moses. As people learned to observe, they also learned to analyze the data from, or appraise, their observations. These observations and appraisals helped them become socialized. Labeling, a common theme of all forms and levels of human life, is derived from appraisal. Each of us during the course of an hour, day, or week instantly gives labels to various things in our environment.

In a review of the literature, many ideas are expressed about the use of the term *labeling*. Although the term is of common use in business, education, and psychiatry, many times the methods of labeling are used without the name calling and stereotyping.

Lemert views labeling from a deviant-social viewpoint and observes that the labeling theory depicts social control as arbitrary, and more or less washes out any causative significance substantive actions one may have for persons who become deviant; as well as denying their objective harm or social damage (1).

Lemert declares that the interaction between the labeled deviant and other group members is unidirectional and unilinear. Further explanation of the labeling theory describes *others* as being the *in* members of a group. These *others,* through their group decisions and actions, reduce certain practices of the group to routinization and characterizations. Persons who choose not to follow or accept the group's practices are identified by labels. These labeled persons are then viewed as deviants and *outsiders* of the group. According to the labeling theory, when extreme, the labeled deviant will lose individuality. As the loss of individuality becomes more pronounced, the more the person is successfully labeled by others (1). The labeled person may resign himself to accept the labeled status. At the same time, this person will attempt to lessen the impact of labeling by trying to reduce those characteristics that give evidence of being deviant and labeled. The labeled person does this by attempting to control the information that is being disseminated about the alleged deviant behaviors and characteristics.

Scheff discusses labeling from the perspective of use or abuse of rules. He views most cases of rule breaking as transitory. Denial is the behavior most often displayed as a reaction to rule breaking. Scheff believes that, at times, the reaction to rule breaking swings to the opposite side. Exaggeration and distortion of the violation occurs. Scheff identifies this pattern of exaggeration as labeling and believes that the "labeling process is a crucial contingency in most careers of residual deviance" (2). From Scheff's viewpoint, the labeled deviant is "rewarded for deviating and punished for attempting to conform" (2). It may be concluded that Scheff views labeling as a process that can create specific behaviors in a person that are reinforced expectations and stereotypes from the greater society in which the person lives.

From a family systems viewpoint, labeling can be termed as what family members have to say about a particular act or behavior of a specific family member (3). This labeling process can serve to stabilize the act or behavior, whether good or bad. According to Goffman, role expectations play an important part in labeling. When a person has a belief as to what another person should be, and when that person turns out to be different and less desirable than this perception, a stigma is developed. Goffman defines a stigma as "an undesired differentness from what we had anticipated" (4). Another labeling process occurs by the use of sanctions. Gibbs defines sanctions as "reactions to deviant behavior" (5). This reaction is an effort by family members to inflict punishment or reward, prevent norm violations, or encourage conformity.

From this review of the literature a nominal definition for labeling would be: a statement of an appraisal of a collective set of information about a person by an individual for the purpose of changing or stabilizing behavior or actions.

How does labeling get its start in a family? Usually, it begins when a family member breaks identified and specific rules of the family. The rule breaking becomes a major issue in the family, and there is pressure on the rule breaker to conform to the expected standards of the family. The more the rule breaking is an issue, the more the family aids the reinforcement of the expected behavior of the rule breaker. The situation becomes circular. What can happen eventually is that the individual begins to accept the very behavior he/she did not want or, perhaps, did not even have. Once the family has publicly declared that this is the type of behavior likely to be seen in this family member, then the labeled person has a difficult time returning to a normal role. Finally, the person is cast into a role that becomes the self-fulfilling prophecy.

Other reasons for labeling are: *(1)* lack of knowledge, *(2)* stereotyping, *(3)* prejudices, *(4)* scapegoating, and *(5)* retribution. These reasons, which are also labels, are intended to eradicate a specific behavior of an individual member. If the desired behavior does not occur, parents may become angry and frustrated. In turn, the person to whom the label was given is more likely to accept the label when the label is made early, is more intense, and is more frequent (3).

SCAPEGOATING

The origins of the term *scapegoat* go back into the pages of antiquity. During the time of Moses, there were many laws regulating the lives of people. With the law of Moses, it was imperative that the sins of the people be confessed to and exonerated by the high priests. Traditionally, during the ritual of confession and exoneration a goat was used as the symbolic expression of these deeds. The high priest held the goat high over the heads of the people as the sins were exonerated by the priest. The goat was then driven into the wilderness, symbolically bearing all the sins of the people. Thus, the term *scapegoat* originated (6).

The word as defined today still bears a relationship to its origin. Definitions of scapegoat or scapegoating have been given as:

any individual or group blamed for the misdeeds or mistakes of others (6).

conflicts between group members that are displaced from a conflictual situation to one particular member of a group (7).

Scapegoating is the collusion formed by two people against a third (3).

the scapegoating process is that someone is assigned an object role by the collusive action of several other members (8).

A nominal definition for scapegoating then would be: an intentional, collusive act or actions by two or more persons against an individual or group by which the designated individual or group takes on the assigned role given by the primary person(s).

Scapegoating is an interesting phenomenon of group interaction, whether the group is a social collection of individuals or a family. According to Francis and Munjas, "The primary function of scapegoating is the maintenance of the family system" (7). The person selected for scapegoating may have some limitations that already make him/her stand out from other family members. He/she may accept the role of *scapegoat* due to a dependent, lower power position and, thus, stay in the role because of reinforcement by others.

Why do people become scapegoats? Some reasons are: masochistic tendencies, a need for relationships with others, doubts of one's ability for genuine acceptance and love, naivety, or a lack of societal skills needed to cope with people that hurt others or with a sadistic person who is pretending to help the person being scapegoated (9). Children are usually the scapegoats in a family. This is due to their powerless position as compared to adults (3). The child's personality can be molded to the role assigned by his parents. Unresolved marital conflicts often lead the parents to place tension on the first available object—a child. For scapegoating to be effective, the behavior must be strongly reinforced by significant others, even though the child has much inward hostility and anger. The child must perceive that the parents have much power over him. Effective scapegoating also occurs when there are inconsistent role expectations and discipline in the family. There are conflicting expectations of the child by the parents, and the child internalizes these expectations.

Once the pattern of scapegoating is established in a family, the family achieves a relatively stable equilibrium (3). However, the difficulty of maintaining family equilibrium in this situation brings forth much guilt and rationalized defensive behavior from family members. Parental conflicts continue, although minimized. Family solidarity is maintained, at least for the moment. The scapegoated person, however, will suffer dysfunctional emotional health.

The scapegoat attempts to find himself relief from this situation by escaping literally and figuratively. This may take the form of either running away, excessive acting out, or suicide. These attempts toward relief upset the family equilibrium.

COMPARISON OF LABELING AND SCAPEGOATING

With a comparison of labeling and scapegoating one can detect that attention is detracted from other family members and directed toward a specific person in order to redirect aggression, refocus attention toward a specific family member, reduce family anxiety, enforce expected norms, and allow the family members (as a group) to assert that a particular family member is different. With labeling and scapegoating, the individual ends up role playing the expected behavior because of family prejudices and dissensions. Many times, the dominant people in the group may have difficulty relating effectively with others due to a lack of social skills. Both these terms use the value systems of a group. They also involve socialization processes, development, and appraisals of accepted norms of specific groups. Eventually emotional changes can occur both in the accuser(s) and the accusee(s). In both labeling and scapegoating, tactics can be redirected and changed by a program developed to offer rewards for appropriate goals and behaviors.

CONTRAST OF LABELING AND SCAPEGOATING

Labeling is not necessarily applied because of faction or negativism. It is an everyday process in socialization and does not necessarily produce bad results in either the labeler or the labeled person. On the other hand, scapegoating has its beginning when specific factions occur in a group and occur under tension and emotionalism of a specific group. The scapegoated person attempts to find relief from the results by escaping literally and figuratively. It is a method of relieving tension or redirecting emotions from a group onto a specific individual, especially if the person is in a one-down-lack-of-self-defense position. Labeling, however, does not necessarily involve tension or anxiety and can occur regardless of a person's position in the group. Any individual can do labeling but the person or group labeled does not necessarily have to accept the label and has alternative ways to escape from further labeling. This is not the case with scapegoating. In this activity, there are usually two or more persons in a primary position who heap verbal assaults on a person in a secondary position. This scapegoated person accepts the assigned role(s) and is generally not able to escape.

The one doing the scapegoating may become the new scapegoat of the group, whereas the one doing the labeling may be able to maintain that title and position. Labeling can both produce and extinguish deviant behavior since its value system is of a longer duration. In scapegoating, one may find reinforced perceived deviant behavior that is not extinguished and a value system that generally is not long lasting.

Aggression is not necessarily involved in labeling, whereas scapegoating may be a form of displaced aggression. Scapegoating is applied to humans, but labeling can be applied to any object, human or otherwise. Thus, labeling and scapegoating are processes used to identify different characteristics of individual(s). There are expectations of changed behavior or characteristics that will be of a long duration and that meet the expectations of other members of a group.

CLINICAL IMPLICATION IN FAMILY THERAPY

Labeling

To break the chain of pathological labeling, the therapist needs to know something of the socialization process, normal child development, and how or what things are learned from other people. The therapist needs to reinforce that the parents are in control of the situation, and by putting forth an effort the parents can institute change. The therapist should cite examples that he/she has observed when the parents have made positive efforts toward change. Have the parents set up a check system to see that the procedure is done as scheduled. Frequently remind the parents to make no negative statements about the behavior and assure them that this method will work.

Labeling can both produce and extinguish deviant behavior. The therapist will need to assess the reason for labeling. If they do not have the ability to handle deviant behavior, the parents will need to be trained. If the parents are not motivated to work with the behavior, they will need to have a program developed to reward appropriate goals and behaviors.

Scapegoating

Many times, a group will use a particular person as an "object for their displaced aggressions" (9). Scapegoating in a group may be the consequence of the "therapist's failure to explore anger directed at a therapist" (10). Thus, even family members (a small group) may vent their anxiety and negative feelings on the scapegoated person.

Ohlsen gives the following advice to a counselor who observes a person in a scapegoat role:

1. Reflect the feelings that he feels the scapegoat is experiencing.
2. The scapegoated person then has a chance to express how he feels.
3. This can rally support and understanding from others in the group.
4. Which in turn helps the scapegoat to discover his impact on others. This can encourage the hurter to seek new ways of relating to others.
5. The hurter may then become the scapegoat of the group.
6. Members of the group must assist the scapegoat and hurter to learn new ways of relating to others (9).

To stop scapegoating and allow for change to occur, new patterns of behavior must influence all members of the family. The therapist can use the following methods of intervention as listed by Smoyak:

(*1*) shifting of traditional roles, (*2*) revision of transactional modes, (*3*) redefining delegation of work roles, (*4*) alternative ways of bargaining, (*5*) substitution of another value system, in the family, that has more lasting satisfaction (3).

SUMMARY

Labeling and scapegoating have many common, yet different, characteristics. Labeling occurs before scapegoating. Labeling is a learned reaction to the appraisals the growing child makes of objects in his/her environment. Scapegoating occurs when people transfer their aggression and negative emotions onto a less powerful person. This redirection brings temporary release of tension between the two people. However, it also keeps the primary persons from having open, honest communications. Labeling, on the other hand, is not necessary to release tension or direct aggression. Both labeling and scapegoating are processes long rooted in human antiquity and will continue to be used by humans.

REFERENCES

1. Lemert, E. M. *Human deviance, social problems and social control* (2nd ed.), Englewood Cliffs, N.J.: Prentice-Hall, 1972, pp. 17–18.
2. Scheff, T. J. *Being mentally ill.* Chicago: Aldine, 1981, p. 81.
3. Smoyak, S. *The psychiatric nurse as a family therapist.* New York: John Wiley & Sons, 1975, pp. 142, 144, 150, 153–154.
4. Goffman, E. *Stigma.* Englewood Cliffs, N.J.: Prentice-Hall, 1963, pp. 3–5.
5. Gibbs, J. P. Sanctions. *Social Problems, 153.*
6. Engle, T. L. & Snellgrove, L. *Psychology: Its principles and applications.* New York: Harcourt Brace Jovanovich, 1974, pp. 285–286.
7. Francis, G. M., & Munjas, B. A. *Manual of social psychologic assessment.* New York: Appleton-Century-Crofts, 1976, p. 39.
8. Boszormenyi-Nagy, I., & Zuk, G. W. *Family therapy and disturbed families.* Palo Alto, Calif.: Science and Behavior Books, 1976, pp. 48–57.
9. Ohlson, M. M. *Group counseling.* New York: Holt, Rinehart & Winston, 1977, pp. 213–215.
10. Longo, D. C., & Williams, R. A. *Clinical practice in psychosocial nursing: Assessment and intervention.* New York: Appleton-Century-Crofts, 1978, p. 227.

23

Family Myth and Ghosts of the Past

Marion Fitzsimmons Briel

Antonio Ferreira and Norman Paul are two psychiatrists who have moved from a psychoanalytic framework to a systems theory approach to treatment. Each of these men has introduced new concepts to the nascent literature on family therapy. This chapter will present Ferreira's concept, *family myth*, and Paul's concept, *ghosts of the past*. The historical development of each of the concepts, their similarities, points of contrast, and implications for clinical practice will be presented.

DEVELOPMENT OF CONCEPTS

The concept of family myth was formulated by Ferreira (1) in response to Jackson's (2) introduction of the concept of *family homeostasis*. Jackson (2) had observed that "the continuous interplay of dynamic forces within the family tended toward the maintenance of certain forms of equilibrium among family members" (1).

Ferreira (1) postulated that the family uses certain homeostatic mechanisms to facilitate equilibrium in the family system. The important homeostatic mechanism introduced by Ferreira (1) was the family myth, which he described as:

A series of fairly well integrated beliefs shared by all family members concerning each other and their mutual position in the family life, beliefs go unchallenged by everyone involved in spite of the reality distortions which they may conspicuously imply (1).

The function of the family myth is to dictate the roles each of the family members plays, as well as the nature of the transactions among the family members. It defines the intrafamily roles and counter-roles and the rules that govern the nature of the relationship. Ferreira (3) states:

It is in effect a blueprint for action, an agreed upon statement about the relationship and its members, a set of programmed patterns and rituals with a definite economic value to the relationship (3).

The heuristic value of the family myth is in its ability to maintain the family homeostasis by dictating the nature of relationships and roles within the family. The family myth prohibits changes in the family that would upset the delicate balance of forces within the system. Like the individual psychological defense mechanisms, which help maintain a balance of intrapsychic forces, the family myth is a group defense mechanism, which helps maintain a balance of interpersonal forces.

The family myth differs greatly from the social facade that a family presents to outsiders. It is not a front or outer image but rather an inner image, an image that expresses the shared convictions of the family about the members' roles, attributes, and relationships. These convictions are accepted by family members without challenge, even when there are apparent contradictions with reality. Rather than risk upset of the homeostasis by questioning the validity of the family myth, the family members strive to ensure its continuance.

Paradoxically, this striving to maintain the myth is coupled with a denial of its existence. The myth requires that the family members exercise a type of selective inattention or limitation of insight. This ensures that there will be no individual insight within the family about the distortions of reality being used. It also results in the individual's fighting and preventing revelation of the nature of the myth to outsiders. Thus, the myth becomes a sort of ultimate truth, which stands above question or inquiry. It is the "repository of the covert rules of the relationship in accordance with which the behavior of family members vis-a-vis each other is prescribed" (3). It explains the behavior of the individuals in the family, while it hides its motives and becomes a formula for actions to be taken at certain points in the relationship (1). Thus, the family myth is the very foundation of family life.

Ferreira postulates that the origins of the family myth date back to the early days of the parents' relationship, courtship, and first two or three years of marriage. During this time the couple is formulating its conceptions about the nature of their relationship and their expectations of family life. Formulations adopted at this time evolve into family myths. For example, the belief that "a baby will solve our marital problems" is likely to evolve into the myth that "we would divorce if it were not for the children."

In the above example, a couple experiencing stress in the marital dyad constructs a belief to decrease the stress (e.g., having a baby). In reality, the child will not decrease the family stress (in all likelihood he or she will probably increase the family stress). The inherent threat to the family equilibrium or homeostasis is too great for the family to handle. Rather than confront the issue head on (i.e., acknowledge the strained situation and consider realistic solutions or alternatives), the parents cling to their belief in the "saving quality of the child or children and reinforce the family myth that they would be divorced if it were not for the children. Ferreira (1) writes:

> Seemingly, the family myth is called into play whenever certain tensions reach predetermined thresholds among the family members and in some way, real or fantasied, threaten to disrupt ongoing relationships. Then, the family myth functions like the thermostat that is kicked into action by the "temperature" of the family. Like any other homeostatic mechanism, the myth prevents the family system from damaging, perhaps destroying, itself. It has therefore the qualities of any "safety valve," that is survival value (1).

Although Ferriera (3) presents much clinical data demonstrating the manifestations of the family myth in families with schizophrenic individuals, he states that family myths are not solely present in pathologic families. He points out that the cultivation of family principles, values, traditions and rituals is a function of the dynamics of family myths. Ferreira (3) concludes that a certain amount of mythology is necessary for "smooth and economic family living" (3).

Ferreira (3) also comments that the concept of the family myth falls on the transition ground between psychiatry and sociology. It deals with individually and socially oriented formulations. That is, it alters the individual's perception of the world, while at the same time having its roots in larger social myths. Manifestations of family myths include individuals who see themselves as "the sick one," "the clumsy one," or "the funny one" within the family. These are examples of the influence of the family myth on the individual's perceptions of himself. Beliefs in the "Irish temper," "Black inferiority," or "Jewish parsimony" are examples of family myths influenced by social myths.

In summary, the family myth is a belief system adapted by a family to promote homeostasis within the family system. It is an agreed on level of compromise that prescribes the roles, counterroles, and relationships within the family. This protects the family system from the threat of disequilibrium and disintegration and thereby serves as a reinforcement for the myth and an avoidance of reality testing.

The concept ghosts of the past is attributed to Norman Paul by Skynner

(4). However, in reviewing the major articles by Paul (5, 6, 7) documenting his work with bereaved clients, one learns that Paul does not use the actual term *ghosts of the past*. Paul writes of the role of unresolved grief in fixated family interactional patterns and treatment of such families. His formulation developed as a result of his work with schizophrenic patients who improved markedly during their hospitalization (but regressed to their prehospitalized state when they returned home. Paul and Grosser (5) observed a common structure in the families of the schizophrenic patients, which included a set of family relationships highly resistant to change, especially observable in attitudes toward the paient. Paul and Grosser (5) describe the attitudes and behaviors as manifestations of a "fixed family equilibrium" and describe this as:

> A relatively unchanging dynamic state to which there is a tendency to return when disturbed. It can be viewed as a pathological homeostasis (5).

Paul and Grosser postulated that the need for such a pathological homeostasis within the family could be related to a family pattern of inability to cope with loss. However, they found a paucity of literature dealing with empirical observations of the actual process of mourning in individuals in either its natural or pathological forms. They found it quite ironic that in a society where we are constantly exhorted to prepare materially for death, we are not prepared psychologically to cope with the loss of a loved one. In contrast to many other areas of the world, which practice elaborate ceremonies to explain the meaning of life and death, our society has become so urbanized and secularized that we have discarded most traditional and emotional forms of grieving. According to Paul and Grosser (5) this results in incomplete mourning and the inability to resolve the loss of the loved ones (pp. 339–340).

Building on the work of Bowlby (8), Paul and Grosser (5) conducted a clinical study of 50 families with schizophrenic members and 25 families with at least one psychoneurotic member. They identified a common feature of variable patterns of maladaptive responses to object loss. Although some of the losses occurred as much as 50 years ago, the inability to cope with the loss was expressed through denial of its significance on an affective level. The style of the family is described as:

> Permeated with varying degrees of denial or "warding off" of losses and disappointments. Major changes in family homeostasis, such as those which might result in separation or independence of its members, were often resisted (5).

Paul and Grosser observed that many times a parent suffered a loss just before the birth of the schizophrenic patient. This has been confirmed. Paul and Grosser (5) documented the projection of the dead relative's characteristics to the schizophrenic patient, as well as the identification with dead persons expressed by the schizophrenic, that is, through references about his own lifelessness (5). Thus, the memory of the deceased relative is a powerful force in the lives of the family members and may thus be labelled a *ghost of the past*. Paul and Grosser (5) also observed the families' resistance to attempts at independence by any of its members. Threatened with another potential loss to the family unit, the members reinforce the symbiotic ties among the members. Based on these observations, Paul and Grosser hypothesized that there is a direct relationship between the maladaptive response to object loss and the fixity in symbiotic relationships in the family.

To overcome the symbiotic fixations, Paul and Grosser introduced operational mourning, that is, the facilitation of the affective discharge of unresolved grief. According to the authors, this process provides a powerful empathic experience, which enables the family members to develop an observing family ego. Displaced hostility and ambivalence from the original lost relative to other family members (e.g., the schizophrenic) can be identified. This results in revelation of previously unknown family secrets.

The family's response to the process of operational mourning is variable. The theme of mourning lost objects is one that is quite difficult to pursue in most families. However, Paul and Grosser (5) found that avoidance of operational mourning is strongest in families with a schizophrenic member. These families want to maintain a fixed role relationship regardless of the inappropriateness of many of the interactions. Paul writes:

> Such fixity, though present for many years appears to be rooted in maladaptive responses to both real and imagined object-and-past-object loss. Furthermore, it appears that such losses and associated sense of deprivation lead to deposits of such affects as sorrow, anger, grief, guilt, bitterness, despair, and regret. These affects, timeless as experienced internally, appear to dictate a restitutive response characterized by the emergence of a perceptual set leading to mate selection. It is as if the prospective mate seeks, in the mate to be selected, both what he had and didn't have in his object relations. These background elements in both partners generate a style of marital harmony and incompatibility. It appears that both factors conspire to promote periodic marital crises. The oscillating marital homeostasis is associated with a denial of or a warding off of real or imagined losses, disappointments, or major changes that require sanctions for and support of greater sense of separation between the spouses (5).

Paul is explaining the circular dynamics involved in the poorly adapted couple and/or family. The unresolved loss in the past drives the individual into a symbiosis with the spouse. There is an intensely interdependent relationship, which magnifies even the slightest attempt at independence as a threat of abandonment. The symbiotic ties are tightened and the cycle continues. Thus the loss of an object in the past, the ghost of the past is in essence the root of the family's problems.

COMPARISON AND CONTRAST

Ferreira's *family myth* and Paul's *ghost of the past* are two terms used to conceptualize the dynamics within the family system. Paul uncovers unresolved grief in an individual and identifies the unresolved grief as a point of fixation for the family. Like Ferreira's family myth, Paul describes the family fixation as a pathological homeostasis. Both men developed their concepts as a result of their work with hospitalized schizophrenic patients and their families. Each therapist observed the phenomenon of patients improving significantly during hospitalization and individual psychotherapy, but failing to maintain their gains after being discharged and returning to live with their families.

The common bond of psychoanalytic training is evident in the development of Ferreira's and Paul's concepts. Ferreira states that the "family myth is to the relationship what the defense is to the individual" (1). Thus, the myth serves as a defense against interpersonal disintegration as individual defense mechanisms serve as a defense against intrapsychic disintegration. Paul's use of the term *fixated family equilibrium* is analogous to the fixations in personality described in the psychoanalytic literature. The unresolved grief results in a fixation in family development.

Although both psychiatrists have a strong psychoanalytic background, they observe the effects the family dynamics have on the individual, but their assessments and interventions center on the family as a system. Ferreira recognizes that to change the individuals within the family, first the covert and overt rules of the family system must be changed. Ferreira's conceptualization of the family myth and Paul's ghost of the past are quite similar to Bowen's (9) family projection system. That is, although the subject matter of the family myth may be focused predominantly on one person, the emotional forces that give it cause and maintenance always involve every family member. In the unresolved grief reaction, the identified patient becomes endowed through projection with a number of characteristics of the lost object. Thus, both Ferreira and Paul see the family, not a particular individual, as the client.

The concepts, family myth and ghosts of the past, relate very closely to Minuchen's concept of enmeshment and Bowen's concept of undifferentiation. Each of these concepts connotes a poorly differentiated family system and subsystem boundaries. As stated earlier, the family myth imposes necessary limitations on the family members' insight. Thus, growth and differentiation and emancipation are viewed as a potential loss to the family. The threat of another loss is too overwhelming and the family members reinforce symbiotic ties.

The lack of differentiation and a high degree of enmeshment result in fixed role relationships among family members plagued by a ghost of the past or a maladaptive family myth. Paul and Grosser (5) describe the structure of the family as "highly resistant to change" and in a state of "fixed family equilibrium," that is, "a relatively unchanging dynamic state to which there is a tendency to return when disturbed." Ferreira (3) discusses the existence of roles and counterroles with the emphasis on "the complementarity of behavior, and the regularities of mutual attitudes in a relationship."

In summary, the terms *family myth* and *ghosts of the past* were coined by Ferreira and Paul, respectively, to describe a systems phenomenon within families. Although family myths are in operation in all families and all families experience loss, Ferreira and Paul use their concepts to assess the dynamics within the family and plan appropriate intervention. They both emphasize the importance of focusing on the underlying structure of the family and not on the superficial symptoms of the individual or "identified patient."

Although Ferreira and Paul share the belief in a family approach to treatment, their concepts differ in a number of ways. The concept of *family myth* is a more general term than the concept of *ghosts of the past*. The family myth can be any set of beliefs held by family members about any image they choose to have. Ghosts of the past, on the other hand, is a concept that specifically deals with the death of a family member. The incompleted mourning affects and can even develop a family myth by resulting in the projection of characteristics of the deceased one to another family member and the establishment of a fixated family equilibrium. Thus, Ferreira's concept of family myth includes the maladaptive family equilibrium resulting from a family's incomplete mourning.

A second point of contrast is the definition of the two terms. Ferreira (1) defines the family myth as a "series of well-integrated *beliefs* . . . beliefs that go unchallenged by everyone involved in spite of the reality distortions which they may conspicuously imply." Thus, the family myth deals primarily with the *cognitive* component of the family members' lives, and interventions focus primarily on these cognitive beliefs.

Paul and Grosser (5) describe the cause of the fixed family equilibrium to be the failure of certain family members to mourn sufficiently the loss of a loved one. As stated earlier, this often results in the projection of certain characteristics of the deceased to a family member and results in a type of family myth. However, Paul and Grosser do not focus on the cognitive beliefs, but rather the repressed affective component of the bereaved individual. Paul and Grosser (5) state that the "abortive mourning or denial of loss seem to be at the core of the fixation." They use operational mourning to induce a belated mourning experience. This results in a shared *affective* experience that is designed to permit all family members, including children, the opportunity to observe the expression of intense feelings. Figuratively, the dam breaks and the flood of emotions is a catharsis for the bereaved. A sense of affective continuity can be identified and dealt with. In short, the shared affective experience facilitates an atmosphere of empathy and understanding of the origin of current relational difficulties.

The ghost of the past is "exorcised" from the position of power in the family, not by discussion, that is, cognitive means, but by the shared expression of emotion, affective means.

A third point of contrast is the role of the therapist in applying these concepts. Ferreira uses his concept of family myth in an abstract way. That is, he makes the reader aware of the existence of the family myth and, generally, how it dictates the behavior of family members. In his articles on the family myth (1, 3), Ferreira does not give specific instructions for interventions. Rather, he points out the resistance to change by the family when a family myth is maintaining homeostasis. As pathologic or maladaptive as the family myth may appear to the therapist, it serves an important function to family. Circumstances and events, for example, the hospitalization or discharge of the "identified patient," can challenge or even destroy a "family myth." When this happens, the family must reformulate family rules. It is at this time that Ferreira believes conjoint family therapy can be of greatest help. Yet, he also cautions that the "help" a family seeks can merely be an attempt to label the "identified patient" and reinforce the family myth. Thus, Ferreira does not give specific suggestions for intervention, but uses the concept of "family myth" as a theoretical framework for assessing the family.

Paul, on the other hand, is much more operationally oriented. (Ferreira has dropped his family psychotherapy practice and returned to a neurology practice in California.) As stated earlier, Paul does not use the specific term *ghosts of the past* in his writings. He does use the terms *fixated family equilibrium* and *operational mourning*. Once Paul has observed fixed role relationships and the evidence of incomplete mourning, he takes a very active role in the therapy sessions. He asks repeated direct inquiries about the reactions to actual losses sustained by specific family members and encourages the expression of feeling of the member directly involved. He then invites other family members to review such feelings as are stimulated through witnessing the grief reaction (5). In his later works, Paul (7) discusses the use of videotapes of other clients expressing their grief about their losses. This technique facilitates the development and expression of similar feelings by the clients watching the videotape.

Thus, Paul's use of operational mourning to free the family from ghosts of the past is an operational procedure, whereas Ferreira's family myth is a theoretical concept. Had Ferreira included more of his specific interventions, he could have developed a more operational concept, for example, "demystification" or "de-myth-ification."

IMPLICATIONS FOR THERAPY

The work of both therapists in dealing with families and in particular, families of schizophrenics is important to family nurse therapists. First, the implication that all "identified patients" are part of a larger system, that is, their family and their behavior must be evaluated in the context of the family dynamics.

Secondly, the family nurse therapist must be aware of the existence and importance of the family myth. The assessment of the family should include the documentation of family beliefs about their roles and their inner image. As discussed earlier, family members strive to keep this concealed. However, exploring the early days of the spouses' relationship and their hopes and beliefs about what a family should be should provide clues to possible family myths. Exploration of relationships will provide data on the existence of roles and counterroles.

Also, when taking the family history, the therapist should document any evidence of unresolved grief in addition to the flexibility of roles. Ascribing characteristics of a deceased relative to a living member is evidence of a ghost of the past influencing the family. Exploration of feelings about past losses will uncover the existence of repressed or unresolved grief reaction. Fears of abandonment, symbiotic relationships, and rigid role expectations can be family symptoms of unresolved object loss. The therapist must serve as a role model for the acceptance of feelings.

The greatest implication for therapy can be found in Paul and Grosser's work from Ferreira's (10) articles on empathy. It appears that the "substance" that can facilitate changes in the family system is the experience of empathy among family members for one another. Although the bereaved family member in Paul's therapy experiences a discharge of emotions, changes are effected in the family when the other family members empathize with the bereaved member and with each other. It appears that empathy for other family members allows a change in role expectations and an increase in role flexibility among all family members. Thus, the family members can grow and differentiate, the family has more alternatives available to it and will be able to maintain an adaptive, not maladaptive or fixed, homeostasis. Thus, the therapist serves as an empathic role model, as well as the facilitator of experiences and discussions to increase the empathic capability of all family members for each other.

SUMMARY

Like many of the therapists since the 1950s, Ferreira and Paul have developed concepts to explain the phenomena encountered by therapists who work with families. The common theoretical framework from which these concepts evolved, namely, the systems theory, is used to examine the similarites between these concepts. The difference in application of the concepts is examined in light of the therapeutic style used by the two therapists. The implication for clinical practice uses both concepts and is built on the liberating force of therapy-empathy.

REFERENCES

1. Ferreira, A. Family myth and homeostasis. *Archives of General Psychiatry,* 1963, *9*(5), 456–463.
2. Jackson, D. D. The question of family homeostasis. *Psychiatric Quarterly,* 1957, *31*(suppl), 79–90.
3. Ferreira, A. Psychosis and family myth. *American Journal of Psychotherapy,* 1967, *2*(21), 186–197.
4. Skynner, A. C. R. *Systems of family and marital psychotherapy.* New York: Brunner/Mazel, 1976.
5. Paul, N. L. & Grosser, G. H. Operational mourning and its role in conjoint family therapy. *Community Mental Health Journal,* 1965, *1*(4), 339–345.
6. Paul, N. L. The role of mourning and empathy in conjoint marital therapy. In G. Zuk, & I. Boszormenyi-Nagy (Eds.), *Pathogenic social systems and family therapy.* Palo Alto, Calif.: Science and Behavior Books, 1966.
7. Paul, N. L. Cross confrontation. In P. J. Guerin (Ed.), *Family therapy: Theory and practice.* New York: Gardner Press, 1976.
8. Bowlby, J. Separation anxiety: A critical review of the literature. *Journal of Child Psychology and Psychiatry,* 1961, *1*, 251–259.
9. Bowen, M. Theory in the practice of psychotherapy. In P. J. Guerin (Ed.), *Family therapy: Theory and practice.* New York: Gardner Press, 1976.
10. Ferreira, A. Empathy and the bridge function of the ego. *Journal of the American Psychoanalytic Association,* 1961, *9*, 91–105.

24

Family Ego Mass and Family Structure

Nancy Lee Nygaard

Murray Bowen's concept of the undifferentiated family ego mass and the degree of individual self-differentiation, and Salvador Minuchin's concept of family structure and boundary function ranging from disengagement to enmeshment represent examples of related theories that have common, but different, focuses. This chapter will examine the two conceptual frameworks. The purpose is to compare and contrast these frameworks and thereby clarify theoretical similarities and differences between these two schools of thought.

HISTORICAL BACKGROUND OF THE THEORIES

Murray Bowen's family systems theory evolved from studies of identified schizophrenic patients and their families. Work with less pathological families and multigenerational studies contributed to further refinement and definition of his theory.

While involved in clinical work at the Menninger Clinic in the early 1950s, Bowen studied mother/child symbiosis and its role in schizophrenia. In 1954 Bowen moved to the National Institute of Mental Health where he conducted a project in which schizophrenic patients and their entire families were hospitalized for observation and research. He participated in the first national meeting where research on family aspects of schizophrenia was presented at the annual meeting of the American Orthopsychiatric Association in March 1957 (1).

The idea of the mother's role in the schizophrenic process extended to the father and other family members. Symptomatology came to be viewed as being reflective of family dysfunction. He realized that the same processes were also operating in less pathological and even normal families (2).

Following termination of this project in 1959, Bowen went to the Georgetown University Medical Center. He pursued work with less pathological families and conducted some multigenerational family research.

He began to focus on theoretical concepts (including differentiation of self) and define his family systems theory, which was first published in 1966. This theory is composed of interlocking concepts of functioning patterns that relate to the family system and cross generational processes. He considers the differentiation-of-self concept a cornerstone of his theory (2).

In 1978 Bowen published his first book, *Family Therapy in Clinical Practice* (3). In this work he discusses the evolution of his theory and presents a collection of many of his papers from 1957 to 1977.

In Salvador Minuchin's structural family therapy, man is viewed in terms of his social context. He describes the development of this approach as a response to twentieth century concepts of man's interaction with his environment (4). With this therapy the family is considered the crucial social context in which an individual functions.

In the early 1960s Minuchin directed a research project at the Wiltwyck School in New York in which low socioeconomic families with delinquent boys were studied. Significant early findings related to family structure, subsystems and functions, communication between parents and children, and influences of the subculture (5). The Family Interaction Apperception Test and The Family Task, tools for study of the family, were developed during the course of this research (6). *Families of the Slums: An Exploration of Their Structure and Treatment* is based on this project (7).

In the late 1960s Minuchin moved to Philadelphia where he became associated with the Philadelphia Child Guidance Clinic and the University of Pennsylvania School of Medicine. He worked with Montalvo, Haley, and others. Here, structural family therapy became formally defined (4).

Minuchin is noted for his work in the treatment of children, psychosomatic disorders, and low socioeconomic families. In 1974 he published *Families and Family Therapy* (4).

DESCRIPTION OF THE THEORIES

Bowen

Bowen conceptualizes an undifferentiated family ego mass that is a fusion of the egos of individual family members. There is a boundary around this ego mass. Bowen describes each person's degree of fusion as his/her *differentiation of self*. This ranges on a scale from a theoretical complete undifferentiation, 0, to complete differentiation, 100 (8).

He also refers to levels of self within each person. The solid self is stable and uninfluenced by the emotional system. It assumes an *I* position and accepts responsibility. The pseudo-self is acquired from others through emotional pressure and becomes involved in the fusion process (2).

Those who are more undifferentiated are more fused with the family ego mass. These people tend to be influenced by emotional forces, and, as the degree of differentiation decreases, the self is increasingly defined by others. They are more reactive to stress and prone to illness.

People with higher degrees of differentiation have more ability to balance emotional responses with intellectual processes. Although they may react to stress, they are better able to regain equilibrium. These people have a better defined self through decreased fusion with other family members. Differentiation does not imply aloofness. A more differentiated individual is freer to move close to others while maintaining the self. While theoretical, complete differentiation is the ideal.

Bowen makes a distinction between *basic* and *functioning* levels of self. The basic level of differentiation for most people remains the same as when they left their parental family. However, the pseudo-self, particularly in less differentiated people, shifts in the relationship system and functional levels of self fluctuate (3).

He has formulated a series of interlocking concepts that relate to the effects of and responses to forces active in the differentiation-of-self concept. These include: (*1*) differentiation-of-self scale, (2) nuclear family emotional system, (*3*) family projection process, (*4*) multigenerational transmission process, (*5*) sibling position, and (*6*) triangles (2, 8). Each of these concepts is related to the manner in which the family and individual members affect and are affected by each other. Anxiety and stress tend to extend the forces.

Bowen later added two other concepts. *Emotional cutoff* refers to emotional processes between generations. *Societal regression* relates to societal responses to anxiety.

Bowen has defined these interlocking concepts in a manner that enables family therapists to understand the dynamics involved in family processes. The overall goal of therapy is to increase the level of differentiation of self. The therapist, while staying out of the emotional system, supports movement toward increased differentiation. Change in one member affects other family members.

Minuchin

Structural family therapy developed by Minuchin is based on an appreciation of the interaction between individuals and their social context. The family is the primary social system of individuals. While fulfilling functions relating to the needs of its members, the family must also be flexible in response to societal forces.

Minuchin views the family from a structural context. The family functions through subsystems that are formed around common purposes. These subsystems may have one to several members. An individual *belongs* to a family, but it is through involvement in subsystems that a sense of identity is gained and differentiated skills are learned. Individuals may be members of more than one subsystem at the same time, and membership in each brings different levels of power and requires different skills.

Minuchin describes typical subsystems and their functions. For instance, the parental subsystem is responsible for nurturance, guidance, and control of children. Within the sibling subsystem, children learn to negotiate, cooperate, and compete (4).

Boundaries regulate participation in subsystems and interactions between family members. Effective subsystem functioning and development of interpersonal skills is dependent on boundaries that permit appropriate contact with others while preventing excessive interference. Boundaries may range from being rigid (inhibiting contact and leading to disengagement) to being diffuse (permitting excessive contact leading to enmeshment).

Disengaged systems (with rigid boundaries) tend toward decreased communication and lack of support and responsiveness. There is an exaggerated sense of autonomy. Enmeshed systems (with blurred boundaries) tend toward a lack of autonomy, with concurrent overinvolvement and reactivity. Most families fall within a normal range somewhere in the middle (4).

The family operates through transactional patterns that are formed over a period of time. Through repetition, patterns of relating to others in the system are established. These transactions may vary, depending on several factors such as developmental influences and stress. The family system's flexiblilty in using alternative transactional patterns affects its ability to adapt to change (4).

In structural family therapy the therapist assumes an active role. The family's transactional patterns are viewed in terms of effectiveness of family functioning. Where appropriate, rigid boundaries in disengaged systems are decreased and blurred boundaries in enmeshed systems are strengthened. Individual subjective experiences change as family structure is transformed.

COMPARISON

It is evident that there are some similarities between Bowen's concept of the undifferentiated family ego mass and the degree of differentiation of self, and Minuchin's concept of family structure, subsystems, and boundary function. The family is viewed as a system with individual members affecting and being affected by others. In both theories, degrees of involvement with other members of the family have implications for functioning (in the sense of autonomy and family function).

Relative degrees of the processes described in these theories do not refer directly to levels of functioning. Rather, these continuums provide a means of understanding tendencies, interactions, and adaptability. While Bowen and Minuchin do describe functional and dysfunctional mechanisms, these are presented as deriving from their concepts but not necessarily being directly related to the level of differentiation or degree of enmeshment versus disengagement. For instance, less differentiated people are prone to being more reactive to stress (2). Similarly, enmeshed families may react strongly to stress in an individual member (4).

Internal and external stresses tend to increase the intensity of the processes described in these theories. Bowen and Minuchin both refer to developmental issues. For example, Bowen identifies circumstances in which a child may become the target of family processes leading to decreased differentiation and the difficulties that may arise when a child (particularly one who is less differentiated) attempts to leave the system. Minuchin describes the variations in boundaries between subsystems as a child (who initially may be more enmeshed with the mother) moves through developmental stages.

CONTRAST

Although there are similarities between these two theories, there are also differences. Levels of self differentiation and degrees of enmeshment versus disengagement are described on continuums. In Bowen's theory, the level of self-differentiation ranges from being low (with tendencies toward dysfunction) to being high (with increasing ability to balance emotional and intellectual processes). One cannot be too differentiated. In Minuchin's structural family therapy, however, extremes of either disengagement or enmeshment (opposites on the continuum) may indicate areas of possible dysfunction.

Specific therapeutic goals and interventions are based on assessment of the family in treatment. In general terms, there is a difference in the focus of these approaches. Bowen's theory addresses interactional processes, but the emphasis is on levels of self-differentiation in relation to family functioning. Therapy is directed toward assisting motivated family members to increase self-differentiation. Change in one member affects others in the family. In structural family therapy, the focus is on interactions in the social context of the family. Minuchin identifies formalized subsystems within the family. The boundaries around the subsystems are critical to the transactional patterns of the family. Therapeutic changes in the family structure alter the subjective experiences of family members.

The focus on past and present relationships also differs. Bowen's family systems theory stresses the importance of understanding past relationships, and time is spent in this effort. The focus of structural family therapy, however, is in the present (9).

The role of the therapist is expressed differently in these approaches. In therapy based on Bowen's theory, the therapeutic role is that of "consultant" or "supervisor," and emotional involvement with the family is minimized (2). In structural family therapy the therapist joins the family (while maintaining the leadership position) to accomplish therapeutic change in the system (4).

SUMMARY

A current difficulty in family systems theory is the lack of unified terminology to adequately identify and express family concepts. Comparing and contrasting related theories clarifies similarities and differences.

A review of the concepts described by Bowen and Minuchin provides evidence of similar views of the family in which symptomatology is perceived as evidence of dysfunction in the family. Both theories take into account the importance of relationships and interactions within the system. However, there are significant differences in focuses of the concepts and perceptions of therapeutic roles.

Assessment, planning and implementation of therapeutic interventions, and evaluation of outcomes are based on the conceptual framework of the therapist. While specific therapeutic goals and interventions depend on assessment of the particular family in treatment, there are differences in the general focuses of the concepts described by Bowen and Minuchin. Bowen's theory emphasizes individual levels of self-differentiation in relation to the family system. In Minuchin's structural family therapy, the individual is viewed in terms of the social context of the family.

While both approaches strive for relief of symptomatology and enhanced individual and family functioning, general goals are described differently. In Bowen's family systems theory, the overall goal is to assist motivated family members to increase self-differentiation. Change in one member affects others in the system. In structural family therapy, changes in family structure alter individual subjective experiences.

A particular difference between these approaches involves the role of the therapist. In Bowen's theory, the therapist consults with, but does not become a part of, the family system. In structural family therapy, change comes from the therapist entering and directly affecting the system.

Professional nurses are becoming more actively involved in the treatment of families. This necessitates educational and experiential preparation based on clear conceptual frameworks. While not all nurses wish to function as family therapists, they often have input into recommendations for treatment and referral services. An understanding of family systems concepts better enables them to assist families in distress to obtain help.

REFERENCES

1. Guerin, Jr., P. *Family therapy: Theory and practice.* New York: Gardner Press, 1976.

2. Bowen, M. Theory in the practice of psychotherapy. In P. Guerin, Jr. (Ed.), *Family therapy: Theory and practice.* New York: Gardner Press, 1976.

3. Bowen, M. *Family therapy in clinical practice.* New York: Jason Aronson, 1978.

4. Minuchin, S. *Families and family therapy.* Cambridge, Mass.: Harvard University Press, 1974.

5. Minuchin, S., Auerwald, E., King, C., & Rabinowitz, C. The study and treatment of families that produce multiple acting-out boys. *American Journal of Orthopsychiatry,* 1964, *34,* 125–133.

6. Elbert, S., Rosman, B., Minuchin, S., & Guerney, B. A method for the clinical study of family interaction. *American Journal of Orthopsychiatry, 34,* 1964, 885–894.

7. Minuchin, S., Montalvo, B., Guerney, Jr., B. G., Rosman, B. L., & Schumer, F. *Families of the slums: An exploration of their structure and treatment.* New York: Basic Books, 1967.

8. Bowen, M. The use of family therapy in clinical practice. *Comprehensive Psychiatry,* 1966, *7,* 345–374.

9. Foley, V. Family therapy. In R. J. Corsini (Ed.), *Current psychotherapies* (2nd ed.). Itasca, Ill.: F. E. Peacock, 1979.

Part **V**

CLINICAL PRACTICE

25

Doing Your Own Family Homework

Margaret McAvoy Trimpey

The beginning family therapist soon becomes aware that many of the relationship problems she sees in the families with whom she works are present, to a lesser degree, in her own family. For the family therapist who uses family systems theory as conceptualized by Murray Bowen (1), part of the learning process that aids the individual to work more effectively with others is to begin "defining a self" within her own family of origin. For instance, L. became interested in working in her own family system following a family therapy conference led by Murray Bowen. She believed such work would increase her understanding of families and the relationships within them. Also, she had become aware of certain patterns in her own behavior in her family that were reactive and automatic, and she wanted to learn how to modify them.

Use of family systems theory in the therapist's relatively open system can be helpful in sorting out relationship problems as they develop within her own nuclear family. This chapter will explore one aspect of Bowen's theory, triangles, and will illustrate the use of the concept with examples from the work of one beginning therapist within her own family.

Before introducing the concept of triangles, it is necessary to present a brief overview of the historical development of Bowen's theory accompanied by definitions and descriptions of related concepts that are necessary to understand the theory. Bowen began his work with families in 1950 at the National Institute of Mental Health in a research project with schizophrenic patients, whose families were hospitalized with them. As a result of the project, Bowen began defining and testing certain ideas that had emerged in the study with families who had less dysfunctional relationships than schizophrenia. In 1959, he also instituted multigenerational family research. A year later, Bowen started gathering data about his own family, and during an emotional crisis in the family in 1966, he used the theory in relating to the members of his own family.

Bowen considers this incident in 1966 as pivotal in the development of his theory, for as he presented the work he had done in his own family to his colleagues at a national conference, he also began sharing what he had learned with the residents he was teaching. They, in turn, began working quietly with their own families. The results were twofold. Not only were these residents more effective clinically than previous residents who had not initiated involvement with their families, but this group of residents was remarkably better able to solve problems and maintain open relationships with their spouses and children.

By 1971, coaching therapists-in-training how to work out relationships in their families of origin had become a highly significant component of Bowen's training program. As Guerin and Fogarty (2) later indicate, when family members are able to communicate openly with one another on emotional issues the "impact of such events on the family system will be absorbed and dissipated."

L. asked a clinical specialist who had completed postgraduate study with Bowen in Georgetown to coach her as she began to explore the relationships in her own family. During the next few years, work was sporadic and intermittent and usually followed some incident in her family that increased L.'s awareness of the need for flexibility and openness in the family system. Work had consisted of becoming familiar with concepts, learning family history from various members of the family of origin, making a

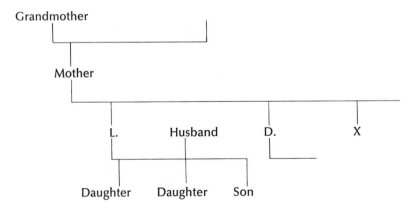

Figure 25-1 L.'s family genogram.

genogram, and beginning to identify the basic triangles and how they work.

L. was the oldest of three children. She had her parents completely to herself for her first 5 years. At that point, several events occurred within a few months of each other that radically changed things. Her sister, D., was born, her mother's parents moved into the home, and the entire family moved to another state.

Bowen (1) warns that family systems theory should not be confused with general systems theory, "which has a much broader frame of reference and no specific application to emotional functioning." His theory does not emphasize cause and effect as in conventional therapy nor work with the identified patient. Rather, as Carter and Orfanidis (3) state, in family systems theory the "emphasis is on the who, what, when, where, and how of family patterns and themes," and work is done with the most motivated member of the family.

In addition, Bowen's theory contains two main variables: the degree of intensity and duration of anxiety with the family and the level of differentiation of self. At the lower level of the differentiation scale are individuals so fused or stuck together with other family members that they "fail to develop themselves or they give up part or most of their autonomy because of their perception that otherwise they will disturb other family members" (3). These people function poorly when anxiety is high or protracted and as a result demonstrate many problems in living. At the other end of the scale, the well differentiated person is self-directed, able to define and pursue personal goals, yet able to remain aware of the degree of dependency in relationships with others. The well differentiated person is thus able to maintain close relationships without losing individual identity by becoming fused with the other person. Most people operate somewhere below or around the middle, where they do more reacting emotionally to others than moving freely in their relationships through the system.

The degree of fusion of two individuals into a "we" depends on the levels of differentiation of the people. Fogarty (4) finds that fusion, or blending, of one into the other increases the level of emotionality between them as well as the level of expectation each one has of the other. The more intense the fusion, the stronger the accompanying feeling that self is being lost. The result is increased anxiety and a need to move away from the other person in an attempt to lower the anxiety. Fogarty (4) states that "the reaction to fusion is distance; the twosome ping-pong back and forth between fusion and distance."

To understand how a person can begin the process that leads to a stronger differentiation of self or "I," it is necessary to understand Bowen's concept of triangles. Triangles are a natural phenomenon that occur in any emotional system regardless of whether the system involved is the family, work, or a social system.

Because the grandmother had been in the home since D.'s birth, and because D. very closely resembled her own daughter, D. became the grandmother's favored child, and a triangle relationship developed that consisted of D., grandmother, and L. A fight would erupt between the sisters and D. would bring in the grandmother to side with her. L. would move to an outside position where she was identified as the selfish, argumentative child. On the other hand, in the triangle between D., L., and their mother, conflict between D. and her mother developed in adolescence that resulted in D. being considered the inconsiderate, selfish one. As adults, neither daughter displayed those identified qualities and both daughters possess many of the characteristics of responsible oldest siblings.

After they reached adulthood, several significant events occurred within a 2-year period. D. and her family moved to the city where L. lived, and their homes were 3 miles apart. In addition, both the mother and grandmother moved in with L. and her family. The move into close proximity activated triangles that had appeared to be dormant. The two sisters continued their conflictual relationship, although on a much lower key and neither was pleased with the quality of the relationship.

Any two-person relationship is unstable, especially in the presence of anxiety and stress. Even in the best of circumstances, it is difficult for two people to discuss or relate to one another on the basis of the issues between them for any length of time before tension increases. The person feeling the most anxiety triangles in a third person or issue. Bringing in a third person results in immediate calm and comfort between the two since it shifts the tension from the original pair but does nothing to improve the quality of their relationship.

Following the grandmother's death, L. attempted to change her and her sister's relationship by initiating a discussion of the issues between them and their relationship with each other and their grandmother. Using "I" statements, L. described how she would behave differently toward D. in the future. Much of their conflict was resolved by the resulting open discussion of the issues, and there was a distinct change in the degree of reactiveness toward one another.

Bowen describes the dynamics of a single triangle as having a comfortable pair and someone on the outside when relationships are calm. The preferred position is to be part of the pair. When the outsider becomes anxious, he/she moves into an inside position and shifts one of the pair to the outside. Each person is "constantly moving to gain a little more close comfort or to withdraw from tension, with each move by one requiring a compensatory move by another" (1).

As an illustration, on one occasion L. consulted the clinical specialist about the acting-out behavior of her son. Her reaction to his behavior was always an intense attempt to exert controls, but she recognized the effects were opposite of what she intended. She was given instructions to leave the relationship with her son alone and start back working on improving the person-to-person relationship within her family of origin. In her attempt to do so, she began, with help, to recognize the activity in the triangle among herself, D., and their mother and how it had affected her relationship with her son.

Within any triangle the emotional forces produce a pattern of reactiveness of members to one another that can be identified and, once identified, can be used to predict the behaviors of any member of the triangle during stress.

Tension had mounted in the relationship between L. and her mother over what L. considered her mother's increasing dependency on her since moving into L.'s home. As the mother became more uncomfortable with the tension, she began calling D. complaining and telling stories about L. Almost simultaneously, D. and mother were in conflict, and their mother told L. stories about D. Then D. and L. would get together and complain, with disparaging laughter, about their mother. As conditions escalated, L. had triangled in her son, who, in an attempt to distance himself, began misbehaving. The original tension between L. and her mother calmed down some as L. focused on controlling her son's behavior since she couldn't control her mother.

Once patterns are identified in a triangle, a plan of intervention can be worked out to stop the motion and allow the members to work out the issues between them. The identification and intervention process is complicated by the fact that triangles grow as the system enlarges. For example, "a five-person system is nine primary triangles" (1). In addition to primary triangles, there are secondary ones that operate on a temporary basis when a particular issue arises, such as occurred when L.'s conflict with her son allowed her to withdraw from the intensity in her relationship with her mother.

In attempting to move herself out of the triangle consisting of herself, D., and their mother, L. humorously began encouraging her mother to become more dependent, a technique known as reversal. She also refused to discuss her son with anyone or to discuss one member of the triangle with the other and suggested that any problems between them be taken up directly with the other. During this period, she spent considerable time with each one separately.

Results were mixed. L.'s son's behavior immediately returned to normal. Her mother did make deliberate attempts to decrease her dependency, and the relationship between mother and daughters was considerably better. Yet, as L.'s husband, who knew nothing of her attempt to de-triangle, told her at the time the issue appeared to be resolving, "Look, if you're angry at your mother, take it up with her. Stop trying to pick fights with me after the two of you have had a talk." L. had attempted to reform the triangle with her husband taking her sister's place.

As in L.'s case, in any attempt a person makes to become differentiated, it is necessary to define self in relationship to the family and begin a process of de-triangling, or changing the motion or direction within the triangle. In essence, de-triangling involves removing one's self from the automatic emotional responses within the triangle. At the same time, the person must develop and maintain person-to-person relationships with each of the other two members of the triangle to prevent them from bringing in another person or issue to reform the triangle.

L. made another attempt in differentiating a self the summer before she left home to go to graduate school 150 miles away. The decision to go had been made months before with the family's encouragement and involvement in all phases of planning, so L. was unprepared for the rise in anxiety and disruptions within the family the last 2 months before she was to leave. In addition, she believed she was overreacting and behaving overresponsibly in her effort to plan for and control every contingency that might occur, as if the entire extended family could not survive without her. In consultation with her coach, she began identifying some of the interlocking triangles that would be affected by her being home only on weekends.

It is necessary to do so because when there are more than three people involved, as in a family, the relationships from a collection of interlocking triangles that span the generations and can become active at any time, especially during periods of change and increased stress. The degree of intensity within the triangles depends on the level of differentiation of the individuals involved. The less closed the relationships and fixed and repetitive the patterns, the less likely one member or the relationship within the triangle is to become dysfunctional.

In her family, L. was the one who ordinarily took over, intervened in conflicts to make things better and sought closeness with other family members, thus allowing her husband to maintain distance. Now he, the three children, the mother-in-law, and L.'s sister's family would have to relate directly and differently. L.'s going to school could serve as an impetus for change in several triangles.

Since she would not consider changing her plans for school in order to return the system to its former equilibrium, she was advised about how to reduce the anxiety within the system and at the same time increase her own differentiation of self.

She would spend time individually and privately with each person in each of the triangles she was involved in within her family. During each talk, she would take an "I" position, taking responsibility for and identifying any feelings, thoughts, rationales, and beliefs that were associated with her leaving and her relationship with the person to whom she was talking.

It was easiest with her two youngest children and husband. Her oldest daughter, who had reacted by moving out immediately after graduation, attempted to aviod any private talk. Yet she responded so favorably that she reinstated personal contact with family members on a consistent basis.

L. and her mother both avoided the talk by setting up barriers or bringing in impersonal topics to discuss. Finally, L. was able to lower her anxiety by planning exactly what she was to say, finding the best time to avoid interruption, and exploring the extent of her emotional fusion with her mother. When she was able to do so and initiated the discussion, her mother responded with her own fears and feelings about being "left" by her daughter. It was the most truly person-to-person communication she could ever remember with her mother.

The results were remarkable. The anxiety and disruptions disappeared and relationships appeared more open. L. no longer felt the need to control events and began to initiate the second phase of her plan. She would attempt to remove herself from the position of delivering messages and facilitating communication between other family members, taking advantage of the fact that she was away during the week.

When one member attempts to change his/her relationship within a triangle, equilibrium within the system is disturbed and the system responds by attempting to stop the process and restore the balance. Carter and Orfanidis (3) describe the process of change as having three stages. The first stage is the change itself followed by the family's reaction to it. The final stage is the person dealing with the family's reaction. The family will react by insisting behaviorally, if not verbally, that the change is bad, followed by a command to change back and a threat of what will occur if the return to status quo isn't accomplished. If the person attempting to de-triangle can maintain the change without resorting to defensiveness or attack, modifications in the function of the triangle will occur, which results in a change in the functioning of the entire system.

L.'s family system actively fought the attempt to change her role. The middle child told tales on everyone, demanding that her mother "do something." Her son and husband argued only on weekends. L.'s mother saved up urgent messages for her to deliver to other family members.

Whether or not L. is able to maintain the change in her behavior toward her family will be influenced by at least two factors. She must resist the family's pressure on her to return to old, predictable behavior without resorting to anger or distance, and she must tolerate the increased anxiety she experiences in association with the pressure. If she succeeds, family members will begin to make changes in their behavior in response to hers.

For L., the use of the family of origin as a source of awareness and growth and as a mechanism for learning has been personally and professionally rewarding. She intends to continue her attempts to avoid becoming enmeshed in the emotional system and, as in the past, these attempts will most likely be intensified during time of family crisis. Her increased knowledge about the workings of triangles will be of assistance in her work with her family as well as with other families in therapy.

Regardless of their sex, beginning family therapists who become involved in the workings of their own family systems can accrue professional as well as personal benefits. Each person, including the therapist, brings personal experiences from the family of origin into the therapy session. Therapists, who have learned to observe what occurs in their own families, become more observant of the processes used by the client family to maintain the system. Likewise they are attuned to the anxiety associated with change and the resistance to change.

Finally, the therapists' family of origin serves as a continuous laboratory for learning experiences that can be generalized into therapy. Since triangles exist in other settings as well as in the family, they can also be expected to develop in the therapy relationship. Therapists are less likely to be triangled by the family in therapy sessions or are more likely to remove themselves successfully from triangles when they have done so in their own family.

REFERENCES

1. Bowen, M. *Family therapy in clinical practice.* New York: Jason Aronson, 1978, pp. 539, 479.
2. Guerin, P. J., & Fogarty, T. F. Study your own family. In A. Ferber, M. Mendelsohn, & A. Napier (Eds.), *The book of family therapy.* N.p.: Science House, 1972.
3. Carter, E. A., & Orfanidis, M. M. Family therapy with one person and the family therapist's own family. In P. J. Guerin (Ed.), *Family therapy: Theory and Practice.* New York: Gardner Press, 1976, pp. 195, 197.
4. Fogarty, T. F. System concepts and the dimensions of self. In P. J. Guerin (Ed.), *Family therapy: Theory and Practice.* New York: Gardner Press, pp. 450, 147.

26

Family Systems: Use of Genograms as an Assessment Tool

Shirley Smoyak

Therapy, of any type, cannot proceed without a plan. Making a plan to treat a simple, somatic disease entity is fairly straightforward and easy. The process in such instances moves from: (*1*) the patient's reporting subjective symptoms; (*2*) the clinician's verifying these by objective tests; (*3*) the clinician's making a diagnosis based on (*1*) and (*2*); and (*4*) finally, instituting a treatment plan. When the problem rests, however, not at the cell, organ, or individual level, but within a complex system of two or more persons living as a unit, the planning requires highly differentiated skills.

The focus of this presentation is on the use of the genogram as a data-recording method. It is indispensable for the planning phase of treatment as well as for recording changes during the entire course of treatment. While its use has been primarily in the area of family psychiatric/mental health treatment, it can also be used by clinicians in nonpsychiatric areas.

Family therapy, as a treatment modality for disturbed individuals and families, will soon begin its third decade as a recognized alternative to intrapsychic or psychoanalytic methods. Most clinicians who switched to this approach found that old systems of record-keeping were as outdated and cumbersome as the archaic views that individuals could be sick by themselves. Using a systems approach clinically demanded shifting to other ways to record the relevant data.

Courtesy of *Proceedings,* a medical symposium, Brooks Air Force Base, San Antonio, Texas, May 24, 1978.

The literature on family therapy—its varieties, techniques, and strategies—has so expanded since the late 1950s that bibliographers are very busy keeping up with the latest books, monographs, reviews, journals, and audiovisual materials. A consensus has emerged, informally, that the best way to portray the family system is by a genogram. While the specific rules may vary among clinicians or treatment and research settings, there is sufficient similarity in the symbols that the diagrams are generally understandable.

The recording system presented here was developed at Rutgers—the State University of New Jersey—Graduate Program in Psychiatric Nursing. It was refined about 5 years ago in the course of a project to scan and select an appropriate record-keeping system for the Rutgers Community Mental Health Center, which is a part of the Department of Psychiatry, the College of Medicine and Dentistry of New Jersey, Rutgers Medical School. People involved in that project reviewed the literature and collected recording examples from a wide variety of psychiatric centers. It is currently used by clinicians on the outreach teams who conduct family therapy, and it is also taught to trainees such as psychiatric residents, psychology interns, pediatric fellows, psychiatric nurses, and social workers.

The value of a genogram over the written paragraph by paragraph, page by page lengthy descriptions of history and behaviors is evident from the first glance. A three-generation family can generally be diagrammed on one $8\frac{1}{2} \times 11$ page. In one picture, all of the relevant structural data are displayed—the names, birth (and death) dates, sexes, ethnicity and religion, occupation or schooling, and health status of all family members. Most importantly, the relationships of key figures by marriage and birth are immediately evident.

The ideal way to learn how to do a genogram is to have the process explained in a *live* seminar. It should be possible, however, to develop initial skills in genogram construction based on information that is included in this chapter.

The following is a set of directions for constructing a genogram that includes a key to the symbols and marks that are used. Figure 26-1 is an example of a three-generation genogram. The reader is advised to study the example and directions and then to construct a genogram of his or her own family of origin or family of procreation. Parents, grandparents, or family elders can provide missing data, lost cousins, "ghosts," or varieties of living arrangements.

The construction of the genogram provides the framework for understanding the family system. It serves as a focus when listening for what the family issue or violation is. As changes occur in the structure and relationship, it can be easily updated.

When the genogram is constructed during the intake session, it serves to give a quick and accurate picture of the structure and relationships of the family members (those absent or geographically distant as well as those

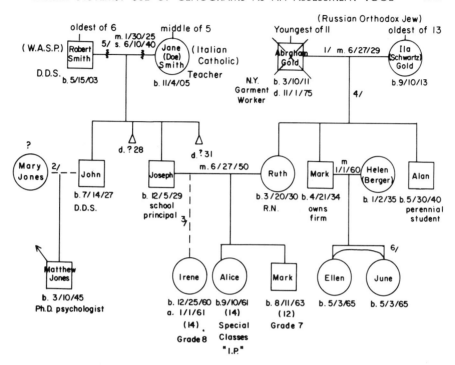

Figure 26-1 Example of three-generation genogram.

present). The therapist, within the time framework of generally 1 or 2 hours, can identify networks of resources and strengths, in addition to gaining a perspective regarding the problem.

Each therapist evolves his or her own style for conducting the genogram construction. Some prefer to have the parents serve as the primary information source; more often, each family member is asked to give the data about self. The genogram session facilitates the development of a therapeutic rapport. The therapist communicates genuine interest, demonstrating this by being able to keep the family details straight.

While much subjective and secondhand-report data emerge during the making of the genogram, the data are more objective than is the case when families are permitted, during an intake, to say what "the problem" is right at the outset. When therapists allow families to begin with stating the problem, it is far more difficult in the long run to gain an accurate view of the total functioning system. Forcing them to contain their problem statement until the therapist knows each member sets the milieu as a positive, organized, systematic one in which the sought-after help will occur.

The manner in which families participate in the genogram construction is an important source of additional data for therapists. For instance,

DIRECTIONS AND KEY

General

Divide paper, lengthwise, into 3 levels.
Begin in the middle, with husband on left.
Males are in squares; females are in circles.
Aborted fetuses, too early to determine sex, are triangles.
Place birth dates below symbol, prefaced by a *b*.
Place death dates below symbol, prefaced by a *d*; mark an X through identity
    symbol.
Place marriage date, preceded by *m* on the paired solid line. Separation $= s$.
    Divorce $= d$.
Adoption date is *a*.
For first generation (the grandparents), indicate the sibling structure by "oldest
    of _____," or "youngest of _____," etc.
Indicate occupation, ethnicity of first generation alongside symbols.
Indicate occupation of middle generation.
Indicate school year or occupation of third generation, (children of major
    couple).

Notations

(Illustrated on genogram and marked as 1/, 2/ etc.)
1/ Solid paired line indicates marriage.
2/ Broken paired line indicates nonmarriage relationship.
3/ Broken vertical line indicates adoption.
4/ Solid vertical line indicates children of the couple.
5/ Broken brackets indicate divorce, separation.
6/ "Rocker" between children indicates twins, triplets, etc.
7/ Date of doing genogram and clinician's name.

the dynamics of dominance, submission, respect, warmth, discounting,
questioning, and so on are quite visible. How each person relates to another and what that person says is very obvious. The therapist can see
whether children, at various ages, are believed or listened to attentively.
The mutuality or lack thereof of parental pairs can be observed. In three-
generation intakes, the dynamics of person as both parent and child can be
watched closely.

A problem-oriented system of notes is the best accompaniment to the
genogram as a data base. The aim of a family therapist is to abstract the
essence of the system's difficulty, defining such in system terms rather than
in intrapsychic language. One cannot use the D.S.M. III in concert with a
genogram; it would make no system sense to assign each family member an

PROBLEM DICTIONARY

I. Internal Stressor
   A. Job/Occupation/Profession
      1. Peer/colleague tensions
      2. Difficulty with superior
      3. Difficulty with subordinates
      4. Loss of work (laid off, fired)
      5. Unemployed
      6. Underemployed
   B. Welfare Agency
      1. Can't get approval
      2. Not enough on which to survive
   C. Legal system
      1. Arrested
      2. Indicted
      3. Convicted
      4. Serving a sentence
      5. On probation
   D. School system
      1. Child (children) identified as problem
      2. Family identified as "noncooperative"
   E. Religious institution
      1. Religious school identifies child (children) as problem
      2. Value system clash between units of extended system
II. External Stressor
   A. Structural Change
      1. Addition of a family member (birth, relative or other coming to join household, adoption)
      2. Loss of family member
         a. death
         b. temporary—job change
         c. temporary—minor hospitalization
      3. Accident (indicate member affected)
         a. resulting in hospitalization
         b. resulting in severe loss of mobility
         c. resulting in disfigurement
   B. Conflict over rules of organization
      (who does what to whom when)
      1. Autonomy vs. solidarity of members
         (issue of separateness/connectedness)
      2. Division of labor
         a. Childbearing
         b. Household maintenance
         c. Spending money
         d. Setting priorities/goals

intrapsychic diagnostic label. The goal is to derive a treatment plan for a dysfunctional system by working on the interactions among subsystems. The formulation of what the difficulty is must be in system language.

A search of existing problematic behavioral classification systems yielded none that seemed to categorize family troubles. There are, of course, isolated and fragmented family system concepts such as coalition across generations, pseudo-mutuality, triangling, and the like that are useful in a descriptive sense. No overall encompassing category scheme exists for use in the problem-generation lists.

Therefore, from family intakes over roughly a 6-year period, the following beginning classification scheme was derived. Its aim is to locate both the source of the difficulty and to describe its nature. The Problem Dictionary is intended for use in problem-oriented records to derive the problem lists for each family. It is to be considered a tool in development. Comments and suggestions by users are welcomed.

The genogram, along with the Family Systems Problem Dictionary, provides a coherent, systematic data base for work with troubled families. The therapist is required to reorient his or her conceptual framework away from viewing trouble as existing inside people and toward a view that questions the functionality or dysfunctionality of human systems. Comments from therapists using these tools in their clinical practices are invited.

27

Three Assessment Tools for Family Therapy

Susan A. Morgan and Mary Jane Macey

Family therapy, a relative newcomer to the practice of psychotherapy, has been increasing in popularity since the 1950s (1). Therapists are becoming more cognizant of the fact that coping with life is much easier when the entire family is made aware of dysfunctional behavior. The family therapist often serves as the catalyst for bringing about awareness of this dysfunctional behavior. As a member of the mental health team and a systems analyst, the therapist is responsible for comprehensive family assessment before she can proceed with family therapy. It is from this viewpoint that the literature has been researched, clinical data have been collected, and family therapy tools have been developed.

REVIEW OF THE LITERATURE

Many authors simply include family concepts in the body of their papers without mentioning family assessment (2–4). There are, however, several definitions of assessment in the literature on family therapy. For the purpose of this paper the following definition of assessment is to be applied.

This chapter is reprinted with permission in its entirety from the *Journal of Psychiatric Nursing and Mental Health Services,* March, 1978.

Assessment is a process that includes the collection of data regarding family health, health habits and health behavior, as well as factors in the community that affect these things . . . The assessment process can be compared to life process itself—a constantly interacting, fluctuating, and changing phenomenon (5).

Also in the literature there is little categorization or consistency of approach to the use of terminology for family therapy. Donald A. Bloch affirms this fact by stating that "there are no clearly defined exclusive tools or techniques" for family therapy (6). Hopefully the assessment tools to be presented will represent pertinent familial information in terminology that can be synthesized by all persons interested in family therapy.

Family therapists must be concerned with an assessment of the family as a whole system, which includes physical health, social, and mental health aspects. For example, in assessing the family, the therapist takes into account each member of the family *and* how that member affects and interacts with all the other family members. This is done with each member and with the family unit as a whole in its community relationships. Therefore, the following assessment tools combine school and Robischon's health aspects, Lickorish's psychological assessment, Westley's emotional aspects of the family, Rice's economic assessment, Ruesch's communication assessment, Ehrenwald's patterns of interaction, and other assessments that are important to family therapy (5, 7–11).

THE ASSESSMENT TOOLS

As stated in the definition of assessment, the process of life itself is constantly changing; therefore, the assessment tools must be flexible and fluid in carrying out the process of implementing family therapy. In the process of family change and growth, marked reactions from each family member will occur that may result in the therapist's need to implement an initial or primary assessment, an ongoing assessment, and a summary or termination assessment.

THE INITIAL ASSESSMENT

In the initial session with the family, the therapist must assess as much of the family system as possible in order to arrive at a better understanding of the family's ability to function. The therapist needs to obtain information concerning the family's background: social, cultural, religious, financial, emotional, psychological, educational, and occupational information. She also needs to acquire information concerning the present status of the family. The present status includes patterns of interaction, family constellation, relationships, living conditions, assets, liabilities, roles, norms and rules, and family functioning. The therapist collects the data, analyzes and assesses this knowledge imaginatively and, in collaboration with the family, they arrive at treatment goals and a prognosis relating to the family's needs. The therapist also keeps in mind that the assessment tools are applicable to all families, but not all sections are necessarily used in every case. The family therapist uses her creativity in applying the necessary tools for each individual family assessment.

One of the pitfalls that the therapist must avoid is the overzealous approach to family therapy without adequate assessment of the family's willingness and readiness to participate. The therapist's entry into a situation may be solicited by only one member of the family. The question may then arise as to whether or not that one member is the family spokesman. The therapist must assess the willingness and readiness of the other family members to participate in therapy. If the therapist's assistance is solicited en masse, further assessment of the family's common effort in therapy may not be necessary. Also the family's cooperativeness in setting up appointment times may be an indication of their desire to participate in therapy. The following is the proposed Initial Family Assessment Tool.

PROPOSED INITIAL FAMILY ASSESSMENT TOOL

I. Background Data
   A. Family compositions—members
       1. Ages (ordinal position of children)
       2. Marital status
       3. Personality
       4. Intellect (level of education)
       5. Physical health status
       6. Culture
       7. Number of persons living in the home
       8. Extended family
   B. Material dimensions
       1. Income (source, amount, and management)
       2. Occupation
       3. Size and nature of house
       4. Neighborhood
       5. Socioeconomic status (number of cars, dishwasher, etc.)
   C. Family–community interaction
       1. Political
       2. Educational
       3. Religious
       4. Recreational activities (entertainment, television, etc.)
       5. Relationship with neighbors

II. Present Situation
  A. Visual data
    1. Dress
    2. Posture
    3. Subgrouping (clingers and loners)
    4. Similarities in appearance (facial expressions, body language)
    5. Initial greeting (verbal/nonverbal)
  B. Number of persons participating in therapy
  C. Communication patterns and levels
    1. Inferences
    2. Affect
    3. Motivation
  D. Relationships
    1. Degrees of warmth and affection
    2. Clients' balance of dominance
    3. Role reciprocity
      a. Kind
      b. Degree
    4. Sexual
    5. Stability
    6. Expectations
    7. Acceptance of responsibility
  E. Social functioning
    1. Marital patterns
    2. Childrearing and development (socialization process)
    3. Family norms
    4. Role of pets
    5. Extrafamilial socialization agents
      a. School (teacher, principal)
      b. Community center
      c. Religious group
    6. Geographical boundaries (family's world of experience)
  F. Psychological–emotional health integration
    1. Status
    2. Power
    3. Acceptance and fulfillment of roles
    4. Autonomy of members
    5. Level of trust
    6. Members' self-esteem
    7. Congruence of family and societal values
    8. Attitudes toward self and others
    9. Reality orientation
    10. Tension management (mediating conflict)
    11. Adaptability (principal defensive operations)
    12. Flexibility
  G. Physical health
    1. Conditions or illness
      a. Acute or chronic
      b. Disabling defects
    2. Growth and development disorders

H. Stress vulnerability
I. Assets and liabilities
J. Family's objectives and goals (individual and family)
   1. Immediate
   2. Intermediate
   3. Long-term
K. Prognosis for family therapy
   1. Willingness for family therapy
      a. Family initiated
      b. Referred
   2. Readiness for family therapy
      a. Cooperativeness
      b. Resistance

THE ONGOING ASSESSMENT TOOL

Ideally, the initial assessment is completed as early as possible in family therapy. It is realized that much of the initial data collection goes on throughout therapy. Therefore, in addition to the initial evaluation, an Ongoing Assessment Tool is proposed as a means of identifying the changes that take place during therapy. During this phase of assessment, it is imperative that at least one home visit be made to promote a realistic evaluation of the home environment and to decrease the artificiality of the interactions that take place in the office visit.

ONGOING ASSESSMENT TOOL

I. Communication Patterns
   A. Active or passive
   B. Ability to express selves
   C. Verbal assessment (coding, example: identifying defense mechanisms)
   D. Nonverbal assessment
   E. Complete-incomplete
   F. Distinctive features
   G. Timing
   H. Effects of interaction
   I. Changes in interaction
   J. Limitations
   K. Direction and response
II. Themes
   A. Recurring
   B. Dominating the session

III. Family Functioning
    A. Sharing
    B. Resistance
    C. Complementary
    D. Contagion patterns
    E. Decision-making process
    F. Functioning as a system
IV. Emotional Overtones of Session
V. Roles
VI. Assets and Liabilities
VII. Seating Arrangement
VIII. Ability to Bargain

TERMINATION ASSESSMENT

The two previous assessment tools focus on the active role of the therapist in the evaluation process. The Termination Assessment incorporates the therapist's identification with the family and their perceptions and progress in therapy. The following is the Termination Assessment.

TERMINATION OF ASSESSMENT TOOL

I. Notable Changes
    A. As seen by family
    B. As seen by therapist
II. Identified Alternatives for Adaptation
III. Areas in Need of Refinement
    A. As seen by family
    B. As seen by therapist

CONCLUSIONS

In this paper the authors attempt to use existing knowledge of the family and family therapy in order to develop a universal tool for family analysis. The assessment tools represent a conceptualization of the three phases of family analysis. Using simplistic guides, such as these assessment tools, should aid the therapist in organizing the overwhelming volume of information that is obtained in a short amount of interviewing time. Again, the assessment tools are only as applicable as the family therapist is imaginative and creative.

REFERENCES

1. Miller, J. C. Systems theory and family psychotherapy. *Nursing Clinics of North America,* 1971, *6,* p. 395.
2. Knox, D. *Marriage happiness.* Champaign, Ill.: Research Press, 1971, pp. 1–144.
3. Bernardo, F. The anthropological approach to the study of the family. In R. J. R. King (Ed.), *Family relations: concepts and theories.* Berkeley, Calif.: Glendessary Press, 1969, pp. 55–78.
4. Handel, G. Psychological study of whole families. In G. Handel (Ed.), *The psychosocial interior of the family.* Chicago: Aldine, 1967, pp. 517–50.
5. Sobol, E. G., & Robischon, P. *Family nursing.* St. Louis: C. V. Mosby, 1970, p. 6.
6. Bloch, D. A. *Techniques of family therapy.* New York: Grune & Stratton, 1973, p. 17.
7. Lickorish, J. R. The psychometric assessment of the family. In J. G. Howells (Ed.), *Theory and practice of family psychiatry.* New York: Brunner/Mazel 1968, pp. 553–585.
8. Westley, W. A., & Epstein, N. B. *Silent majority.* San Francisco: Jossey-Bass, 1970, pp. 22–66.
9. Rice, A. S. An economic framework for viewing the family. In F. N. Ivan, & F. M. Bernardo (Eds.), *Emerging conceptual frameworks in the family analysis.* New York: Macmillan, 1966, p. 255.
10. Ruesch, J. Synopsis of the theory of human communication. In J. G. Howells (Ed.), *Theory and practice of family psychiatry.* New York: Brunner/Mazel 1968, pp. 227–266.
11. Ehrenwald, J. Family diagnosis and mechanisms of psychosocial defense. In J. G. Howells (Ed.), *Theory and practice of family psychiatry.* New York: Brunner/Mazel, 1968, pp. 390–399.

28

Family Rules: Planning Intervention to Enhance Family Members' Understanding

Anita Turner Kinslow

Systems theory has been presented in a previous chapter. Reference is made to that information to gain a more thorough understanding of how a system functions. In particular, the rules of transformation, called family rules in the family system, should be reviewed.

The purpose of this chapter is to define family rules and to offer a strategy for planning interventions during family therapy sessions whereby each family member gains an understanding of family rules and of their impact on family interactions.

DEFINITION

Family rules are relationship agreements within a family unit that govern the interactions of individuals, thereby prescribing and restricting their communications and behaviors such that over a period of time, organized, repetitive patterns of interacting develop. In considering the family as a system, family rules are those rules of transformation that govern the process prescribing the system's response to input. The concept of family rules is a descriptive metaphor imposed by an observer on the family's patterns of behavior as a means of understanding and practicing behaviors and communications. Family rules play a very important part in determining the nature of the family system—that is, a closed or an open system—and how it operates. In an open system, family members are constantly weighing the pros and cons of alternative ways of thinking, behaving, and feeling; and as a result, the members are constantly changing and growing within the family system. In a closed system, family members are quite rigid regarding changes and are threatened by environmental influences that are different.

Even the family participants are not completely aware of their rule-governed system of interacting as family rules emerge with little or no conscious thought being given to them. When a therapist observes a pattern of interaction at least three times, he can be reasonably sure that a family rule is involved; and by supporting the rule, the family is preserving the homeostasis of the family unit regardless of the effect on an individual member. According to Burr, family rules govern interactions and are concerned with the family member who offers benefits in return for other benefits from one or more family members (1). Family rules can also be concerned with the restrictions that are placed on family members.

REVIEW OF LITERATURE

The concept of family rules was developed in 1965 by Don Jackson based on Bateson's report-command theory of communication (2, 3). Jackson focuses on the relationship level, rather than the content level, of communication in developing his theory about family rules. He speculates that within a family unit, the relationship agreements, which he calls rules, prescribe and limit the individuals' behaviors or communications over a wide variety of content areas, organizing their interactions into a reasonably stable system (homeostasis) (2).

According to Jackson, a trained observer can study many family behaviors and then infer what general rules exist. In turn, these rules explain the family's behavior and interaction patterns. These family rules are not known completely even to the participants. A whole family system can be run by a relatively small set of rules governing relationships; then all the complex behaviors of a family may turn out to be patterned, understandable, and perhaps predictable (2).

Lederer and Jackson (4) describe the formation of family rules. First, a couple behaves randomly and explores a wide variety of behaviors as each probes, vacillates, and juggles actions and reactions in an attempt to determine the limits of acceptable behavior. In a workable relationship, the maladaptive patterns of behavior die out, and eventually the couple works out mutually acceptable ways of interrelating so that each individual feels that he/she is an equal. Further, Lederer and Jackson label this largely unconscious pattern of operating as a quid pro quo pattern, implying a shared, or exchanged, behavior. The equality of the relationship may not be apparent to outsiders; it may be based on values meaningless to anyone else, yet serve to maintain the relationship because the individuals involved perceive their behavioral balance as fair and mutually satisfying. Whether the actions are cruel or loving is irrevelant; both partners accept them, once the pattern is established. This provides some sense of security and protects both partners' dignity, self-respect, and self-esteem.

Lederer and Jackson also offer four circumstances in which the quid pro quo becomes destructive: (1) during courtship a set of rules is developed, but after marriage, one or both partners do not accept these rules as workable; (2) one or both partners may be incapable of understanding verbal and/or nonverbal communications; (3) one partner may break the rules after these have been consciously or unconsciously accepted by both; (4) if the behavior, creativity, or growth of one or both spouses is limited by the rules, the couple may break up the marriage or continue in a rigid, unchanging, and negative relationship. One technique to diminish a destructive set of rules is to bring it from the unconscious to the conscious level (5).

Wertheim presents a hierarchical organization of rule networks that reflect the family system's values. In such a hierarchy, ground rules prescribe concrete behavior (for example, "Each family member comes and goes as he pleases"); and the first-, second-, and third-order rules (called meta-rules) define principles of behavior (for example, "Family must allow individual development") (5).

The structural morphostatic properties of the family system are reflected in its rules and their organization into rule networks. The reader is referred to Wertheim's article in order to gain a more thorough understanding of Wertheim's concept of the structural characteristics of the family system (rules) viewed as a control system (5).

Cromwell and Olson discriminate between three different types of family rules: that is, rules of direct distribution (example, the family budget), rules allocating authority (example, who gets to make the decision in various content areas), and rule-bound negotiation (example, specifies how contested decisions may be negotiated). Further, these authors suggest that a family does not operate consistently in a simple mode, but within a short span of time may use all of the different levels of governance (6).

Grinder and Bandler (7) consider family rules as limitations imposed by the family system on themselves and on each other; many rules are restrictions on the input and output channels of communication. Furthermore, Grinder and Bandler imply that specific rules are not developed by people who are trying purposefully to create pain for each other.

Kantor and Lehr (8) consider family rules to be "strategies" or recurring patterns of interactional sequences among all family members for the purpose of regulating and shaping relationships between and/or among the members. Rules, defined and momentarily redefined, lead to message confusion and chaos; a pattern of excessive repetition of any one behavior, such as a consistent scapegoat, makes for inefficiency and perhaps inhibits the transmission of new information into the family system.

Ford and Rarrick describe family rules that reflect the overriding lifestyle of the family and the manner in which they approach the world. Five family rules or styles are described: (1) children come first, (2) two against the world, (3) share and share alike, (4) every man for himself, and (5) until death do us part (9). These authors also suggest that therapy should focus on the constant, explicit restatement of diffuse, inappropriate rules.

CONCEPTUAL FRAMEWORK

In planning interventions for destructive family rules, it seems that each family member must be able to consciously recognize such rules, both constructive and destructive, before he can fully understand their effects on interactions within the family. As the therapist repeatedly explores specific examples of a more general rule, each family member gives reasons for his actions and, in doing so, gains a basic understanding of the formation and use of rules within the family system. Furthermore, once the general rules for behavior within the family are understood, the family members can then be directed toward the predictive value of rules in future interactions.

As the therapist guides each family member through such a step-by-step process, his final goal is to enhance family members' understanding of family rules and their effects on interactions so that changes can be made to alter the destructive patterns. Basically, the process involves: (1) exploring with each member several specific examples of behavior used by him to earn rewards (recognition, acceptance, approval, etc.) or punishments (no recognition, no acceptance, no approval etc.); (2) asking family member to state his reasons for specific behavior mentioned in step number 1; (3) relate specific examples of individual's behavior to more general rules governing family interactions; (4) teach members the predictive value of family rules.

By exploring a specific example of behavior and by stating reasons for such behavior, each family member is helped to bring rules from the unconscious to the conscious level. This is a slow process, and the therapist may need to point out and explore specific examples repeatedly before a member is able to become consciously aware of the rules that are being used in interactions. The emphasis here is on the process of interactions between members as well as the actual content of interactions. For example, a therapist may observe that in the process of interacting, no one answers a question until the father has been given a chance to speak first; at a later time, one member may verbalize that in this family, the father is allowed always to speak first when a question is asked and that each member remains quiet until the father speaks.

The second step, stating reasons for a specific behavior and a specific rule, teaches family members to reason out the consequences of their own behavior as well as to question why a rule is formed within the family in the first place. Listening to the words that connect actions with consequences allows family members to understand when each member is supposed to do what. Later, when the therapist is planning changes in the family rules, the understanding gained during step number 2 may assist family members to make better choices of rules, that is, more constructive ones rather than destructive ones.

Next, specify several examples or specific incidents observed by the therapist that relate to the more general rules of the family. The two cases given above are specific examples of a more general family rule; that is, in this family, the father is the one with the power.

Family rules provide guidelines for all family members to follow, and rules provide a consistent pattern of interaction between family members. By understanding that every family has a predictable system of operations and a set of expectations and by understanding particularly how the family operates, family members not only can be helped to see destructive patterns in their rules but also can be taught to plan changes so that rules are equitable to all members in the relationship. The implication is not that all family rules can be put through such a process during a short sequence of sessions with a family, but that the family learns the process well and can initiate the step-by-step process by themselves in order to continue to understand their interactions and to plan appropriate changes in destructive patterns, when needed, after the therapist has terminated therapy sessions with the family.

IMPLICATIONS FOR PRACTICE

An overall plan of the therapeutic process relating to family rules includes: (*1*) defining for the family what is meant by family rules, (*2*) assessing the family's "desired" state of rules, (*3*) observing and identifying "present" patterns in family interactions, (*4*) specifying treatment goals, and (*5*) providing experiences for the family to be able to change rules in order to accomplish the "desired" status. The strategy proposed in this chapter helps the family not only to learn what is meant by family rules but also to identify and understand the present patterns in family interactions and the impact that such rules have on future interactions.

The therapist must specify treatment goals with the family, "changing those areas of the family members' models which are impoverished in some way which prohibits the evolving of the desired reference structure" (what the family wants) (7). The therapist's task is to expand the system so that rules will not interfere with the needs of individual members and to move the family toward the ideal open system of coping with situational and developmental stresses. In order for the family system to survive as a system, "no one member of the family can be left behind with the old set of rules, and no one member can be outside the rules" (7). It seems that if more time is allowed initially to enhance family members' understanding of family rules and their overall impact on family relationships, the therapist will meet less resistance from the family in changing old, destructive or maladaptive rules into more adaptive patterns of interaction.

The nature of the family system is determined by its rules, patterns of behavior, and homeostasis. Clinically, the opposite extremes on a continuum, that is, rigid and chaotic rules and patterns of interaction, are the problematic areas that the therapist needs to evaluate and plan treatment goals so that the family can be moved away from these extremes to a more functional level.

REFERENCES

1. Burr, W. R. et al. (Eds.), *Contemporary theories about the family*. New York: The Free Press, 1979.

2. Jackson, D. The study of the family. *Family Process,* March 1965, *4*(1), 6–19.

3. Bateson G. Information and codification: A philosophical approach. In J. Ruesch, & G. Bateson, *Communication: The social matrix of psychiatry*. New York: W. W. Norton, 1951.

4. Lederer, W. J., & Jackson, D. D. *The mirages of marriage*. New York: W. W. Norton, 1968.

5. Wertheim, E. S. The science and typology of family systems II: Further theoretical and practical consideration. *Family Process,* 1975, *14,* 285–308.

6. Cromwell, R. E., & Olson, D. H. *Power in families*. New York: John Wiley & Sons, 1975.

7. Grinder, J., & Bandler, R. *The structure of magic II*. Palo Alto, Calif.: Science and Behavior Books, 1976. Reprinted by permission of the author and the publisher.

8. Kantor, D., & Lehr, W. *Inside the family*. Washington, D.C.: Jossey-Bass, 1976.

9. Ford, F. R., & Rarrick, J. Family rules: Family life styles. In L. Fisher (Ed.), On the classification of families. *Archives of General Psychiatry,* April 1977, *34,* 424–433. Copyright 1977, American Medical Association.

BIBLIOGRAPHY

Becker, W. C. *Parents are teachers.* Champaign, Ill.: Research Press, 1971.

Erickson, G. D., & Hogan, T. P. *Family therapy—An introduction to theory and technique.* New York: Jason Aronson, 1976.

Luthman, S. G., & Kirschenbaum, M. *The dynamic family.* Palo Alto, Calif.: Science and Behavior Books, 1974.

Olson, D. H. et al. Circumplex model of marital and family systems: I. Cohesion and adaptability dimensions, family types, and clinical applications. *Family Process,* April 1979, *18*(1), 3–28.

Satir, V., Stachowiak, J., & Taschman, H. A. *Helping families to change.* New York: Jason Aronson, 1975.

Smoyak, S. *The psychiatric nurse as a family therapist.* New York: John Wiley & Sons, 1975.

29

A Developmental Perspective for Treatment of Families with Young Children

Deane L. Critchley

As discussed in previous chapters, there are a variety of family therapy models from which the therapist may choose a framework for intervention. However, most models do not take into account the early experiences of the parents, especially those of infancy and early childhood. Parents with unsuccessfully resolved developmental problems have limited capacities to relate to their own children other than in terms of their own needs (1–3). Much of the family therapy perspective is derived not from the naturalistic environment of the home but from office visits. Family therapists expect a capacity for verbal interaction and children are often excluded from therapy sessions until they are old enough to behave and to participate in adultlike verbal exchanges. Family therapy training does not emphasize child development. Some family therapists avoid seeing children altogether and work only with and through the adults who are seen as the main holders of power and definers of family structure and function. Thus, those aspects of adult functioning that are derived from and relate to early childhood developmental issues appear not to have relevance for family therapy.

This chapter presents a developmental approach to examining family systems and interventions. Such a model is based on the developmental needs of all family members both as individuals and as a family system. A developmental perspective can be used in conjunction with any of the family therapy models. The psychopathology and conflicts seen in the family and its members are the result of many etiological factors (multicausal). A developmental approach illuminates one of the major causal factors. The historical perspective provides an indepth understanding that helps to clarify existing interactional patterns as well as cross-sectional views of individual behavior.

Such an approach is based on the following assumptions:

1. Family behavior is a result of the past life experiences of the family members as expressed in the present as well as in their goals and expectations for the future.
2. Families follow similar and broadly consistent patterns in their development and change over time.
3. The child's development and developmental needs impinge on deficits in the family's capacity to meet these needs. The deficits may often be a result of one or both parents having unsuccessfully negotiated a particular developmental task themselves.
4. The current family environment may be sufficiently stressful, for any number of reasons (such as severe chronic illness of a family member), to produce inadequate family support for a child's developmental needs.
5. At times, factors involved in both three and four above may combine to produce an acute family crisis—for example, a family where the simultaneous developmental needs of an infant and an adolescent serve to create intense stress on a previously functioning family. Such stress serves to reveal developmental deficiencies in the parents that were previously compensated for.

This approach looks at individual families against the broad patterns of family structure and development over time (4). It contrasts with those approaches that focus on the internal dynamics of the family system operating only at the point of therapeutic intervention (5, 6).

ENTRY AND ALLIANCE ISSUES

The therapist must gain entry into the family system and establish a therapeutic alliance with the family and its individual members. When the identified patient is a child, these objectives are both critical and difficult as previously indicated. Usually the child's unmet developmental needs result in conflicts that in turn create disturbances in the family system that bring the family into treatment.

The therapeutic goal is to help the family identify and meet developmental needs in ways that are growth producing for the child and conflict reductive for the family. Family members are frequently helped to identify and to increase their own mastery of earlier unaccomplished developmental tasks. This chapter focuses on methods of entry into the family and family treatment techniques appropriate to the particular age and problem the child patient presents.

Discussion of certain critical developmental stages will illustrate how one or both parents' vulnerabilities may be activated as indicators that the parents have residual difficulties from negotiating that particular developmental phase.

The developmental stages of infancy and early childhood will be discussed in this chapter with clinical illustrations as they are rarely dealt with in family therapy. Infancy is focused on because of the infant's intense need for nurturance, responsive attentiveness, and total depedency for survival on the parents. Early childhood is discussed because the child's conflicting needs for dependence and autonomy, as well as beginning sexual identification, are often troublesome for parents. Early school age brings the most referrals for behavioral problems to clinics and for family therapy. Adolescent problems due to the recurring tasks of sexual identification, individuation, and independence from the family also are frequently referred for family therapy. School age children and adolescents are obviously more familiar to family therapists, although they usually are not worked with from a developmental vantage point.

OVERVIEW OF ISSUES AND TECHNIQUES OF FAMILY INTERVENTION

The child's problem behaviors as recognized by social institutions (usually school) personnel, are often the impetus for treatment referral. These problems are often seen as individual and idiosyncratic, while the parents are frequently seen as responsible for the child's problems.

Historically, child mental health professionals tend to blame the problems of the children on the parents. Families often reach the point of self blame after frustrating, fruitless attempts to alter the situation with or without help. To establish an alliance with the family and, more importantly, as a genuine effort to ease the family pain, the therapist must attempt to deal with issues of blame. A focus on the needs of the parents as well as those of the child makes it possible to diminish the blaming quality, while stressing the importance of the family interaction and the parents' vital role in the family. The therapist needs to highlight the parents' and family's successes in dealing with other children or other life situations. Thus, the therapist can support a basic image of competency for the family. Engagement then becomes a process based on helping the family recognize the child's developmental needs and the family's role in enhancing the development and functioning of all the family members.

The needs of the child and the family are presented in terms of normal developmental theory. The parental and family developmental tasks are normative ones. This approach assists in minimizing the sense of blame and responsibility the parents feel about having created the problem.

The therapeutic focus is essentially a task-oriented one, to assist the family members to interact with each other in ways that will promote the child's emotional growth and positive family functioning. Helping parents to identify their own histories of developmental problems helps them understand and overcome the obstacles to carrying out their parental roles in child development. This is not to imply that the process is purely one of education. Knowledge alone is insufficient to identify and resolve the conflicts experienced by the parents as activated by their child's behavior. Thus, problem identification and conflict resolution is the major therapeutic task (7). The child who is able to participate is necessarily included. The child's behaviors that stimulate and reverberate with the parents' conflicts and continue the dysfunctional patterns of development need to be identified. The child requires help to recognize, understand, and accept his or her responsibility in reducing these behaviors in a supportive, reinforcing family context. The next step is to work through the inevitable individual and collective resistance to change. Blocks to planning and carrying out tasks agreed on by therapist and family members are focused on to foster individual and family changes in behavior.

The psychiatric nurse has a particular advantage in using a developmental framework in family therapy. It is a framework widely understood and used in psychiatric nursing. In addition, the nurse is identified as a helpful person to the entire family, neither intrusive nor blaming as may occur with teachers and school counselors. As a health professional, she is identified as being helpful to both the identified patient and the family in the acute and recovery phases of an illness. The variety of helpful roles associated with the nurse and the fact that the nurse routinely interacts with families facilitates her acceptance by the family in the role of therapist. Developmentally oriented family therapy is a natural extension of a nurse's work with families.

ILLUSTRATIONS OF CRITICAL DEVELOPMENTAL PHASES WITH ACCOMPANYING PROBLEMS

Infancy

Infancy presents a critical period of development both for the infant and the other family members.

The literature documents that the attitudes of the parents around the decision to have a child, their fantasies of what to expect, and the disparity that occurs between fantasy and reality have a tremendous influence on parent-child bonding and interaction. In addition, the work of Escalona and Thomas and Chess have shown how influential the fit between the parent and child is for optimal child development (8, 9). Problems in fit occur when the individual characteristics of the infant do not mesh well with or cannot be adapted to easily by the primary caretaker. Or, if there is little recognition and support given to these differences by other family members, then the repercussions for the infant's development are crucial and there is greater probability of dysfunctional behavioral patterns developing.

When a developmentally immature or premature infant is constantly fussy, has erratic feeding and sleep patterns, and does not respond to soothing, it often creates great feelings of frustration, inadequacy, rage, and depression in the mother. She may, without help at such a crucial time, withdraw from the infant and thus aggravate the infant's sense of not being cared for in the face of its great needs.

Clinical Example. In one instance, a mother's depression following the death of her own mother affected her relationship with her own infant and her husband. Her husband withdrew out of his own jealous anger resulting from his unmet needs. The mother was unable to respond to her infant's normal cries and irritability when he needed food, cuddling, and stimulation. Over several months the infant became apathetic, withdrawn, and unresponsive to the mother's tentative efforts to interact.

Both parents came from large, disorganized families where the children received little attention let alone nurturance from the parents. Both parents viewed their own parents and older caretaking siblings as harsh, punitive persons who reacted with anger to their 4- and 5-year-old attempts at play. They had married while still young. Theirs had been a loving marriage where each was able to give to the other and to be playful together until the mother's pregnancy and the death of the mother's mother. These two events seemed to exacerbate not only each parent's needs from the other but also their subsequent mutual anger and withdrawal as these needs were not met.

The birth of a helpless, needy, and demanding infant increased each parent's painful feelings of being asked to give what they needed themselves, with accompanying feelings of estrangement and withdrawal.

The mother's depression and problems with her infant came to the attention of the nurse practitioner at the local Well Child Clinic. The infant's apathy, listlessness, and failure to gain weight along with the mother's helplessness aroused the nurse's concern. She made a home visit and noted the estrangement between the parents.

The nurse suggested a local infant stimulation program that included a child development seminar for the parents. In the infant program the mother learned to sing to, play with, and enjoy cuddling her infant. In the parent's group, the discussion on infant and child development made clear what an infant and child needed from both parents. After the third session the group leaders noted the increased depression of these parents and suggested counseling with a psychiatric nurse.

During the initial, as well as subsequent sessions, the nurse obtained answers to questions basic to identification of the central family patterns and dysfunctions. These questions included: who is the primary caretaker; how much eye contact and physical contact occurs between infant and parents; are the parents aware and do they take precautions for the infant's safety; how much anxiety do the parents experience in their care of the infant/child. These observations are critical in identifying developmental needs of all family members and permit the therapist to understand the family's interaction from the infant/child's point of view. These issues are often ignored by family therapists (10).

In their first session, the parents were helped in describing their own very deprived childhoods. The therapist empathized with their feelings of being burdened and overwhelmed by an infant's needs when they had just begun to be able to meet each other's needs. In ensuing sessions they began to talk about how frightening it was to feel responsible for a new life and their uncertainties about being good parents. With the therapist's encouragement, one home visit helped the father learn some of the ways to play with and to interact with his baby as the mother was now doing more effectively. The infant's responsiveness to these stimuli was rewarding to both parents. In subsequent sessions the parents were helped to focus on how each parent could make the other feel helpless and angry by making demands that could not be met. For example, the father would want to make love at the infant's feeding time making the issue "whom do you love most." In turn the mother would demand that the father bottlefeed and quiet the angry baby at mealtime because she was tired and did not want to breastfeed the infant. After having ignored the baby's cries in order to finish making supper, the mother felt martyred and made the father feel he was ineffectual because the baby continued to cry. By this time, the wife's efforts to get the meal went unrecognized and neither parent could quiet the baby. As each parent was helped to acknowledge the bind in which they placed the other they began to reduce these and other adversarial interactions.

The therapist's task was, first, to help each parent describe the intended effect of their behavior and to recognize its perception by their spouse. The father said his objective was to make his wife aware that they rarely had sexual relations since the baby's birth, thus his timing. The mother felt her husband was behaving like his greedy infant son and felt the two demands as overwhelming. She was more relaxed and felt comfortable about having sex when the baby went to sleep in the early evening. Her husband usually turned on a ball game then and the mother felt rejected. The father wanted sexual relations but also some acknowledgement that the baby's presence interfered with their relationship. His wife found this difficult to acknowledge. As the overt and covert communications were discussed in terms of what each wanted to say by their behavior and how each piece of behavior was perceived, the pair began to slowly make their way out of innumerable double binds.

At the end of 8 months of therapy, both parents could give to each other and to the baby so that most of their interactions were loving and supportive of mutual growth and the baby's continued normal development.

Early Childhood

This stage can be a critical one for both child and parent due to the child's increasing motor activity and independence. His continued, though lessening, dependency and his beginning identification with the parent of the same sex with competition for attention from the parent of the opposite sex leads to increased family tension. For a parent who has had difficulty in meeting a child's early dependency needs there may be continuing problems. While the parent welcomes the child's increasing autonomy and independence and verbal proficiency, there may be unrealistic, adultlike behavioral expectations of the child. In fact, parents often turn to the child to meet their needs for nurturance and care. Parents may then react with anger, hostility, and abuse toward a child who cannot meet these needs. Parents may respond to the child's need to explore and to master the environment as willful attempts to aggravate. Such perceptions can then result in rage and a determination to show the child who is in charge, often leading to physical abuse. The child then requires individual treatment in order to reduce the impact of the trauma. The new relationship with an adult allows the child to experience a noncoercive, trusting person who fosters creative and spontaneous play and the enjoyment of fantasy.

The purpose of family treatment would be to help the parents understand and alter their role in their own and their child's development around the issues of dependency, need gratification, support, and sustenance.

Clinical Example. The identified patient was a petite doll-like 4½-year-old girl, Carlotta. She was the second of three children in a young Chicano family. The other children were Juan, 6 years of age, and Esteban, 14 months of age. The mother was also 3-months pregnant. The family was referred to the nurse by Children's Protective Services. Carlotta was then in foster placement. The court's placement occurred because of severe abuse by the mother.

Agency referrals are very common both with this age group and older school age children. Frequently, however, the family denies the need for referral and is extremely resistant to treatment.

The parents, Rose and José, were both in their early twenties. Taking numerous courses in early child development and child psychology at the local college had helped Rose get time away from her children. José had held a number of unskilled jobs since their marriage and was unemployed for 6 months before the referral.

At the initial interview the couple requested to be seen without their children. Both Rose and José expressed great anger at being forced to see someone when there was no need—all parents had the right to discipline their children. Carlotta's injuries had been accidental. The nurse did not focus on the issue of intent, but rather on the current reality factors that could be stressors for any family: the age and spacing of the children, the mother's need for relief from child care and the difficulty in finding such relief, the father's unemployment, and having a child removed from the family against their wishes.

In the course of therapy sessions with both parents and later with Carlotta, the parents were familiarized with the normal developmental tasks of a 4-year-old girl as well as with the indicators of Carlotta's difficulty in achieving these tasks. As each task was discussed the mother and father both recounted their own childhood experiences, which made it difficult for them to understand Carlotta's needs and to alter their behaviors to promote her development. Thus, around Carlotta's strivings for autonomy and mastery, the mother talked of her own childhood, which was brief since she was expected to care for all her brothers. The father had experienced girls and women as looking after the males. He resented Carlotta's demands to play with him and his wife's requests for assistance in child care.

The mother expressed anger both that Carlotta let her brothers take away her playthings and that, at times when the mother expected Carlotta to help her care for the boys, Carlotta was equally passive. The mother saw the passivity as defiance and punished Carlotta.

Carlotta, in individual therapy, became more verbal, assertive, and spontaneously playful. Both parents expressed their unease and displeasure with such behavior. On the one hand they were pleased at her increased ability to defend herself and her toys from her brothers. However, each parent reflecting their own childhoods, saw the assertiveness and spontaneity as defiance toward them, which aroused their retaliatory anger. In each instance the origins of the parents' feelings from their pasts were explored and understood with them. Ways of dealing with Carlotta and beginning to enjoy her new age-appropriate behaviors were negotiated. Obstacles to each parent's relating to Carlotta's new behaviors were anticipated and discussed. The father who felt closer to Carlotta was first able to play with her to the mother's discomfort. Later, the mother and Carlotta could cook and shop together. The mother, for the first time, could watch her daughter play with dolls without feeling anger at this waste of time and envy that she had not been able to do the same as a child. As the father was helped to take more responsibility for his sons and they became less a burden on the mother, her anger at Carlotta for not caring for them lessened.

When Carlotta joined the parents for family session it was to permit the therapist to model how adults can relate to and play with children and enjoy it. Taking turns, each parent was helped in playing a board game and some fantasy play from "Little Red Riding Hood" with their daughter. The father was especially pleased with his acting of the Wolf.

In family therapy, the father, first in looking at how to interact with Carlotta, began to recognize his importance to his sons' development. He slowly accepted the idea that playful yet realistic interactions with them enhanced rather than detracted from his male role. He also accepted the idea that this promoted a more positive male identification for his sons. The mother had previously depreciated the father because of his unemployment and constantly compared him to his "worthless and troublesome" sons. Both parents slowly recognized their past roles in blaming the other for their troubles. They began with specific suggestions from the nurse to try to alter their behaviors. Such alterations resulted in greater mutual enjoyment and life in the family became more peaceful. The father's search for work intensified and became successful since he no longer had to fail at jobs because he saw them as beneath his real capabilities. The development of each parent as a more playful, interactive, and participating family member was evident along with Carlotta's marked developmental gains.

SUMMARY

This chapter has described a developmental approach to treatment of families with young children. The child's symptoms bring the family into treatment. The engagement of the family in therapy and certain treatment techniques used are different from other family therapy approaches. Because the parents view the child as the patient and feel blamed for the child's problems they are more difficult to engage. A developmental treatment approach focuses on normal developmental goals for the child. A task-oriented process helps the parents foster the child's development and feel effective as parents. Simultaneously, the treatment process addresses the parents' own developmental deficits that prevent their facilitating their child's maturation, produces conflicts in the family and symptoms in the child, and deprives the family of productive, enjoyable living. Treatment then helps the parents recognize their problems stemming from childhood and approach their current problem child in new ways. It engages the child, siblings, and parents in altering their behaviors, thus fostering mutual development.

From the literature it is clear that family therapists are more comfortable with school age children and adolescents. With both these age groups a developmental approach would facilitate family therapy and resolution of stage specific problems for the school-age child, adolescent, and family.

REFERENCES

1. Framo, J. L. Rationale and techniques of intensive family therapy. In I. Boszor-menyi-Nagy, & J. L. Framo (Eds.), *Intensive family therapy,* New York: Harper & Row, 1965, pp. 143–212.

2. Beavers, W. R. A theoretical basis for family evaluation. In J. M. Lewis et al. (Eds.), *No single thread,* New York: Brunner/Mazel, 1976, pp. 46–82.

3. Bowen, M. *Family therapy in clinical practice.* New York: Jason Aronson, 1978.

4. Aldous, J. *The developmental approach to family analysis* (Vol. 1). Athens, Georgia: University of Georgia, 1974.

5. Minuchin, S. *Families and family therapy.* Cambridge, Mass.: Harvard University Press, 1974.

6. Haley, J. *Problem solving therapy.* San Francisco: Jossey-Bass, 1976.

7. Boszormenyi-Nagy, I., & Spark, G. *Invisible loyalties.* New York: Harper & Row, 1973.

8. Escalona, S. K. *The roots of individuality.* Chicago: Aldine, 1968.

9. Thomas, A., & Chess, S. *Temperament and development.* New York: Brunner/Mazel, 1977.

10. La Perriere, K. On children, adults and families: The critical transition from couple to parents. In J. K. Pearce, & L. J. Friedman (Eds.), *Family therapy,* New York: Grune & Stratton, 1980, pp. 81–92.

30
Family Therapy: A Case Study

Joan Soulier Adams

Family therapy is a currently accepted method of treating social and psychological problems of individuals. Although these problems occur more commonly among the poor (1), there is a dearth of literature about the problems and treatment of low income families. In *Families of the Slums,* Minuchin, Montalvo, Guerney, Rosman, and Schumer describe the results of a research project in working with the families of delinquent boys in New York City (2). The project focused on the family systems, rather than the individual boys, and the authors defined these families as disorganized, low socioeconomic families.

This chapter describes the process of family therapy with one low socioeconomic family, the Grays, using the theory proposed by Minuchin et al. Described first are some of the authors' findings in dealing with poverty-stricken families, as related in *Families of the Slums.* These findings will then be applied to family therapy with the Gray family, using the theory proposed by Minuchin et al. and will include comments on findings that are not applicable to the Grays. Finally the therapists' experience and implications for nurse therapists working with the poor will be discussed.

Families of the Slums was arbitrarily organized into three main areas of family interaction: (*1*) self-observation and communication; (*2*) structure; (*3*) socialization of affect (mood). This chapter will follow a similar pattern.

FINDINGS OF MINUCHIN ET AL.

Self-Observation and Communication

In overcrowded living conditions, constant kaleidoscopic stimuli exist. Parents tend to ignore individual children. Parental rules are random, depending more on the parents' mood at that moment than on the child's action. Therefore, the child does not internalize the rules, but must seek constant contact with the parents in order to know what the correct behavior is at any given time. In addition, the child learns that the most certain way to gain his parents' attention is to be louder than his siblings. Conflicts are resolved by escalated threats. Responses are not content oriented, but hierarchical, with the most powerful member deciding the outcome (2).

Individuals who want to speak deliver their monologues without expecting to be heard, giving rise to constant, abrupt shifts in content. Family members deal with these content shifts in one of three ways: by following the new content, by changing the topic again, or by disengaging, that is, mentally withdrawing from the scene. It is not uncommon to see children daydreaming or falling asleep amidst these swirling monologues (2).

There are fixed communication pathways, with the gatekeeper usually being the mother. All of the children are involved with their mother, and most sustained dialogue is with or through her. There is an emphasis on negatives, with the word *don't* used frequently. Good behavior, exploration, and achievement are not acknowledged or encouraged. The spouses rarely talk to each other, and the father, if one is present, may have to compete with the children for his wife's attention (2).

By the time the children begin school, they have learned to disengage from those around them. They have also learned that achievement will not yield a reward and that the way to gain attention is to loudly interrupt others. In school, their only active behaviors, interrupting and distracting, are usually rewarded by attention, thus fostering their continuance (2).

Structure

The husband/wife subsystem usually consists of a vague, undefined relationship. These two adults, who had failed to define their own roles when younger, now have the roles of parents. Their conflicts are parenting conflicts. Their children are seen as useful sources of feedback, extensions, and reflections of themselves. Although the spouse subsystem functions primarily as a parent subsystem, the nature of the parents' power is confusing. At times, they exhibit autocratic control and, at other times, helplessness. They may relinquish their executive function through physical or emotional abandonment or by allocating authority to a child. There is a breakdown in communication between parents and children; the sibling subsystem becomes the socializing agent, with the child who is most parentlike acting as a source of reference for guidance, control, and decision making (2).

Socialization of Affect

The two main affects or moods in these families are anger and affection. The parents often see their role as synonymous with "I am able to give" (3). They do not consider the appropriateness of the child's demands or the need to delay satisfaction. The child comes to believe that his parents owe him gratification, and the parents experience guilt if the child feels he has not received what is due him (3).

When the mother becomes completely overburdened with nurturing duties she is likely to withdraw her attention completely, or to react to a relatively minor incident with violent anger. For the child, who has been unable to internalize rules, the violence is unpredictable. He learns to adapt with the mood as it shifts from affection to aggression and back again. The undifferentiated quality of his experience prevents him from being in touch with his feelings. There are no expressed gradations of emotions; when asked how he is feeling, the child is likely to respond "good" or "bad" or "I don't know." Furthermore, feelings become externalized; instead of saying "I am angry," this family member will say "You are bad" (2).

The two modalities of contact are *enmeshment* and *disengagement*. When the family is enmeshed, all transactions go through the mother, and she is responsible for all behavioral control. When she becomes overburdened, she disengages, and will accept no responsibility for any actions of the children (2).

THERAPY WITH THE GRAYS

The therapists were graduate nursing students—one man, one woman.* Family therapy consisted of eight sessions with the Grays in their home. Mr. and Mrs. Gray had been married for 23 years. Seven years before the sessions, Mr. Gray had quit his job as a fireman because of muscle spasms in his lower back. When the sessions began, he was spending all of his time at home except for occasional trips to the grocery store. Shonda, the eldest child, had married and left home at age 14. Two months before the sessions began, Shonda's marriage had dissolved, and she and her two children had

* The author of this chapter was one of the therapists in this case summary.

come to live with her parents. The family was living on welfare and Shonda's earnings from working nights as a waitress. They lived in a dilapidated three room house, which was heated by a large coal furnace in the living room. Water was obtained from a well in the front yard. A brief description of family members follows:

Mr. Gray (42) complained of constant anxiety and back pain but seldom appeared anxious or in pain; he talked in rambling monologues, was talented in carpentry and painting, was taking Valium and Tofranil and smoked cigarettes constantly.

Mrs. Gray (35) complained of nervousness, was afraid to go out, waited on family members, even putting food on their plates and washing clothes by hand nightly, was attractive and articulate.

Shonda (19) was attractive, gentle and soft spoken and was the only one who drove a car and worked outside the home.

Trish (15) interacted with all family members, supported but questioned her parents, had frequent illnesses and difficulty with schoolwork.

Ricky (14) performed what was considered *male functions* in the family: drawing water, going to the store, etc.

Jason (8) was epileptic, was on Dilantin and Tofranil and had difficulty in school.

Billy (2) had leukemia; he was active and playful.

Shannon (1) was active and playful.

Intervention

A central goal in work with the Grays, as in that of Minuchin et al., was "re-establishing appropriate parental function in the special areas of executive control and guidance . . . and the appropriate use of nurturing" (3). To accomplish this goal, the therapists joined the family system, took a directive role, and demonstrated appropriate parental behavior. Focus on pathology was avoided, with emphasis on "finding, enhancing and rewarding competence" (4).

In describing the implementation of Minuchin's theory, the divisions of (*1*) self-observation and communication, (*2*) structure, and (*3*) socialization of affect will be continued. However, this division is arbitrary and artificial, and there is much overlap.

Self-Observation and Communication

Minuchin et al. noted that communication in such families is hierarchical and goes through the mother; whoever is loudest gets her attention (2). In the Gray family, loudness was replaced by sickness. Every family member had several ailments requiring Mrs. Gray's attention. These included sinus problems, migraine headaches, ringing in the ears, sore throats, earaches, hip, leg, and back pain, and injuries from accidents. When more than three people were sick at once, Mrs. Gray described her nerves as getting worse.

During the initial sessions, Mr. Gray would spend up to 15 minutes in a monologue on his illness. By the third session, the therapists gained his permission to interrupt him and focus on family interaction. Mrs. Gray soon imitated that behavior, allowing Mr. Gray to speak for a few minutes then redirecting the conversation. This intervention changed the content from illness to another topic and promoted family interaction.

Initially, each member spoke individually to the therapists. When one member mentioned another, he/she was redirected and was asked to speak to that person. Members were willing to do this and, with some coaching, they began to clarify communication. The following conversation exemplified this: (Note: the communication technique used by the therapists in each intervention is identified in parentheses.)

TRISH:	(to therapist) I hope you can help Mama and Daddy get better, so I won't have to worry about them.
MRS. GRAY:	(to therapist) I didn't know that Trish was worried about us.
THERAPIST:	(to Mrs. Gray) Tell Trish. (Redirect)
MRS. GRAY:	I didn't know you were worried about me.
TRISH:	Well, Mama, I can't stay over Kathy's 'cause you're nervous.
MRS. GRAY:	That's not why I don't want you to go.
TRISH:	Well, that's what you told me. You said your nerves were bothering you.
MRS. GRAY:	Well, there's someone staying there . . .
TRISH:	He ain't even there no more. Who do you mean?
MRS. GRAY:	(to therapist) She said he's not there, and she don't even know who her mama's talkin' about. She's gonna do what she wants anyway.
THERAPIST:	Mrs. Gray, let's go back a little. You get nervous sometimes, and that's not related to Trish. But when you're worried about her, you say you're nervous. It sounds like she has to stay home because you're nervous. (Clarify)
MRS. GRAY:	Oh, I see what you mean. I didn't think of that.
THERAPIST:	So, "nervous" and "worried about your daughter" are two different things. (Clarify)
TRISH:	She's always worried about everything.
THERAPIST:	I can understand her worrying, Trish. I have a teenage daughter, and I worry when she's out at night. (Support parent)
MRS. GRAY:	Yeah!

(Discussion about worrying and responsibility ensued at this point)

Later:

THERAPIST: Mrs. Gray, you said something before that I don't understand. You said that "Trish is going to do what she wants anyway." It sounds like you don't think very much of her. (Confront)

MRS. GRAY: Well, she's going to do what she wants.

THERAPIST: That sounds like you expect her to get into trouble. (Clarify)

MRS. GRAY: No, I don't expect that. I know she's a good girl. But she's going to do what she wants.

THERAPIST: Did you say she's a good girl? (Find and focus on positive)

MRS. GRAY: Sure she is.

THERAPIST: Mrs. Gray, tell her that. (Redirect)

MRS. GRAY: She knows I think she's a good girl.

THERAPIST: Mr. Gray, tell her, not me. (Help parent to support child)

MRS. GRAY: I think you're a good girl, Trish. You won't get in no trouble.

In the above section, the therapists guided communication, supported family interaction, clarified statements, stressed positives, and encouraged family members to support each other. Family members soon began to imitate that behavior and use these communication techniques with each other.

The family members avoided disagreement. The therapists attempted to focus on a theme and deal with conflict by taking sides and verbalizing the apparent problems. For example: Shonda was working nights and chauffeuring family members during the day. Mrs. Gray was trying to take care of five children. It was pointed out that Shonda was exhausted and Mrs. Gray was overwhelmed. Both replied, almost in unison, "I don't mind. I want to do it 'cause I love them." The therapist took sides:

THERAPIST 1: Shonda, I'm feeling too much pressure for you. I want to be on your side and say to my family, "Hey! I need your help!" (Shonda starts crying)

THERAPIST 2: Mrs. Gray, I think you have too much to do. You don't know when Shonda's going to change the diapers or when you have to do it. You have to do the housework, cook, and take care of the babies too.

The above dialogue by the therapist led to discussion, some clarification of roles, and assistance from other family members.

In order to focus on a theme, one therapist would stay out of the content. Therapist 1 would enter the conversation, clarifying, redirecting, and confronting. When the topic changed, as it frequently did, Therapist 2 would say, "We started by talking about who does what job. Perhaps we better get back to that."

The therapists relabeled things. Mrs. Gray, as the communication gateway, had control over the whole family. However, she was not labeled as controlling, but as overburdened. It was pointed out that she was doing such a good job of parenting that it was wearing her out and that she would be doing an even better job by helping the children to take some responsibility. With encouragement, she enlisted the help of other family members. By the eighth session, Mr. Gray was getting up in the morning with the children, Trish was helping with the babies, and the children were all taking care of their own clothes.

Structure

The seating arrangement during the first session illustrated the structure of the Gray family. Mrs. Gray sat near one end of the couch, with a child sitting closely on either side, a child at her feet, and one in her lap. Mr. Gray sat in the opposite corner of the couch. This seating arrangement continued through the next session. However, at the third session, Mrs. Gray, who had been under stress, was seated at a distance from everyone. She had withdrawn from her central position; the therapist capitalized on this and encouraged dialogue between the parents. When Mr. Gray said that the children should take care of their own clothes, he was helped to discuss this with his wife and come to an agreement. An attempt was made to strengthen the parental subsystem by encouraging them to make a job list for the children. They did make the list, but were unable to enforce it. During a later session, discussion revealed some of the difficulties the parents had with their executive function: Mrs. Gray did most of Trish's job "to help her"; Mr. Gray did Shonda's job "to get some exercise." Jason was given the job of carrying out the garbage, but he couldn't lift it, so Ricky did Jason's job. The therapists spent parts of the sixth, seventh, and eighth sessions discussing jobs. It was apparent that, with support and direction, the parents could have taken a more parental role. However, there were to be only eight sessions, and termination was anticipated. This problem will be discussed later.

Socialization of Affect

Minuchin et al. describe the two main moods in poor families as anger and affection (2). When the therapists began seeing the Grays, the expressed mood, or affect, was nurturance. In fact, it was not unusual to see Shonda

(19) and Trish (15) curled up in a fetal position with their heads on Mrs. Gray's shoulders. Anger and conflict were never verbally expressed in the therapists' presence, but they were apparent in behavior. For example, Mrs. Gray verbally expressed concern and understanding for her husband; yet she seemed to avoid sitting near him or touching him. Although she did not interrupt his monologues, her facial expression was one of anger and irritation. Mr. Gray verbally expressed love and admiration for his wife; yet he seemed uninterested in the children's welfare, which was her greatest concern. During the course of therapy, the parents began to verbally discuss conflicts with each other and to resolve them. With assistance, Mrs. Gray asserted herself, tactfully interrupting her husband's monologues. Mr. Gray became more of a participant in child care, affirming that the children needed rules and discipline. Once they could express anger verbally, their behavior became more mutually supportive. During the eighth session, Mrs. Gray was sitting near her husband, touching his arm as she talked to him, and Mr. Gray was holding one of the children in his lap.

THERAPISTS' AFFECTIVE EXPERIENCE

Working with the Grays, the therapists became part of the family. The evening visits were anticipated by everyone, including the therapists. In addition, the therapists spent several hours each week listening to tapes, identifying problems, planning strategies, and consulting with colleagues, who awaited a weekly report and offered helpful suggestions.

The therapists took active roles in the famly sessions and felt deep concern for each member of the family. The therapists were elated at the achievements and frustrated at relapses. Minuchin et al. sum up this kind of experience:

> The therapist can also find himself exhausted when a session ends. . . . A variety of transactions have occurred, seemingly without any connection to each other, and he has tried to weave what was being transacted into some unity, hoping to maintain a theme with some family members while keeping the others engaged in active listening. And he has been continuously thwarted in the process. . . . But at other times he can feel elated because of some evidence of "registering." . . . His feeling of superfluousness, at this point, is replaced by a keen sense of potency and centrality in the family, as if it were in him and in him only that any possibility of family organization resides (2).

The therapists were exhausted after each discussion, but particularly after the eighth session. Although the Grays had experienced many positive changes, it was apparent that the family would need support and encouragement for this growth to continue. The therapists felt like traitors who had introduced many changes into the family system and were now exiting before these changes had time to gel and become habits.

DIVERSIONS FROM THE THEORY OF MINUCHIN ET AL.

The most obvious difference between the Gray family and those of *Families of the Slums* was that the Grays did not live in the slums. They were poor, but they lived in the country. Their home was crowded, but the neighborhood wasn't. One could go outside to escape the bombardment. A second difference was that illness was substituted for loudness to gain attention. A third difference was that the people in *Families of the Slums* were unable to conceptualize, and the therapists had to use concrete actions and expressions a great deal. The parents in the Gray family were unusually articulate and able to conceptualize; although nonverbal behavior was used, it was possible to get ideas and opinions across with verbal statements.

The greatest difference between this work and that of Minuchin et al. was the length of time spent with the family. The fact that there were only eight sessions greatly restricted interventions. It wasn't until the third session that the therapists became *part of the family,* and, by the sixth session, termination was anticipated. Because of the short duration, the focus was on the family as a whole, while Minuchin et al. had separated each session into three separate meetings: one with the parents, one with the siblings, and one with the entire family. In retrospect, these therapists would have liked to have done the same thing. Mr. and Mrs. Gray were left to deal with the children's reactions to the changes. In separate sessions with the children, their disengagement from their mother could have been supported, and interaction among them could have been promoted.

IMPLICATIONS FOR NURSE THERAPISTS

Nurses often contact disorganized, low income families in the mental health and out-patient centers. In order to effectively work with them, it is necessary to understand their values, their modes of communication, their structure, and affect. In working with them, it is necessary to use one's self fully, by joining with the family, directing communication, supporting individual members, introducing new affect, and finding and rewarding competence.

One important aspect of the above case study was home visits, which gave a real appreciation of the problems with which the family had to deal. The therapists felt the overcrowding, the lack of paint on the walls, the lack of running water, and the lack of other necessities. After each session, Mr. Gray would put on a heavy glove, unscrew the one light bulb, and screw it in the porch socket for the therapists to see as they left. Home visits also demonstrated the therapists' interest in the family, and facilitated sharing "authority" with them, since it was their home turf.

Another important aspect of this work was the use of cotherapy. One therapist would have become overwhelmed by the family system. Minuchin et al. report the use of three therapists: two to work with the family, and one to observe from behind a one-way mirror, entering the room occasionally to get the family and therapists back on track.

Minuchin et al. state that *family* with these families is *not* short term. The therapists' own frustration about the short duration in this case study supports that statement.

REFERENCES

1. Burgess, A. W., & Lazare, A. *Psychiatric nursing in the hospital and the community.* Englewood Cliffs, N.J.: Prentice-Hall, 1976.
2. Minuchin, S., Montalvo, B., Guerney, B., Rosman, B., & Schumer, F. *Families of the slums.* New York: Basic Books, 1967.
3. Minuchin, S., Auerswald, E., King, C., & Rabinowitz, C. The study and treatment of families that produce multiple acting-out boys. *American Journal of Orthopsychiatry,* 1964, *34,* 125–133.
4. Minuchin, S. The plight of the poverty-stricken family in the united states. *Child Welfare,* 1970, *49,* 124–130.

31

Family Conflict: A Comparison of Ackerman and Satir

Eva Benson

Both Nathan Ackerman and Virginia Satir frequently refer to the presence of conflict in the family. Family differences, according to Ackerman, cause conflict, and solutions to that conflict may be achieved by obtaining complementarity of roles. Satir speaks of conflict as the result of differentness in the family and suggests that with congruent communication differences may be negotiated to a satisfactory solution.

In studying the writings of these two family therapists in an effort to understand their views, the terms *complementarity* and *differentness* appear again and again. Both writers agree that differences in family members cause conflict. Ackerman identifies complementarity as the positive solution to conflict. Resolution of family differentness may signal complementarity according to Ackerman, and conversely, the absence of complementarity may indicate unresolved differences. However, these terms are a bit confusing, so for clarification it seems appropriate to examine a sampling of the authors' statements that include the terms "complementarity" and "differentness." This comparison is not intended as a comprehensive review but rather as a representative statement allowing a comparison of the authors' views on family conflict and of the clarity of their presentation.

DEFINITIONS

Initially, the author's own definitions of their respective terms should be considered. Ackerman defines complementarity thus:

> The term *complementarity* refers to specific patterns of role relations that provide satisfactions, avenues of solution of conflict, support for a needed self-image, and buttressing of crucial forms of defenses against anxiety (1).

Satir plainly states her meaning when using the term "differentness."

> I mean the term *differentness* to cover the whole area of individuality, how each person is innately different from every other person (2).

Historically speaking, Ackerman's writing on *social roles* and *complementarity* first appeared in the literature in 1951 (3). He expanded the terms further in books published in 1958 and 1966 (1, 4). Satir used the term *differentness* in her books published in 1964, 1972 and 1975 (2, 5–6).

Satir was probably influenced by Ackerman, who is known as the grandfather of family therapy (7). She quotes Ackerman, and this influence likely led to the similarities apparent in Ackerman's and her statements.

COMPARISON OF STATEMENTS

Six statement sets will be compared addressing the following areas: cause of conflict, dealing with conflict, self-esteem and conflict, marital relation and conflict, parent–child relation and conflict, and goals for family growth.

In each instance, the quotation of Ackerman will be followed by that of Satir with a note of comparison after each set. The quotations in each set are generally in agreement, but those of Satir are more concrete.

> When differences within the family group are felt as a menace instead of being prized, conflict brings a rift (4).
> Treat the presence of differentness as an opportunity to learn and explore rather than as a threat or a signal for conflict (2).

Ackerman leaves us wondering what the direction of conflict resolution should be. Satir points to a first step—differences must be allowed expression.

> Self-esteem, the satisfaction of emotional need, the control of conflict, and the growth and fulfillment in life depend on what is done with elements of sameness and difference in family relations (4).

. . . The more covertly and indirectly people communicate the more dysfunctional they are likely to be. . . . if they are dysfunctional to an extreme degree, . . . [they] will have low esteem, high hopes and little trust (2).

In mentioning self-esteem, once again Ackerman leaves us wondering just what should be done with sameness and difference. Satir links dysfunctional communication to low self-esteem and thus suggests a possible solution: improvement of communication.

Disturbances of marital relationships are characterized by two salient elements: (*1*) failure of reciprocity of satisfactions and (*2*) conflict (1).

As I have said before, when one of the partners in a marriage is confronted with a differentness in the other that he did not expect, or that he did not know about, it is important that he treat this as an opportunity to explore and understand rather than as a signal for war (2).

Ackerman speaks about the causes of marital disturbances; Satir agrees but is more specific in delineating what can be done to prevent the disturbance.

The psychological identity of the marital and parental pair shapes the child to his identity, but the child, in turn, also shapes the parental pair to his needs (4).

Our parents are our first teachers. We get ideas of how to behave from what we see, what we experience and what we are told, and all this comes to us from our first teachers (2).

In considering the parent–child relationship, Ackerman states that each shapes the other. Satir goes further to state how the shaping is done by learning from each other.

In defining the goals for family growth Ackerman states:

In family process, growth is forward movement . . . It is embodied in a progressive shift of dynamics of family role adaptation. It is the ability to accommodate to new experience, to cultivate new levels of complementarity in family role relationships (4).

Satir is more definitive and succinct. She states:

A person's reaction to differentness is an index of his ability to adapt to growth and change (2).

and,

In the congruent, integrated state, when there is a difference you negotiate (6).

ANALYSIS

After comparing this limited sampling from the writings of Ackerman and Satir, it seems apparent that they agree that differentness may cause conflict in the family and that how the conflict is handled is the key to successful family relations. They differ in their stated recommendations for handling the conflict. Ackerman speaks of role complementarity and Satir of negotiation and congruent communication.

Of the two, Ackerman appears to have the greater depth of thought and breadth of vocabulary. However, for sheer clarity of presentation and for readily applicable information, Satir is outstanding. Though her writing seems less sophisticated, Satir has further developed the concept of differentness and family conflict provided by Ackerman. She has progressed beyond Ackerman's rhetoric, bypassing his *social role* and role *complementarity,* and has documented her own concrete, workable solutions to family *differentness.*

In applying the results of this comparison to the nurse in family therapy, two observations come to mind. They are concerned with the presentation and content of the quotations.

First, Satir's statements demonstrate the effectiveness of her translation of basic philosophy into concrete examples. Illustrations and examples can be powerful tools for the nurse in the education of family members or colleagues. Their use enables the audience to visualize what goes on in practice.

Second, there is repeated reference to the importance of congruent communication. Not only is congruent communication important to family function, but it is imperative in the family therapist. The nurse in family therapy must constantly monitor his/her own communication for congruence. The nurse serves as the model for communication when working with the family.

Borrowing the technique from Satir, the following will illustrate the observations:

A family therapist had been meeting with a family for several weeks with no apparent progress and was beginning to become discouraged. She kept these feelings to herself, however, and continued to present a facade of cheerful professionalism. Her verbal communication was at odds with what she really wanted to say.

Finally, after an unfruitful half-hour session in which no one in the family would share his/her problems, she threw up her hands in desperation and confessed her frustration.

> This family doesn't want to share their problems. I feel useless and frustrated coming here week after week. Is there any need for me to come?

Her communication had become congruent.

Family members reacted by accusing each other of driving away their one source of help. Problem areas were finally opened for discussion. One family member told the therapist that for the first time that night she had seemed to be a *real* person with needs and feelings and with, perhaps, the capability of understanding their family.

On another occasion, a different family group was having difficulty understanding the concept of family negotiation and bargaining.

The therapist checked with the family members for possible points of illustration. The father was an active union member, and all the family members were very aware of union negotiations. The family therapist described family bargaining in relation to their knowledge of union activities.

When the family therapist gave them concrete examples of negotiation and bargaining, they were able to understand and apply the concepts in their family interaction.

SUMMARY

In conclusion, two recommendations are indicated. One is a plaudit to Satir for her clarity and brevity. If a message can be stated in fewer words or those words can be made more explicit, let it be done.

Second, much has been written regarding both congruent communication (8) and negotiations and bargaining (9). The nurse involved in family therapy must be aware of significant differences and trends in published works regarding family conflict.

This chapter reviews some representative statements comparing the views and clarity of presentation of Satir's and Ackerman's work on family conflict. It concludes that there is a general agreement between the two authors, but that Satir presents the more concrete statement, providing definite direction regarding conflict resolution. From this, recommendations for application can be made to the nurse in family therapy.

REFERENCES

1. Ackerman, N. *The psychodynamics of family life.* New York: Basic Books, 1958.
2. Satir, V. *Conjoint family therapy.* Palo Alto, Calif.: Science and Behavior Books, 1967.
3. Ackerman, N. Social roles and total personality. *American Journal of Orthopsychiatry*, 1951, *21*, 1–17.
4. Ackerman, N. *Treating the troubled family.* New York: Basic Books, 1966.
5. Satir, V. *Peoplemaking.* Palo Alto, Calif.: Science and Behavior Books, 1972.
6. Satir, V., Stachowiak, J., & Taschman, H. *Helping families to change.* New York: Jason Aronson, 1975.

7. Foley, V. D. *An introduction to family therapy.* New York: Grune & Stratton, 1974.

8. Bandler, R., & Grinder, J. *The structure of magic.* Palo Alto, Calif.: Science and Behavior Books, 1975.

9. Lederer, W. J., & Jackson, D. D. *Mirages of Marriage.* New York: W. W. Norton, 1968.

32

Adaptation: The Patient and Family Response to Long-Term Hemodialysis

Deborah Williams

Because long-term hemodialysis is a stressful procedure and chronic renal failure is stressful, many patients of hemodialysis have difficulty adapting. Adaptation is difficult not only for the patient but also for the family of the hemodialysis patient. Therefore, if families could be helped to adapt, then the patient could adapt with far less difficulty. This problem will comprise the major focus of this chapter.

The first section of the chapter will define adaptation. The next section will include a literature review on the topic of patient and family adaptation to long-term hemodialysis. The succeeding section will include narration and verbatim interviews of one family in which the wife/mother is the patient on hemodialysis. This clinical example will be viewed in light of the adaptation process. Recommendations will be offered for working with families with a hemodialysis patient. Topics needing additional study and research will be discussed.

ADAPTATION DEFINED

Adaptation has been defined as "fitting or conforming to the environment typically by means of a combination of . . . maneuvers which involve a change in the self and . . . maneuvers which involve alteration of the external environment" (1). Another definition of adaptation is the "change in quality, intensity, or distinctness of a sensation which occurs after continuous stimulation of constant intensity" (2).

LITERATURE REVIEW

Abram has stated that adaptation to long-term hemodialysis occurs in four phases or stages: First, the uremic syndrome, which has been described as "Prior to the beginning of dialysis the patient suffers from severe uremia, characterized by fatigue, apathy, drowsiness, inability to concentrate, depression and instability" (3). Second, the shift to physiological equilibrium "characterized by a return from the dead type of revitalization" (3). There are three subcategories under this stage: "(a) apathy, occurring as the patient approaches physiologic equilibrium; (b) euphoria, the patient realizes he is not at death's door; (c) anxiety, this is transient and lasts only one or two dialyses" (3). The third stage according to Abram's classification is *Convalescence—The Return to the Living* and is characterized by depression since the "problem of living with dialysis becomes apparent" (3). The fourth stage is the *Struggle for Normalcy* that involves "the problem of living rather than dying" (3).

Adaptation has three stages according to Reichman and Levy. They are: the honeymoon, disenchantment, and long-term adaptation (3). The first stage, the honeymoon stage, is "characterized by improvement of both physical and emotional state" (3). The second stage, disenchantment, "shows a relationship with some external event (usually the planning or resumption of an active role in society)." And the third stage, long-term adaptation, is "characterized by the patients arriving at some degree of acceptance of their own limitations" (3).

Other authors describe adaptation as involving the defense mechanism of denial. Wright and associates have used the MMPI to show that the dialysis patient uses denial quite effectively. They saw changes in three scales of the MMPI that have been frequently interpreted as indicating the existence of denial (4). These researchers also noted an elevation of repression and simultaneously a lowering of anxiety that indicated the effective use of denial (4).

Short and Wilson talk about family denial and community denial as mechanisms for adapting to the presence of a family member receiving long-term hemodialysis. These authors say that many changes are made initially by the family of the hemodialysis patient and that these changes are made in "good faith" and "with sincere motivation," however, the changes necessary never end (4). Marital roles change and the closeness once seen becomes less. In addition to the shift in marital roles, parent–child relations change also. Short and Wilson describe the denial pattern of the family quite vividly in the following manner:

> In order to maintain a degree of self-protection, the spouse, who initially supports the dialysis program for their mate, begins to question the validity of the decision to continue the dialysis. They recognize the changes occurring in their loved one, who is no longer the person they married. They see their children moving away from the disabled parent, making decisions at the exclusion of the dialysand. Initially, attempts are made to correct these reactions, but the problem persists. In an effort to maintain some degree of balance in the household, these changes become ignored and situations producing them are avoided by the family (4).

As stated previously, Short and Wilson address community denial. This involves the patients of hemodialysis giving up their activities in the community; and in turn the community members aviod the dialysis patient (4). These actions make the use of denial even greater.

It is known that many people use food and/or sex as ways of dealing with stress of physical illness or as a preliminary step in the adaptation process. However, these two avenues cannot be used effectively with the dialysis patient. Food restrictions are very much a part of the treatment plan as are fluid restrictions. Dianne Anger addresses the sexual problems associated with the long-term hemodialysis patient in stating that the sexual drive and sexual performance decrease with the progression of renal disease (5). These factors bring about feelings of guilt in the patient since the handicap means that he is not able to sexually satisfy the marital partner (5). She also addresses, very briefly, the issue of the family's adaptation. She tells us that some families are overprotective of the ill member and thereby they "reinforce the sick and dependent role" (5). She says that other families react to the dialysis with "an opposite manner by totally ignoring or avoiding the patient, leaving him with feelings of abandonment. This situation, in turn, frequently precipitates depression and suicidal behavior" (5) in the hemodialysis patient.

Levy has also addressed the sexual issue of long-term hemodialysis patients. Levy's survey "showed that hemodialysis patients of both sexes (but particularly men) reported substantial deterioration in sexual functioning" (6). Abram has established statistically that frequency of sexual intercourse decreased remarkably from the time before uremia to the time after dialysis began. Although these studies suggest decrease in sexual frequency, the primary focus is directed toward man's response to hemodialysis rather than the sexual response of women on hemodialysis.

Other sources give another viewpoint of adaptation of patients and their families. Johnson says that "an emotionally stable home environment and a high degree of motivation toward a specific goal" are "essential prerequisites for successful adaptation to long-term dialysis therapy" (5). Sand supports this view with the following conclusions: Patients with "(1) higher intelligence, (2) a less defensive attitude about admitting to anxiety or emotional difficulty, (3) less reliance on emotional defenses that involve the use of physical symptoms, (4) more satisfactory emotional support from family members" more successfully adapted to dialysis (1).

Clinical Example

Family therapy was suggested to the F. family by the dialysis center because there were problems with the grades of the youngest son. This was an indication that the family had not effectively adapted to Mrs. F.'s hemodialysis.

Bargaining was the therapeutic technique used with this family since it is a systems approach. The systems approach is one of the most effective family therapy approaches, since it emphasizes open communication among family members and correctly identifies the problem as a family problem and not one person's problem within the family

The family discussed here will be identified as the F. family. (Names have been disguised by using initials which do not correspond with the actual names of the family of the study.) The family includes the father, C., age 43, the mother, J., age 43, and the son, M., age 14. She has been receiving hemodialysis for 5 years and goes to a local clinic three times per week to be dialyzed. The family is judged to be of the lower middle socioeconomic group.

Since J. has been receiving dialysis for 5 years, many of the early processes of adaptation are no longer obvious; however, C. relates the following as being initial changes of the family in response to J.'s dialysis: "Well, at first it was hard, J. was having to go to the clinic for dialysis, and I was taking her in the mornings and then going to work, leaving work to pick her up, and then going back to work. J. used to work but she hasn't worked since being on dialysis."

C. also related to the therapist that he works two jobs but not as a consequence of the dialysis. He said he has worked two jobs for the majority of his adult life.

J.'s response to the question of the effect of hemodialysis on the family was "We've adjusted to it; I don't see any real changes in the family." In an earlier interview she related that when she was working, she was able to save a substantial amount of money and that she has contributed to the family income through her savings since ceasing to work outside the home.

M. was quiet during the discussion of changes or effects of hemodialysis on the family. M. maintained a pattern of quiet behavior throughout the beginning sessions with the family.

J.'s present activities include driving herself to and from the dialysis clinic three times per week. She is involved with the neighbors and babysits for the next door neighbors from time to time. She described herself as being involved also with her stepdaughters, shopping, etc., and J. drove one stepdaughter to work until just recently. C. says his wife "always gets up and makes breakfast for me, has supper ready when I come home, and always has some kind of dessert made."

From the preceding verbatim interview and from information gained throughout several sessions with this family, it can be seen that although J. has chronic renal disease, she is quite independent and highly values this quality. C. and M. are supportive of J. and have many positive things to say about J. To illustrate these two observations further, C. and M. had difficulty in the second and third bargaining sessions coming up with things they would like for J. to do for them. They both indicated that J. met their needs effectively.

In the fourth bargaining session J. expressed a need, as did M., for the family to spend more time together. The suggestion was made to use bargaining to meet this need. A family bargain was made that all three of them spend 10 to 15 minutes on a daily basis discussing with each other their activities of that day.

The family was unable to do this on a daily basis due to C.'s work schedule and J.'s dialysis; therefore, the family altered and decided to spend 30 minutes together three to four times per week discussing each person's day or in playing a game including the whole family. The game playing was included in this bargain since this had been expressed as a desire of both J. and M.

By the end of the eight sessions, the family was spending more time together both in talking about each person's activities and in playing games. M. was more talkative during the sessions, and there was increased interaction among M., J., and C. M.'s grades had also improved dramatically.

This family's adaptation phase closely resembles Reichman and Levy's third stage, that of long-term adaptation, since J. seems to have accepted her limitations. This family's stage also resembles Abram's fourth stage called *the struggle for normalcy* since J. is involved with life rather than with an outward concern for death. Her activities support this. Data collected during the sessions with this family also support Johnson's conclusions of successful adaptation due to a stable home as well as Sand's conclusions that higher intelligence and support from family members are essential for successful adaptation.

Since this family had no problem identifiable with adaptation during the initial interview or in succeeding sessions, the focus of the sessions was directed toward further opening lines of communication through the technique of bargaining. With this approach, the family could use the technique if future problems occurred regarding adaptation to long-term hemodialysis.

IMPLICATIONS FOR NURSING

When working with families in which one member is a patient of hemodialysis, the therapy sessions should start as soon after the dialysis begins as possible so that the family and the patient may be helped to understand the steps that occur in the adaptation process. Anger has listed three guidelines that any nurse working with these families should consider:

> The nurse should work closely with the family by (*a*) determining what effect the patient's illness and dialysis has had on the family unit, (*b*) encouraging them to support, yet allow the patient to remain as independent as possible by continuing to involve him in family affairs and decisions, and (*c*) encouraging the patient and spouse to discuss their feelings related to changes in the marriage brought about by dialysis, such as loss of sexual function, role reversal, patient and spouse responsibilities (5).

If these guidelines were followed, the nurse would address very important aspects of family relationships and support each family member more fully.

Further research should be done regarding the woman's response to hemodialysis. Much of the research available is directed toward the male response, especially in the area of sexual functioning. It cannot be assumed that both men and women respond in the same way. Another area in which the male response is discussed predominantly is in role reversal; that is, the man is forced to decrease his working hours and financial security is threatened, and as a result the wife assumes the role of breadwinner. The female response to loss of financial security brought about by her loss of employment is given less attention.

SUMMARY

Adaptation is a dynamic process that occurs with the person receiving hemodialysis as well with the other family members. There are various stages in this process as pointed out by the literature. The family discussed here is in the long-term adaptation phase or the struggle for normalcy phase. This family works well together at this point, and C. and M. are very supportive of J. Bargaining was used as the technique to further improve their relationship. From the data presented here it can be seen that bargaining is an effective tool in further opening lines of communication and is a tool that the family can use after the therapist terminates the relationship.

REFERENCES

1. American Psychiatric Association. *A psychiatric glossary*. New York: Basic Books, S.v. adaptation.
2. Clayton, T. L. (Ed.). *Taber's cyclopedic medical dictionary*. Philadelphia: F. A. Davis, 1973, S.v. adaptation.
3. Abram, H. S. Survival by machine: The psychological stress of chronic hemo-dialysis. *Psychiatry in Medicine*, 1970, *1*(1) p. 40.
4. Short, M. J., & Wilson, F. P. Roles of denial in chronic hemodialysis. *Archives of General Psychiatry, 20,* 434–435. Copyright 1969, American Medical Association.
5. Anger, D. The psychologic stress of chronic renal failure and long term hemo-dialysis. *Nursing Clinics of North America,* 1975, *10*(3) 453–458.
6. Anderson, K. The psychological aspects of chronic hemodialysis. *Canadian Psy-chiatric Association Journal, 1,* p. 387. Reprinted with permission from the Canadian Psychiatric Association Journal 20(5): 385–391, 1975.

33

Therapy in Action: Strategies

Marjorie Fox

Verbal communication skills have become the goal of our educational system and the focus of our attention in therapy. Verbal communication is "communication by means of words written or spoken" (1). Communication, in its many forms, can be defined as "an act (or behavior) and a process" (1). If indeed actions speak louder than words, and communication is a behavior, techniques that require only verbal forms of communication are not the only methods of approaching the dynamic family system.

Regardless of which family treatment model the therapist uses, she/he must make use of techniques that relate space, time, and also movement. The individual in a system "can change only if he can transcend the system which is his context, and he cannot transcend it until he knows how it works" (2), that is, until he can see how it works.

There are techniques available that can allow the family to see the dynamics at work within its system. Some of these techniques will be reviewed and related to clinical practice in this overview: role playing, choreography, and videotaping. Research has been conducted on each technique, and therapists should familiarize themselves with the technique before employing it.

ROLE PLAYING

Role playing involves the symbolic representation of roles as they are perceived by the person playing them. It is more commonly referred to as sociodrama in employment and social counseling and as psychodrama in counseling and psychotherapy. J. L. Moreno has promoted the application of this technique more than anyone else while working with groups (3).

Role playing can be used both in data collection through observation and in intervention with the family. That is, in role playing, a person reveals two facts to himself: (1) He demonstrates he had more facts about the situation than he thought he did. (2) He discovers he knows more than he thought he did (2). Further, families often stumble with words trying to describe what has happened; when explaining the family problems, they attempt to choose the perfect words, which offend no one. They are so touched with a problem that they cannot describe the relationships without bias. The therapist realizes that a self-report and/or the question and answer techniques are not productive to understanding the family at this point, nor are they effective as intervention techniques. Hence, the nurse therapist can introduce the role playing technique.

Two types of role playing are most widely used in families. Family members may play themselves or each other in the role play. Role playing increases self-understanding when a person plays himself. Olsen says when a person puts himself into another's role, "he can perceive better the person's feelings within the relationship" (3).

Clinical applications of role playing emphasizes two points that should be remembered when using this technique. They are (1) the necessity of an appropriate introduction to role playing, and (2) the need for feedback discussions after the role play. First, *when* role playing is introduced is important. It cannot be used because the therapist simply finds it fun and likes the technique's reception with the family. The family can perceive its use as a gimmick and not as a way to understand their problems. Role playing must be spontaneous and appropriate for the subject area. For example, the therapist had previously used role playing with the E family to clarify the family problem. Everyone found it informative and enjoyable. It was the third meeting and the family was working on bargaining. The parents were attempting to clarify a behavior of the children that they saw as a problem and part of the bargain. After 10 minutes of disussion the children suddenly shouted, "I know, let's just role play it so we can see what they mean." "No," said the therapist, "I believe this point can be understood if you continue to talk with your parents." The therapist realized at this point that the behavior being discussed was easly understood verbally. The children were being playful, and role playing at this point would be inappropriate and would destroy the credibility of using role playing.

Second, when role playing is used time should be provided to discuss what happened during the role playing. Each person should have "a chance to reveal his feelings about what happened during the role playing, to comment on whatever he may have discovered about himself and/or the relationships, and to consider the possible benefit of role playing the scene" (3).

One advantage in using role playing is that it is easily understood.

For example, when it was introduced to the Allen family, the parents immediately responded, "okay" with great enthusiasm. "What's role playing?" asked the child, 14 years old. "It's a play without a written script," replied the mother. "What is it?" asked the 10-year-old child of his sister. "It's playing parts without lines written down," she answered. "Oh, okay." No more explanation was needed to explain the role playing. Another advantage is that role playing can also be a fun experience, for therapy, like learning, need not be all pain to be enlightening. Children, because they are naturally spontaneous, enjoy and learn from spontaneous role playing. Last, role playing provides a feedback mechanism in discussion time that is not as threatening to a person's integrity as confrontation.

Some disadvantages of this technique are that members may refuse to participate in the experience; there must be an objective observer who will also direct the discussion; and the enthusiastic therapist may overuse the technique.

Clinical Example Using Role Playing

Role playing can be used as an observation technique that helps to clarify the problem on which the family wishes to work. A clinical example of an interaction follows. Comments are in parentheses.

> MR. K: I'd like to see something done about mealtimes.
> (Introducing a topic that he feels is a problem.)
>
> NURSE THERAPIST: What specifically about mealtime is a problem?
> (Clarifying)
>
> MR. K: It's really hard to say. We just seem to get into a hassle around meals and about what we're going to eat.
> (Having difficulty being specific.)
>
> MRS. K: Well, I don't know if that's a problem. Like I'm not so sure that meals just aren't a place where the problems come out.
> (Does not understand that meals are really a problem.)
>
> MR. K: Well, I guess I do see a problem at meals though.
> (Reiterates his point.)
>
> NURSE THERAPIST: Is there something specific going on you can describe?
> (Attempting to clarify for specifics.)
>
> MR. K: Well, like, I give the boys this food to eat. Then there's this hassle.
> (Struggling to be specific.)

> NURSE: What happens?
> (Attempting to understand through request for description.)
>
> MR. K: I tell them how good in protein it is and they make faces.
> (Explaining the behavior he sees.)
>
> A (SON AGE 10): I just don't like that food.
> (Sons don't see a family problem.)
>
> M (SON AGE 14): I don't know if there's a problem. We just don't like some foods.

At this point the nurse therapist felt the language was not explaining any behaviors that would be observed at mealtime. Therefore, she introduced the technique of role playing. The family accepted this suggestion and moved to the kitchen to act out a meal. After the role play, the therapist rejoined the family for discussion. During the discussion the meaning of the nonverbal behavior was expressed to the father.

> A: I get angry at Dad when he makes me eat that food.
>
> MR. K: You never told me that.
>
> M: Well, you could see how angry he was. I can tell by his face and all.
>
> MRS. K: Yes, I knew he was angry too. It seems like really M and I stay out of it, but there is a battle between A and you.
>
> MR. K: The food is high in protein—good for you and I think you should eat it.
>
> A: But you yell and you force me.
>
> MR. K: Well, I didn't know how you felt. Maybe something else would be high in protein too.

The next meeting the family told the therapist this problem had already been worked out, and the father and son were no longer getting angry at each other.

Role playing is also useful as an intervention technique to explore the subject of authority and power.

The family was asked if there were more bargains on which they would like to work in the fifth meeting. The father introduced the discussion of a bargain the children had made with neighbors and explained the children were not keeping this bargain. The children protested. The mother quipped angrily, "Well, it's your responsibility, and you all are just not taking it." The children explained they had missed only one day of following the agreement made with the neighbor. The father continued to reiterate that it was the chidren's responsibility. One child summed up the feelings of both, "I just don't see what we did wrong."

The children negotiated not to complain or mention their agreement with the neighbor at all. The parents continued by pointing out more reasons why they were irresponsible. The children became silent. "Well, what else can we say?" one boy finally said.

The therapist at this point asked the family to role play reversing roles—parents playing children, and children playing parents.

This role playing was not effective because in the children's roles the parents retained their own personalities. The loudness of the parents overshadowed the children in the parents' roles. The children became discouraged and quiet.

Two recommendations for the successful use of role playing should be made. The therapist should not tell the family how to interact with each other during a role play. However, the therapist should not fail to point out inconsistencies in a role during role reversals.

CHOREOGRAPHY

A second technique similar to role playing is choreography. David Kanton in 1950 introduced the technique derived from the information on sculpturing. Choreography added movement to the elements of space and time used in sculpturing. It uses no verbal language. It "choreographs transactional patterns, alliances, triangles, and shifting emotional currents and projects them outward as a silent motion picture" (2).

The use of choregraphy is predominately for intervention. The nurse therapist generally gets an understanding of a problem through conversation and uses choreography so that members can experience an old problem in a new way. Family members are usually surprised when they *see* the problem, whereas they are seldom surprised at each other's descriptions. In other words, the family has heard it all before, and choreography introduces the element of the unpredictable or of spontaneity. When used in intervention, alternative patterns of interaction can be explored "but in terms of movement and position" (2). Choreography as an intervention allows each member to change things as he would like it or to practice changes. The therapist may also suggest changes and let members try them. For example, the therapist had discussed the father's role with the family, and the father often introduced the topic himself, including during bargaining. Through choreography the family related to the father how they saw his role. Then the nurse suggested the wife assume the central role. Based on this change, the choreography of the family showed marked differences in how everyone related.

The introduction of choreography is also very important. One suggestion on how to introduce it is to "ask each person to show a visual picture of the way he or she experienced a problem" (2). Family members can also be asked to show how they see their family or how they would like their family to be. These introductions are effective with children or family members who are less verbal. Second, feedback time is also very important in this technique. Since choreography is used to introduce changes in interacting, it is important to allow members time to express verbally how each sees the change or what he discovered about the interaction or relationships.

One advantage in using this technique is that it is a nonverbal medium and can be quite appropriate for the less literate families and for quieter family members. Unlike role playing, the term *choreography* may not be familiar to the family; however, this technique can be explained as a silent movie. Last, families are experts in using words to maintain a homeostatic family system, and thus the power of words is decreased. A new power of understanding is gained "through seeing and physically moving through the situation" (2).

Some disadvantages in the use of choreography are: (*1*) it is often difficult for articulate families not to talk; (*2*) an objective observer should be present and nonverbal also, during the choreography; and (*3*) the therapist must be knowledgeable enough to handle "fallout" from changes in interaction and relationships (2).

Clinical Example Using Choreography

The West family had previously discussed the father's role in the family in the last two meetings. In the fifth meeting, the nurse therapist decided to use choreography to illustrate how each family member related to the father's role or how they had demonstrated approaching or avoiding behavior in relation to the father.

The nurse therapist asked the family to illustrate in movement how each member approached the father. To illustrate more clearly ties with each other and with the father, towels were given to the father to hold as contact points to the family.

The family members approached the father hesitantly. The son closest to the father moved toward him first. The father agreed to a request to play with the son. The other child moved toward the father slowly, took a different towel as contact, released the towel and moved away again. The wife also took a different towel and made a request of the husband as she moved close. The husband indicated agreement with the wife's request. The son became frustrated and shouted, "You can't do both, which one are you doing, playing or doing something with her?" The family stopped at this point and began to discuss what had happened. They talked about how they related to each other and about their thoughts and feelings as they choreographed relating to the father. The father pointed out the difficulty he had trying to meet all the requests of family members.

Next, the central role was given to the wife who now held the towels. The choreography was repeated. Afterward, discussion revealed that the wife enjoyed the role of more leadership and the father was "relieved not to hold the towels." The children discussed why they just never thought to go to the mother with their requests. The family agreed they better understood how the father must feel sometimes and how things could be changed to relieve the pressure on him.

Some recommendations for the use of choreography based on this experience are:

1. Use choreography without profuse verbal introduction.
2. Move out of the family's field of vision to prevent distraction and allow freedom of movement.
3. Do not talk to the family during a choreography set.
4. Allow the family to terminate a choreography set on their own.

VIDEOTAPING

Videotaping is the third technique in which the action of human drama can be recorded. It is another medium to incorporate elements of space, time, and movement. One of the important elements in this medium is that a person's "observing self is totally separated from his participating self" (4). He can change his verbal communication about his past behavior but his drama is recorded and can be observed and no longer influenced.

This technique can be used, therefore, both in data collection and intervention. Forgotten observations are no longer a problem for the therapist nor are incomplete notes. However, assessing change in behavior can be difficult. Videotaping assists the therapist by recapturing the past and retaining the present at the same time. In intervention then, the videotape can be used in many ways according to the therapist's ingenuity. For example, one therapist may record 15 minutes of a session, replay it, and move to the discussion of the taped interactions. Therapists have recorded whole sessions and replayed them and have used many other combinations of time and feedback. Thus, the replay or feedback represents the use of videotaping in intervention. There are many special effects that can be achieved with videotaping. It can be used as face to face self-confrontation, profile self-confrontation, or juxtaposition of images.

All of the different effects that can be created sound like an expensive project. Videotaping can become quite expensive using special effects. However, since 1965 less expensive equipment has been developed. Some of the basic equipment recommended in literature include a videorecorder, a camera, suitable lenses, and power lighting (4).

Introduction is not as much of a problem in videotaping as in other techniques previously discussed. Most family members have never seen themselves on any type of videotape and are often quite curious and open to the process. If the therapist has any doubts concerning the family's reception to the use of video, a matter of fact approach is effective. For example, the therapist may say, "You see this camera and videorecorder, and television set. I find it useful to make videorecordings of our sessions, so from time to time we can look together at what we are doing" (2). In videotaping, feedback is provided by playbacks and discussions and remains an important element of this technique as in other techniques. It is true that videotaping can be used strictly for recording sessions; however, in doing so the therapist is limiting intervention techniques. Literature demonstrates that the patient feels more a part of the therapy when he, along with the therapist, runs the video equipment and evaluates the taped behavior.

One advantage to videotaping is that it is a medium with *image impact* (4). That is, the family sees itself as it really is, perhaps for the first time. The impact of this image opens up clarification of the dynamics within the family. Second, videotaping provides the family with a second chance (4). Specifics of a past experience are clearly recorded by videotaping, and by reviewing the tape the family more clearly sees changes or the need for changes.

Some disadvantages to videotaping are that some therapists find any technical equipment a drawback. With improper use the equipment could shadow the therapy. In addition, "some people may have a negative reaction to their own image" (2).

Clinical Example Using Video Playback

It was the ninth session, and the nurse therapists in cotherapy were planning to use videotaping for the first time.

The family arrived early at the media center where the taping was to be. They expressed their feelings about "being on TV" by joking and asking questions.

During the time the camera was being set up and focused, the boys entertained by making faces and gestures on the television. The camera was put in place, and close-ups were done on everyone, which brought laughter and gestures from the entire family.

The nurse therapists began the meeting with the family, and the camera was soon forgotten as they moved into discussions of changes in the family.

The meeting progressed as usual and afterward the family moved to the video screen to review the tape. The parents pulled up chairs directly in front as the children lay on the floor. The family watched with concentration even though the boys could not resist laughing and mimicking their previous behavior.

During the discussion, family members pointed out and explained their nonverbal behavior to each other. Questions about what was happening at different points on the tape were introduced by the therapist. The father became aware of his change in position during the meeting in which he turned more toward the rest of the family. The father and son compared their speech patterns, which were similar in loudness and rhythm. The father also explained why the therapist moved toward one son when he said, "I thought it was to let him know you identified with what was happening with him."

In addition, the therapist became aware of how the family members cue each other on talking and mimicking nonverbal behavior between themselves such as touching the chin when speaking.

Some recommendations for the use of videotaping based on this experience are that videotaping should not be used to replace the therapist's role. In addition, the therapist should become familiar and comfortable with the equipment. Video should be used earlier than the ninth session with the client or family. Therapists should be sure to allow enough time for discussion and ask for feedback on the experience of being videotaped.

SUMMARY

There are many techniques not mentioned here that are equally effective as action techniques. Verbal communication is certainly not being discounted, but it can be enhanced with nonverbal techniques.

Change is the indictor of growth in therapy. It means moving from one phase to another, giving and receiving, and becoming different. Only those techniques that combine space, time, and movement can capture a changing dynamic system called family. Such techniques are role playing, choreography, and videotaping.

Therapists must become aware of the availability of methods in therapy that allow each family member to reexperience interactions and that provide greater objectivity to the data collection process. If the therapist is interested in using one of these techniques, additional research and investigation is recommended since the purpose of this chapter is to provide only an overview of these techniques.

The use of these techniques and similar ones is limited only by therapists' lack of imagination. This awareness should provide therapists with a new enthusiasm at the possibilities in therapy and a greater understanding of the words *becoming* and *changing* in a dynamic system.

REFERENCES

1. Travelbee, J. *Interpersonal aspects of nursing.* Philadelphia: F. A. Davis, 1971, pp. 94–118.

2. Guerin, Jr., P. *Family therapy.* New York: Gardner Press, 1976, pp. 465–501, 530–547.

3. Ohlsen, M. *Group counseling.* New York: Holt, Rinehart, & Winston, 1974, p. 153.

4. Haley, J. *Changing families.* New York: Grune & Stratton, pp. 237–246.

BIBLIOGRAPHY

Ferber, A., Mendelsohn, M., & Napier, A. *The book of family therapy.* New York: Jason Aronson, 1972, pp. 318–337, 278–314.

Kaplan, H. S., & Sager, C. J. *Progress in group and family therapy.* New York: Brunner/Mazel, 1972, pp. 135–149.

Satir, V. *Peoplemaking.* Palo Alto, Calif.: Science and Behavior Books, 1972.

Sedgwick, R. R. Role playing: A bridge between talk and action. *Journal of Psychiatric Nursing and Mental Health Services,* November 1976, pp. 16–21.

34

Comparison of Two Forms of Family Bargaining

Jane Kreplick Brody

The area of decision making and conflict resolution within the family is an important factor in the stability and functioning of individual family members and the family as a whole. The basic skills required for these two processes are often lacking in families. Unresolved conflicts of inadequate decision making manifest a wide range of symptomatology: alcoholism, psychosomatic illness, and mental illness are common examples (1). Therefore, it is critical that families learn the skills of decision making. It is also imperative that nurses who engage in family practice should be aware of techniques available to help families learn these skills.

Two theories proposed to assist families in the decision-making process are Thomas Gordon's "No Lose Method" described in *Parent Effectiveness Training (P.E.T.)*, and William Lederer and Don D. Jackson's "Quid Pro Quo" outlined in *Mirages of Marriage* (2, 3).

GORDON'S NO LOSE METHOD

Gordon's no lose method operates in the following manner.

When a conflict between parent and child occurs, the parent asks the child to participate in a joint search for some solution acceptable to both. Either may suggest possible solutions, which are then evaluated. A decision is then made on the best solution. They then decide how it is to be carried out. No coercion is required, hence no power is used (2).

This process is actually the final stage of a longer decision-making process constituting the core of *P.E.T.*

The foundation of Gordon's method is the concept of problem ownership. First, the child's behavior is divided into acceptable and unacceptable categories. Usually, acceptable behavior creates no parent–child conflict. However, some behaviors that are acceptable to the parents may cause conflict within the child; for example, whether the child should try out for a sports team or use the time to earn extra money. The child owns this problem and the parents should only be facilitators in the child's decision making process. In the parent–child relationship, conflict can occur with acceptable child behavior only when the parents interfere by taking responsibility of the child's problem (2). They rob the child of the opportunity to test his decision-making skills, reinforce that the child is a dependent, inadequate person, and take responsibility away from the child for the outcome of the decision.

When the child's behavior falls into the unacceptable category, the child's actions interfere with the parent's needs. The amount of unacceptable behavior can be reduced through improved communication. Gordon suggests techniques like the "I-message," which is an assertive statement of need by the owner of the problem who is the parent in this case (2).

Only when the child's behavior is unacceptable and improved communication is not effective is the "No Lose Method" needed. Here, neither parent nor child forces his will on the other. Both truly accept the solution and their needs are met (2).

The chronological steps of the no lose method are:

1. Define the real problem. Parents and child must agree that a problem exists and specifically what behavior is being discussed.
2. Seek more than one possible solution.
3. Allow the child to begin to suggest solutions but have parental suggestions for solution also. This is a joint endeavor.
4. Do not stop to evaluate suggestions until "brainstorming" period has ended.
5. Modify the suggested solutions when necessary. If the agreed upon solution is not satisfactory when implemented, begin the whole process again (2).

Although Gordon's no lose method is effective in resolving conflicts about behaviors, it is not applicable in resolving conflicts about values. Often there is not a tangible concrete way in which one person's values interfere with another person's meeting his needs. In conflicts about values, parents should reexamine their own values, model these values, and act as a consultant to their child only at the child's request. Finally, parents must accept what cannot be changed as part of the maturing process of the child who is separating from the family to establish his own personal identity (2).

LEDERER AND JACKSON'S QUID PRO QUO

Lederer and Jackson envision their bargaining process, quid pro quo (which means something for something) as functioning within a marriage to:

1. prevent constant repetition of old, destructive patterns;
2. stop small problems from becoming big problems;
3. point to broad relationship goals;
4. force spouses or prospective spouses to explore certain areas that they have avoided (3).

Before the bargaining process begins, the couple must determine their commitment to their relationship and accept that bargaining is not winning or losing on a particular issue but is a long-term pattern of negotiation. Next, the couple improves their communication patterns by learning to send complete unambiguous messages, consisting of statement, acknowledgment, and second acknowledgment (3).

The overall theme of quid pro quo can be described as follows:

> Both spouses are saying 'I can't have everything I want and you can't have everything you want, but let's arrange our behavior in such a manner that we each get the maximum' (3).

By using their improved communication skills, the couple build a quid pro quo during a series of bargaining sessions. Maintenance bargaining sessions are recommended to accommodate the inevitable changes that occur.

Analysis

Many similarities exist between the no lose method and quid pro quo. Both methods attempt to improve familial relationships by modifying behaviors. Each bargaining process is based on the mutual respect and concern of the bargainers for each other. This assumes that some commitment and positive feelings are present within the relationship. The no lose method and quid pro quo reach decision by consensus. No coercion is permitted. Also, Gordon and Lederer and Jackson see their decision-making strategies as only part of a larger process of the family system. Finally, both the no lose method and quid pro quo are on-going processes rather than one-time events.

The differences between quid pro quo and the no lose method point out the advantages and limitations of each system, as well as the differences between a marital and a parental–child relationship. A marital relationship usually begins when two adults, independent people, choose to develop a long-term interdependence that is mutually satisfying. In the parent–child relationship, the child only becomes an equal partner in the relationship after a slow maturing process. The child moves from total dependence on the parents to a point where the child looks beyond his parents to satisfy his needs.

The no lose method is the final step in a long decision-making process. It is only a small part of the parent–child relationship. In contrast, quid pro quo is the basic decision-making process in a marriage and forms the underpinnings of the relationship.

Quid pro quo is truly a bargaining technique because both parties are giving up something in return for a gain. In the no lose method the parent and child reach agreement on how the child's behavior will be modified but often without the parent having to give up something in return.

The no lose method is here-and-now–oriented, working with parent–child behaviors as they occur. It deals only indirectly with goals and values. Quid pro quo is more future-oriented, setting up a framework of interaction for the spouses. Although mostly a behavioral approach, it can be used to explore marital goals and values.

Since the no lose method focuses on one specific behavior or pattern, its results are seen more easily and more quickly. In contrast, quid pro quo takes longer to establish, and its results are less immediate.

Gordon tries to teach the parents to make decisions more effectively, but Lederer and Jackson work equally with both partners in the relationship. As a child matures, he would use the decision-making skills he sees modeled and the no lose method would be initiated by him.

Clinical Applications

Families seeking therapy may have a wide range of symptoms. However, despite the various manifestations of dysfunction, the root is often unresolved conflict. Families trying to cope with life stresses, such as death or divorce, often find adaptation difficult because of poor decision-making capabilities.

It is imperative that nurses who work with families learn methods to assess how each family makes decisions and resolves conflicts. Gordon's no lose method and Lederer and Jackson's quid pro quo provide models for assessing decision-making processes and their sequelae. The nurse can use these models to interpret the patterns developing within a family and then can intervene by teaching one of these techniques and by aiding its implementation. As the family assimilates the model and uses it independently, the need for intervention by the nurse will often diminish. By helping families gain better modes of decision making and conflict resolution, the nurse can enable families to meet more fully the needs of its members.

SUMMARY

Although families may come to a nurse with a variety of problems and issues, at the root of many families' problems lies poor decision-making skills. Inability to resolve conflicts prevents families from adapting to stressful situations and limits the families' abilities to meet the needs of their members. Two methods of decision making were presented, Gordon's no lose method and Lederer and Jackson's quid pro quo. A brief explanation of the no lose method within the entire concept of *P.E.T.* followed. Quid pro quo was then introduced and contrasted with the no lose method. Although many similarities were apparent, there were also some important differences. It was suggested that nurses teach bargaining techniques to families to improve the functioning of the family. Once the family incorporates bargaining techniques into its interactions, the need for nursing intervention should diminish. The area of decision making and bargaining within a family is an area that needs more research and documentation. Nurses who use techniques such as quid pro quo and the no lose method should try to extend the present knowledge of this area through research.

REFERENCES

1. Satir, V. *Conjoint family therapy*. Palo Alto, Calif.: Science and Behavior Books, 1967.
2. Gordon, T. *P.E.T. in Action*. New York: Bantam Books, 1976, p. 176.
3. Lederer, W., & Jackson, D. D. *Mirages of marriage*. New York: W. W. Norton, 1968, pp. 262, 286.

35

Paradoxical
Interventions
in Family Therapy

Mary Ann Woodward-Smith

This chapter will explore the therapeutic use of paradox in family therapy. The first section of the chapter includes a review of the literature regarding paradoxical interventions along with an explanation of why paradox works. The last section of the chapter includes a clinical example of paradoxical intervention drawn from the author's clinical practice with recommendations regarding the therapeutic use of paradox in family therapy.

Hare–Mustin defines paradox as "any seemingly self-contradictory or absurd event which in reality expresses a possible truth" (1). Papp defines a paradoxical intervention as accomplishing the opposite of what it seemingly intends to accomplish (2). The success of the intervention depends on the family's response, either in defying the therapist's instructions or in following instructions to the point of absurdity.

REVIEW OF THE LITERATURE: THE TERMINOLOGY

Eighty-seven years ago Freud was consulted about a young woman who was unable to feed her newborn infant. She vomited all her food, was unable to sleep, and became extremely agitated when the infant was brought to her bedside. Freud used hypnosis and paradoxical injunction to help the patient gain control over her symptoms (3). The term *paradoxical injunction,* however, was not actually coined until many years later. Dunlap used a technique that he termed *negative practice* (4, 5). Negative practice involves instructing a client to maintain or exaggerate his symptoms, with the emphasis on subjective change. By practicing the symptom under instruction and with a different feeling, the client achieves voluntary control of the symptom resulting in its remission. Rosen discussed the same techniques in his work with schizophrenics. He termed it *reductio ad absurdum* or *re-enacting the psychosis* (6).

Watzlawick et al. define having the client display symptomatic behavior as applying a *be spontaneous* paradox (7). Jay Haley and Milton Erickson often use *scheduling of symptoms by the therapist* to make it impossible for the client to use his/her symptoms as a way of controlling the treatment (8–10). The client can defeat the treatment only by giving up the symptom, but, in doing so, he has helped make the treatment a success. Farrelly and Brandsma frequently encourage clients to practice their symptoms in an exaggerated fashion (11). This serves to point out the client's irrational beliefs about him/herself. Frankl describes what he terms *paradoxical intentions* in the treatment of phobic and obsessive conditions (12, 13).

REVIEW OF THE LITERATURE: THE METHODOLOGY

The following is an example of how paradoxical intention works:

A symptom evokes a fearful expectation in the client that the symptom might recur. Fear tends to make true precisely what one fears. Therefore, the anticipatory anxiety is liable to trigger the symptom of which the client is afraid. A self-sustaining circle begins. The purpose of paradoxical intention is to intervene in this vicious circle of fears. The client is encouraged to do or wish to happen the very thing he/she fears. This helps the client to stop fleeing from his/her fears. The pathogenic fear is replaced by a paradoxical wish and the vicious circle of anticipatory anxiety is broken (13).

Gerz reported a 75 percent recovery rate using paradoxical intention with his phobic patients and a 66 percent recovery rate with his obsessive and psychoneurotic schizophrenic patients (14). However, it should be noted that along with paradoxical intention Gerz used prescription of symptoms, chemotherapy, and a variety of verbal therapeutic interventions. Solyom et al. conducted a pilot study using paradoxical intention in treatment of obsessive thoughts. In this study there was a 50 percent decrease in the obsessive thoughts (15).

The paradoxical procedures of reframing, emphasizing the positive, resistance, and double bind are employed with hypnosis (8, 9, 16). Erickson and Rossi also discuss a number of double binds used in hypnosis and psychotherapy, such as offering the client a free choice among alternatives, one of which *must* be chosen; for example, asking the client if he would like to go into a trance *now* or *later* (10).

The use of paradoxical methods in dealing with children is discussed by Haley (9). He gives the clinical example of a 5-year-old boy who had never been toilet trained and soiled his pants several times a day. The parents were a young, middle class couple who were overly concerned about doing the right thing with their child. The family was treated by restraining the family from improving. The therapist adopted the posture of being benevolently concerned about what would happen in the family if the child became "normal." The family became highly motivated to solve their problem and prove that they could be "normal." Within 4 weeks the child was completely toilet trained. According to Haley this approach of restraining the family from changing is most effective with sensitive, over-concerned, middle class families. Haley attributes this to the fact that the family must be keenly sensitive to the therapist's opinion of them in order for this approach to work.

Jessee and L'Abate also discuss the use of paradoxical intervention with children (17). They feel this method is advantageous with children on an inpatient unit because it: (1) induces quick problem resolution, (2) requires limited verbal ability and insight, (3) allows the child to assume responsibility for change, which increases his/her self-esteem and ability to control his/her behavior, and (4) focuses on the problem rather than the diagnosis, which, in turn, decreases the child's feelings of being *sick*.

Soper and L'Abate point out that straightforward interpretations by the therapist are frequently expected and therefore easily ignored; whereas a paradoxical communication, which presents the familiar in an unexpected light, has a greater chance of being heard and evoking change (18).

Greenberg discusses the use of the paradoxical technique of *anti-expectation* in dealing with resistant clients (19). Greenberg breaks into the closed system of resistant clients by aligning himself with their negative comments and greatly amplifying the views that they feel certain any therapist would oppose. This makes it extremely difficult for the client to be resistant since there is no one to resist. Unable to use old defenses and confronted by the humor of the unexpected, the client is forced to look at his/her behavior from a different perspective.

Of the aforementioned works, the best known paradoxical methods are those associated with the work of Jay Haley (8, 9) and Milton Erickson (10). They use a directive therapy approach that focuses on accepting the client's view of him/herself, understanding the communicative value of the symptom, and overtly or subtly rechanneling the patient's life so that the symptom becomes unnecessary or more constructively useful.

CLINICAL EXAMPLE OF PARADOX IN FAMILY THERAPY

The author's experience is that paradoxical methods are useful in family therapy, especially in working with resistant clients. The following case summary is an example of how paradox can be used in family therapy:

A middle-class family with parents in their early forties and four teen-age children was referred by a private physician to two cotherapists. The family was referred for family therapy because of multiple somatic complaints, tension, and stress. Initially, the family was very resistant to family therapy maintaining that they were very close and did not have any family problems. Using paradoxical techniques, one of the therapists stated, "That's great. It will be nice to work with a normal family and not have to deal with problems. We don't want you to talk about problems. By working with you, we can learn a lot about how a normal family communicates. And, being a close family, I'm sure you're interested in ways to improve your communication. This is an ideal opportunity for us to do family enrichment instead of family therapy." This paradox served to break through the family's initial resistance. Now, in order to continue resisting, they would be impelled to discuss problems and, conversely, would be cooperating if they resisted. If, however, they chose not to resist, they would be learning about their communication patterns, therefore helping to make the family therapy a success. By labeling them a normal family, resistance was also reduced. The family was in the position of being unable to resist family therapy because it was termed *family enrichment* with the implication that all close families wanted family enrichment. The family responded by stating that they were always interested in improving their family communication and would be interested in family enrichment. They further responded to the paradox by stating that they certainly had their problems just like any other family. The family, therefore, did discuss various problems throughout the sessions.

Although the family had agreed that they had problems and were interested in family enrichment, a great deal of resistance was encountered, especially from the father. During one session when the father was being particularly resistant to the therapists' suggestions, the following paradox was used: After he told one therapist all of the reasons one of the suggestions would not work, the therapist responded, "It's all right for you to say no to our suggestions; maybe in time you'll open up to them." Giving him permission to resist served to reduce his resistance.

Due to the father's strong resistances, prescribing the symptom was a very useful technique. During the fourth session, the father was talking about how there was no way to reduce his stress since everyone in the family brought their problems to him. He repeatedly stated that the therapists' suggestions regarding stress reduction simply would not work. The therapists stated that in order to have a clear picture of the stress he was experiencing, he should delve into it more deeply. For the next week everyone in the family was instructed to bring *all* their problems to the father to solve. He immediately responded that the family always did that. The therapists emphasized that, although a lot of problems were brought to him in the past, now *all* of the family's problems should be brought to him. The teen-agers enthusiastically agreed to follow the instructions, but the mother indicated that she did not feel that her husband could tolerate any more stress. The husband immediately started figuring out ways to avoid handling everyone's problems. The next week, when asked how things had gone, the father stated, "Real good. I just took it easy." When asked if other family members brought him their problems, he stated, "I let them take care of their own problems." This exercise helped him to understand that he could indeed control the stress in his life.

The use of paradoxical methods was very helpful in reducing this family's resistance. The family responded well to the *confused therapist approach* (20). Since the father wanted to remain in control, he was allowed to do so and was asked to help the therapist understand the family.

RECOMMENDATIONS REGARDING USE OF PARADOXICAL METHODS

Watzlawick et al. indicate that an essential ingredient of a paradoxical injunction is an intense relationship involving a high degree of physical and/or psychological dependence (7). In light of this, it is recommended by some that the therapist set up binding conditions before the paradoxical prescription. For example, the therapist would have the client promise in advance that he will follow the therapist's recommendations. However, Viaro states that an explicit contract is not necessary (21). Viaro does stress the importance of not criticizing the family and of using a systems approach with the family. Greenberg points out that in using antiexpectation techniques the therapist must be able to deliver the antiexpectation message without sarcasm and initially refrain from responding to the humorous or absurd aspects of the interactions (19).

Drawn from Haley's work (9), some guidelines for the effective use of paradoxical methods are:

1. The therapist should not oppose or confront the family with what they are doing wrong but should accept their behavior and facilitate change within that framework.
2. The therapist should not make interpretations to help the family understand their behavior.
3. The therapist should focus on the present.
4. The therapy should be brief and intensive intervention with rapid disengagement.

Papp recommends that the decision to use or not use paradox be based on the family's degree of resistance to change (2). According to him, paradoxical intervention should be reserved for long-standing, repetitious behavior patterns that do not respond to direct interventions. Papp does not recommend paradoxical intervention in crises such as acute grief, attended suicide, or other situations in which the therapist needs to quickly provide structure and control. Jessee and L'Abate also recommend that paradoxical intervention not be used in an intense crisis with children (17). They further recommend that paradoxical intention not be used with people who are mentally disorganized or mentally retarded.

Papp further emphasizes avoidance of two common errors made by beginning therapists who use paradoxical intervention (2). The most common mistake is prescribing the symptom without helping the client understand the symptom. The technique of redefining the symptom in positive terms is essential. The second error is to unconvincingly deliver a paradoxical message. The beginning therapist is often self-conscious and delivers the message in a way that makes the family feel he/she is being facetious. In order to be effective, the message must be delivered in a sincere manner.

SUMMARY

Paradoxical interventions that consist of seemingly self-contradictory and, sometimes, even absurd therapeutic methods are frequently very effective in family therapy. As several authors have pointed out, the novelty of paradoxical interventions appears to be part of the key to success. Another reason that this method of therapy works is because most clients are resistant to change, and paradoxical interventions do not fight the resistance. The client is invited to resist, and the resistance is used to evoke change.

Paradoxical interventions are not recommended in intense crises in which the therapist needs to take immediate control.

REFERENCES

1. Hare-Mustin, R. T. Paradoxical tasks in family therapy: Who can resist? *Psychotherapy: Theory, research and practice,* 1976, *2,* 128–130.

2. Papp, P. The greek chorus and other techniques of paradoxical therapy. *Family Process,* 1980, *19*(1), 45–57.

3. Sander, F. M. Freud's "A case of successful treatment by hypnotism (1892–1893)": An uncommon therapy? *Family Process,* 1974, *13,* 461–468.

4. Dunlap, K. A revision of the fundamental law of habit formation. *Science,* 1928, *57,* 360–362.

5. Dunlap, K. Repetition in breaking of habits. *Science Monthly,* 1930, *30,* 66–70.

6. Rosen, J. N. *Direct analysis.* New York: Grune & Stratton, 1953.

7. Watzlawick, P., Beavin, J. H., & Jackson, D. D. *Pragmatics of human communication.* New York: W. W. Norton, 1967.

8. Haley, J. *Strategies of psychotherapy.* New York: Grune & Stratton, 1963.

9. Haley, J. *Uncommon therapy.* New York: Ballantine Books, 1973.

10. Erickson, M. H., & Rossi, E. L. Varieties of double bind. *American Journal of Clinical Hypnosis,* 1975, *17,* 143–157.

11. Farrelly, F., & Brandsma, J. *Provocative therapy.* Fort Collins, Colo.: Shields, 1974.

12. Frankl, V. E. *Psychotherapy and existentialism: Selected papers on logotherapy.* New York: Washington Square Press, 1967.

13. Frankl, V. E. Paradoxical intention and deflection. *Psychotherapy: Theory, research and practice,* 1975, *12,* 226–37.

14. Gerz, H. O. Experience with the logotherapeutic technique of paradoxical intention in the treatment of phobic and obsessive compulsive patients. *American Journal of Psychiatry,* 1966, *123,* 548–553.

15. Solyom, L., Garza-Perez, J., Ledwidge, B. L., & Solyoim, C. Paradoxical intention in the treatment of obsessive thoughts: A pilot study. *Comprehensive Psychiatry,* 1972, *13,* 291–297.

16. Andolfi, M. Paradox in psychotherapy. *American Journal of Psychoanalysis,* 1974, *34,* 221–228.

17. Jessee, E., & L'Abate, L. The use of paradox with children in an inpatient treatment setting. *Family Process,* 1980, *19*(1), 59–64.

18. Soper, P. H., L'Abate, L. Paradox as a therapeutic technique: A review. *International Journal of Family Therapy,* 1977, *5,* 10–21.

19. Greenberg, R. P. Anti-expectation techniques in psychotherapy: The power of negative thinking. *Psychotherapy: Theory, research and practice,* 1973, *10,* 145–148.

20. Weakland, J. H., Fisch, R., Watzlawick, P., & Boddin, A. M. Brief therapy: Focused problem resolution. *Family Process,* 1974, *13,* 141–168.

21. Viaro, M. Case report: Smuggling family therapy through. *Family Process,* 1980, *191,* 35–44.

36

Use of Structural Strategy in Systems Approach to Family Therapy

George A. Lee

Salvador Minuchin is the leading proponent of structural family therapy. The purpose of this chapter is to translate Minuchin's theory into nursing process strategy and operation, incorporating clinical practice and family systems theory. Examples are drawn from an actual family in therapy. The nursing process sequence of assessment, planning, intervention, and evaluation will follow (1).

THEORY AND METHOD

Minuchin distinguishes between (1) family models and types of operation, a *theoretical* orientation, and (2) goals and strategies, a *pragmatic* orientation to specific families. His models and operational types are part of his family systems theory (2). Individuals within families within social context are in flux in relationship to their interdependencies. This change process has aspects of normalcy and pathology. When the pathology outweighs the normalcy, symptomatic signals may lead family members to seek the help of a family nurse therapist. A variation of this helping process is to have another nurse therapist assisting.

As background for this chapter, cotherapists, male and female mental health nurses, conducted family therapy for 8 weeks with the Craigs. The Craigs were referred for counseling by a crisis intervention center as the result of alleged child molestation and wife abuse. Reluctantly, the husband agreed to participate in family therapy sessions with his wife. The young children of the family, aged 2 and 6 years, were also present, playing in the living room where family therapy sessions were conducted. Corresponding to family system theory, the children were present with their parents in order to observe the interaction of the whole family.

PRELUDE TO THERAPY: JOINING AND ACCOMMODATION

Minuchin feels that to be therapeutic, a therapist must first *join* the family system (2). This means that the family nurse therapist needs to act and react as a member of the family system. The therapist should resonate to "currents" flowing through family members. Such currents include personality interactions, the effect of ethnic identification, family life-style and tempo of conversation. The family therapist, like a social anthropologist, is a participant-observer (3, 4). As participant-observer, the therapist *joins* the dramatic set of the family production.

By a series of small *accommodations* the therapist lets himself experience some of the "pulls and tugs" of the family he is attempting to aid. These accommodations include feeling the pain of being caught in family quarrels, feeling the pride of new home ownership, or struggling with the family as they try to decide whether the husband should take a new job. Joining and accommodation operations pave the way for nursing intervention, letting the family know that the therapist understands and appreciates their life together. The dialogue with the Craig family in the second interview proceeded as follows.

> WIFE: Last weekend we spent a whole day camping out, playing softball, and riding our bikes. Only he plays too rough and hard. You'd think he hadn't spent the whole week working.
>
> HUSBAND: My gosh, Linda, you have to make up for all week. It was the first weekend we had together in a while.

The husband's physical, boisterous quality is already indicated. The therapist let this early indication pass by in an attempt to join and accommodate.

MALE COTHERAPIST: You both really know how to enjoy yourselves. It's really great that you have so much fun when you have time off together.

In session number four with the Craigs, the mood was different.

WIFE: You can't tell him anything. He just *sits there*. I don't really expect him to do much work around the house. But I'd like just once if he'd ask if I wanted help.
(Silence)

In an attempt to join the husband in a coalition the therapist responded as follows.

MALE COTHERAPIST: Ted, I feel pretty uncomfortable right now, kind of frustrated. I sense this is the way you may be feeling just now.

ACTUALIZING FAMILY TRANSACTION PATTERNS

If the nurse therapist has done a good job in the process of joining and accommodating, the stage is set for therapeutic restructuring efforts. Assuming the nurse therapist is accepted and is beginning to blend into the family, *assessment,* the first step in the nursing process, can take place with minimum bias. The therapist observes the family in action and transaction as conversation and nonverbal behavior occur in the fourth session (2). Observations are made, for example, that the children climb all over the mother, rather than the father, and ask her to identify pictures in a book. The therapists also observe, since the couple is no longer on their "best" behavior, that the wife looks up and shouts at the husband. The husband in turn looks down and mutters a derogatory remark, barely audible.

The second step, *planning,* follows from assessment. Planning for family intervention is only as valid as the observation of the patterns. In the example above, the mother is in subsystem alliance with the children and needs to be weaned away from this tight bond. The husband–wife team have one-way, incomplete communication. The plan in this case is to bait the conversation to establish the one-way communication, then, quickly point this out to the family.

The third step is crucial for Minuchin and the nursing process. *Intervention* by the therapists can underline, through the process of enactment, the true course of family patterns. This type of intervention is subtle, in that the nurse therapist can direct it merely as an extension of what is already going on. Having observed that the children gravitate to their mother, the nurse therapist plans and clarifies this pattern by asking the children to "See what your parents say about staying up this late." He expects the children to look to their mother for the answer. When they do this and the matter has been decided, the nurse-therapist and the family have another evidence of this family pattern.

With regard to the one-way, incomplete communication between the husband and wife, this intervention was tried.

FEMALE COTHERAPIST: Linda, you've been telling us about the schedule of housework you have after you get home from work. Some couples share some of this. Could you talk to Ted about this now?

WIFE: (Taken aback) Ain't no use talking to him. (Looking at her husband and shouting) Isn't that right, Ted? You never want to do nothing around here!

HUSBAND: (Softly, fighting for control) I don't know what you're talking about. You never ask me.

WIFE: (Again loudly) And you never want to! Isn't that right Ted. Come on now, admit it!

HUSBAND: (Tightly) No, I won't.

The fourth step, *evaluation,* for Minuchin and family therapists is sometimes problematic. The process of therapy does not end with evaluation. Problems are like a skin disorder that becomes invisible for a month, only to flare up again. Positive evaluation suggests that the intervention succeeded. In the above cases, intervention was successful. But the goal was a modest one, appropriate for the first few occasions when the therapist gets acquainted with the family. Data must continue to be gathered. Family patterns are seen, plans are made, and interventions made by staging the family drama. The therapist is looking for a specific confirmation, and having obtained it, he shares his finding with the family. The wife was told she "sets up" an argument by anticipating her husband's response before he gives it to her. In this way, the family and the therapist share in the nursing process.

MARKING BOUNDARIES

Each family, according to Minuchin (2), has its own unique map, but there are enough similarities among families to develop patterns and rules. The patterns and rules are not so rigid as to prohibit change from taking place. At least this is the operating premise of the nurse therapist; families that are relatively unable to change receive far less benefit from family therapy.

Part of the mapping of a family involves the *assessment* of boundaries around each person and subsystem of the family. The boundary establishes the relative individuality or autonomy of family members or subsystems. Families in which the members are close to each other have permeable boundary systems. Those families having members who operate independently of each other can be referred to as disengaged (2).

The family studied, the Craigs, is (nearer) the disengaged end of the spectrum. Both husband and wife work in administrative positions in retail sales. Linda and Ted are also partaking liberally in the materialistic benefits involved with working wives (7). Both have expectations of moving up a career ladder in their present line of work.

At work and at home, Ted is a "prizewinner" type, feels that he deserves to win, and has little self-doubt or guilt. If things go wrong, he blames others. Linda has only partly embraced the world of work. Not long ago she only worked part-time. At home she plays the victim role. The victim has low self-esteem. She anticipates trouble, stores resentment, walks a tightrope, and is easily thrown off balance (6).

Linda is particularly proud of the bonuses she has received for her excellent sales record. Ted has been told several times that he is on the list to be promoted from assistant store manager to store manager. Ted is ambivalent, however, about the responsibilities of managing a store and having to go back to school to take further training. The children further separate and disengage this couple. The two children living in the home are not Ted's. Ted has two children, and they are in the custody of his exwife. The activity that does pull Ted and Linda together at least 1 day a week is their leisure time pursuits, such as motorcycle riding and boating.

The *planning* step here is to open the boundary separating the husband and wife. Ted needs to express his affection more openly. The mother is very close to the children, as noted above, and ideally should reduce the permeability of the boundary between herself and her offspring. A rearrangement of family space and positioning during the therapeutic sessions was deemed desirable.

Intervention proceeded as follows. In the sixth session the female cotherapist preempted Ted's favorite seat. Usually the female cotherapist sat with Linda on the couch. The male therapist took another chair. This left the couch open for Ted. Ted did sit on the couch with some encouragement from the therapist but stayed at the far opposite end from his wife. The male cotherapist played with Bud, the 2-year-old son, while the female cotherapist played with Robin, the daughter.

Evaluation of this modest intervention can be seen partly in terms of nonverbal behavior observed. Ted at first was with his wife seated on the couch and nothing more. He looked nervous and disconcerted. He spoke little, did not watch his wife as she spoke, and alternately watched the children playing with the therapists and a television screen, which was on without sound. Later, however, he became much more involved with his wife nonverbally. She was dealing with the problem of her anger with the co-therapists. As she spoke this time, late in session six, Ted extended his hand to her on the top of the couch and held it, occasionally giving her little squeezes while she was listening and talking.

ESCALATING STRESS

Escalating stress is one of the most radical strategies in Minuchin's re-structuring repertoire. Stress is not in itself dysfunctional in the family sys-tem. Stress in fact can be used to demonstrate differences or to challenge a family system that is not functioning properly. The therapist may ally him-self with one member of the family to precipitate a crisis during the family session (2).

In *assessing* the Craig family it was discovered that the wife talked about the troubles the family was having to a number of relatives and friends. She did not admit this openly, however. Since these troubles in-cluded accusations of child molestation and wife beating, the nurse thera-pists knew this was a very sensitive area for the Craig family. The husband briefly expressed that he did not think her talking to others was a good idea. But the wife did not really pick up on this. She was silent and sulked. There was a disparity of modes that the family was neglecting. Tension or stress was present but was not being completely expressed.

The *planning* step had to include both spouses. The wife had to be free enough to express her self further. But the husband was usually the one who was put down. He is the "identified patient" who is accused of bring-ing trouble to the family. So he needed support to take this issue back to the wife and make a stand.

The *intervention* was for the male therapist to escalate the tension of this problem area by continuing the spouse dialogue with the female co-therapist in psychodrama mode.

MALE COTHERAPIST: Ann, I think I agree with Ted; I wouldn't want my wife talkin' about our marital problems to just anybody. What do you think?

FEMALE COTHERAPIST: Well, different people do have different ideas on this. Usually women confide more in people than men do. I sometimes feel I need someone I can talk to and share things with.

MALE COTHERAPIST: The thing that upsets me so much about this is that she talks about such *personal* things in our family to others and I have no control over this.

HUSBAND: That's her! She just runs off her mouth to every-one.

WIFE: (Quickly and with anger) I *do not.*

HUSBAND: (With considerable force and anger) You lie! (Silence)

MALE COTHERAPIST: I'm having a little trouble deciding who is right here. (Turning to wife) You mentioned having to pick up your husband's clothes a bit ago. Do you ever talk to anyone about that?

HUSBAND: (Laughing in a gloating fashion) Oh, yeah!

WIFE: (With anger and hurt) I did not!

HUSBAND: Every time we're down at my Mom's I hear you talking to her, "I just have to pick up everything of his. He doesn't do anything to help me." I've heard you say this to her.

WIFE: I never have. I think you're exaggerating.

HUSBAND: (Softly) I don't think so. (Silence)

FEMALE COTHERAPIST: Linda, I have the feeling that you have something else you want to say.

WIFE: (Extremely upset) I . . . I can't say nothing, or . . . or I get in trouble. I can't talk to anyone or I get into trouble.

HUSBAND: (With anger) What do you mean by that?

WIFE: (Still very upset) Just what I said.

HUSBAND: You're spoiling for a fight woman. (Wife cries and leaves the room)

When the wife returned, an *evaluation* of what had happened took place. The husband and wife acknowledged that stress had built up between them because the wife was unwilling (and afraid) to share with the husband problem areas in their marriage. The husband also admitted that he does not discuss these with his wife because he does not like to get put down and is afraid he will get mad and start hitting her. It was also pointed out to the wife that she uses denial, and she anticipates trouble and her husband's negative attitude without communicating directly with him. The mood was turned around, and the family was more receptive to suggestions after the disagreement was dramatized.

ASSIGNING TASKS

In the last two family sessions with the Craigs, the nurse cotherapists determined that unfinished business included (*1*) confronting the family with the anger and physical violence that led to the charges of child molestation and wife beating and (2) understanding better how the children fit into the family. Minuchin defines tasks as the actualization of a problem area. In assigning tasks, the therapist becomes a rule setter. The family is not graded on how well it performs. It does provide another opportunity to see the family at work in its own system (2).

In *assessing* the physical violence charges, data were used from the backgrounds of the spouses and from direct questioning. A time was chosen during the seventh session when the children were not present. By that time a good rapport had built up between the nurse therapists and the family. The husband was reminded by the female therapist that she understood that legal charges had been made against him for child molestation and wife beating.

FEMALE COTHERAPIST: Ted, I'm just going to ask you straight out, did you ever hit your wife?

HUSBAND: (hesitantly) Yes . . . I did. I'm not proud of it. It happened quite awhile ago and I don't want it to happen again.

MALE COTHERAPIST: Ted, when you get angry, do you ever do something before things get out of hand?

HUSBAND: Yes, I leave the house.

WIFE: And he doesn't come back all night. I don't know where he is sometimes.

HUSBAND: You know I'm at my Mom's.

WIFE: Well, I couldn't do anything like that. Do you think that's right to stay away at night? That isn't working on the marriage.
(Husband is silent.)

This remark by the wife was picked up later in the assigned task intervention.

A little later in the session the wife is asked about the charges of sexual molestation.

WIFE: Well, Robin has this, I don't know how to put it, redness around her . . . well, you know . . . privates, and I have to use special soap and all. I know my husband didn't do it, that's ridiculous. But I wouldn't put it past her real daddy. He sleeps in the same bed with her on weekends.

FEMALE COTHERAPIST: I'm not sure I understand. Who made the charges?

WIFE: My exhusband, her real daddy. But I think his mother put him up to it.

HUSBAND: Yeah, that's right.

It seemed to the cotherapist that there was denial going on, but the matter was deferred for later exploration.

To get a more complete picture of the violence, the spouses were asked about their parental home life. Both husband and wife come from homes where beatings were common between husband and wife and of children. Ted admitted his brothers were wild, even wilder than he. Linda pictured herself as a tomboy who fought physically any time she wanted to.

Insight was gathered about the children from play therapy. Robin, the girl, played house with Barbie and Ken dolls. She said that they were the Mommie and Daddy and had no children. They went motorcycling and played softball on weekends. When they grew up, they would have children. Picking up a book, she pointed to insects and fierce animals as men, fathers, and the male cotherapist. She says they were "scary and mean." But, the 2 year old, seems to be taking the "bad man" role on by bedeviling his sister with a frightening picture of the "Kiss" rock group. On occasion Bud pushes and shoves his sister around. Ted disciplined Bud, once hitting him briefly and sending him to his room. Robin did not need discipline during the therapy sessions. Ted admits that he leaves the disciplining of her to his wife.

The cotherapists *planned* to assign homework tasks to the family. These were to be done between sessions seven and eight. Homework tasks allow therapy to continue beyond the time of the scheduled sessions. The nurse cotherapists then check the following session on how the family performed the tasks.

The *intervention* with regard to the children was to have the father spend at least 15 minutes each day he was home playing with Robin in a game of her choice. The wife could be present, but she was not to participate. If possible, the wife was to keep Bud otherwise occupied during this 15-minute time period. The other assigned task was for the spouses to discuss the anger that Linda, the wife, felt at Ted for spending a whole day visiting with his children in Clarksville. The couple was instructed not to spend more than 20 minutes on just one occasion talking about this. If it seemed that an argument might ensue, the couple could stop for a minute or so, but neither should leave the room or the house.

Evaluating the assigned tasks, it was found that Ted managed to spend four 15-minute periods with Robin. He read a book to her in two of the sessions, watched a television program once, and helped her play with dolls on the fourth time. Ted stated he really enjoyed this time and felt a little guilty about not spending more time with her.

The couple was less successful with their other homework assignment. They both laughed and said they didn't see much of each other during the past week. When asked for other reasons, they suggested that maybe they were getting along better. The cotherapists pointed out that it is sometimes very difficult to face a sensitive issue. The nurse therapists stated again that better communication was needed to avert continuing anger, Ted's leaving the house, and physical violence. Linda was asked whether she was sometimes afraid of Ted. She admitted that she was on occasion. Linda and Ted were both reminded by the therapists about their resolve to keep the marriage together and to solve difficulties by better communication rather than leaving the house or physical violence.

SUMMARY

This chapter has demonstrated how Minuchin's restructuring techniques can be used in the nursing process. The Craig family was exposed to a comparatively brief therapeutic process. During this time the nurse therapists dealt with anger, one-way, incomplete communication, and disengagement as family characteristics. Although the therapy is by no means complete, the Craigs have seen a number of their difficulties dramatized and a few correctives suggested. The prognosis for this family is not a good one, especially without further family therapy.

REFERENCES

1. Marriner, A. *The nursing process: A scientific approach to nursing care* (2nd Ed.). St. Louis: C. V. Mosby, 1979.
2. Minuchin, S. *Families and family therapy.* Cambridge, Mass.: Harvard University Press, 1974.
3. Bruyn, S. *The human perspective in sociology: The methodology of participant observation.* Englewood Cliffs, N.J.: Prentice-Hall, 1966.
4. Humphreys, L. *Tearoom trade: Impersonal sex in public places.* Chicago: Aldine, 1970.
5. Bird, C. *The two paycheck marriage.* New York: Rawson, Wade Publishers, 1979.
6. Goldstine, D. et al. *The Dance-away lover and other roles we play in love, sex and marriage.* New York: Ballantine, 1977.
7. Hopkins, J., & White, P. The dual-career couple: Constraints and supports. *The Family Coordinator,* July 1978, 253–259.

37

Operational Mourning: An Intervention Strategy for Dysfunctional Families

Marion Fitzsimmons Briel

Mauksch and David (1) state "the nursing process enables a nurse to realize her potential as an independent decision-maker, who has command over competencies, which heretofore were not used in carrying out predominantly assistance-type functions." In the area of family therapy, this is particularly true. The nurse therapist uses the nursing process to enhance the family's communication and functioning. She uses her observation and evaluation skills and plans intervention strategies in a manner similar to other nurse practitioners. However, the problems that the nurse therapist deals with in family therapy are often less tangible than those dealt with by nurse specialists in other areas. The clinical specialist in the coronary care unit has sophisticated equipment to aid her in assessing the status of her patient. The nurse midwife has clear-cut protocols to aid her in planning the care for her patient. The nurse therapist in family therapy has less developed assessment tools and no clear cut protocols for planning intervention. The therapist must assess the dynamics of the family as a group, the process of emotional integration of the individual into his family roles and the basic reciprocity of role relationships, and the internal organization of individual personality and its historic development (2). However, therapists such as Smoyak (3) and Barnhill (4) decry the lack of systemization of assessment parameters, clearly identified goals, and effective implementation strategies. Although the general concepts of the theorists are easily available, the specifics of intervention are not. Often the beginning therapist is able to present an adequate assessment of the family dynamics but is unable to develop a specific plan of action for intervention. This chapter will present a specific intervention strategy developed by Norman Paul and the rationale for its use in family therapy.

OPERATIONAL MOURNING

While working with schizophrenic patients in the late 1950s and early 1960s, Paul and Grosser (5) observed some similarities among the families of the schizophrenic patients. Among these similarities was a set of family relationships that were highly resistant to change. This was particularly evident in the family members' attitude toward the patient. Any new behaviors exhibited by the patient were met with resistance from other family members. Paul and Grosser (5) describe this as a "fixed family equilibrium, a relatively unchanging dynamic state to which there is a tendency to return when disturbed." Similar patterns of inflexible interactions within families and resistance to changes in the family system have been described by Jackson (6) as pathologic homeostasis, by Ferreira (7) as family myth, by Minuchen (8) as enmeshment, and by Bowen (9) as undifferentiated ego mass and family projection process.

Each of the above theorists gives a clear conceptual presentation of the state of the family. None of them gives as specific an etiology as does Paul. Paul (5, 10) states that the fixed roles and resistance to change is a result of the family members' inability to cope with loss. Minuchin (8) and Bowen (9) also state that increased individuation and differentiation by family members is a threat to the family homeostasis. However, they do not clearly state why family members are threatened. Paul suggests that losses within the family have been negated or warded off by refusal of family members to deal adequately with loss on an affective level. This pattern of denial of losses or disappointments often existed for generations in families. The observed pattern was most severe in families of schizophrenic patients. Based on the clinical observation of his schizophrenic patients and their families and Bowlby's (10) work with separation anxiety, Paul and Grosser (5) hypothesized that there is a direct relationship between the maladaptive response to object loss and the fixity in symbiotic relationships in the family. The authors developed a treatment technique that would help the family members mobilize the repressed affects of their earlier losses. They named this technique operational mourning.

Paul and Grosser (5) postulated that the family members' denial of loss in the past had resulted in "abortive mourning." Like Lindemann (11), Paul and Grosser believe that there is a certain amount of grief work necessary to cope with losses adaptively. However, unlike Lindemann (11), Paul and Grosser deal with the grief work within the family, not on an individual basis. Parents, grandparents, siblings, and other family members are seen together during the operational mourning procedure.

The goal of operational mourning is to aid the expression of the affective elements of mourning. According to Paul and Grosser (5) the therapist uses direct inquiry about the reactions to actual losses sustained by specific family members. In his clinical data, it appears that Paul often focuses on the losses of the parent of the identified patient. Often he will discover that a parent or grandparent has not resolved the loss of their own parents. As a result of this, displaced hostility from the original lost object to other family members, usually the identified patient can be brought to the awareness of all family members and dealt with in subsequent meetings.

The direct inquiries go beyond mere recounting of the cause of the loved one's death. Paul encourages the client to recall specific details. This seems to help the client go beyond the fixed cognitive images they have developed and kept over the years as a defense against the emotions associated with the loss. When forced by direct inquiry and prodding from the therapist to review the circumstances and events surrounding the loss, clients who had not talked about the incident for over 50 years, shared minute details as if the event had happened yesterday. Having bypassed the client's defense mechanisms and gotten him to share this material, Paul then focuses on the client's feelings. He will use questions such as "How do you feel as you recall this experience now?" If a client begins to share thoughts, Paul keeps the focus on the affective, for example, "But I want to know how you feel now," or he will help the client clarify his feelings, for example, "In a certain sense, you must have felt like your life ended," or "Do you feel a sense of sadness inside?"

Although these questions focus on the individual, Paul is very aware of the presence of the other family members. He believes that the observation of the expression of such intense and real feelings by one family member provides a powerful empathic experience for the other family members. He describes it as a sense of "affective continuity"; secrets that the family members were aware of but had covertly learned were "taboo" to talk about are finally brought into the open. For many families, it is the first time they can openly share affective experiences with each other. Paul encourages the observing family members to give the bereaved member feedback. For example, when one usually staid father asked, "What effect does it have by talking about it?" Paul encourages him to ask the other family members. Again, he helps the other family members to focus on their affective experience during the expression of such deep feelings by another family member. Throughout the sharing of feelings, Paul reassures the family members of the normalcy of such emotions.

The overt expression of such deep rooted feelings is contrary to the rigid rules and inflexible roles dictated by the fixed family equilibrium. The deviance from past behavior made possible by operational mourning is an interruption of the pathologic dynamics of the family. Paul has found that such new behavior exhibited by family members will cause strain within the family system. Like the person who undergoes temporary personal disorganization during Bowlby's (20) second phase of mourning, so too, does the family undergo a temporary period of increased tension and disorganization. Lindemann (11) has shown in his work that during this period of crisis, the individual is more open to alternative behaviors. Thus, the therapist can use the next few sessions to teach and encourage new behaviors and interactions among the family's members.

Not so surprisingly, Paul and Grosser (5) found that the families with the most severe schizophrenic patients were the most resistant to operational mourning. However, being a creative therapist, Paul further developed his technique to overcome such strong resistance. In an article entitled, "Cross Confrontation," Paul (10) discusses his use of videotapes to help resistant clients get in touch with their own feelings. He will show a videotape in which a family member is relating the loss of his parent and the feelings he experienced as a result of that loss. Paul will then stop the videotape and capitalize on the viewer's empathic experience. He will ask, "What are you feeling when you hear him talking about his father?" The client, who is capable of such an empathic experience, will usually respond with a comment like, "I was thinking about the death of my own father/mother." Paul then pursues this opening, as above, encouraging the recollection of the client's loss and emphasizing the experiential elements of the grief process.

In summary, operational mourning as presented by Paul and Grosser (5) and Paul (10) is a specific intervention strategy designed to encourage identification and expression of repressed feelings regarding loss. By bringing these feelings to the conscious level of the person and to the awareness of other family members, perceived threats of loss can be identified and displacement and projections can be dealt with.

RATIONALE FOR THERAPY

Paul and Grosser (5) discovered that losses were usually suffered by one or the other parent often before the birth of a schizophrenic patient (p. 341). Walsh (12) found that the death of a grandparent two years before or after the birth of a child occurred in 41 percent of families with a schizophrenic child as opposed to 20 percent of cases of nonschizophrenic psychiatric disorders and only 8 percent of the families in the control group. Parents of the schizophrenic children revealed unresolved mourning and a confusion and denial as to the simultaneity of the death/birth events.

As an explanation for these findings, Walsh (12) postulates that the parent was emotionally unavailable to the other spouse and child because of his/her own bereavement or that attention to the child may block mourning and absorb painful feelings, with the child assuming a special replacement role. Bowen's (9) construct of family projection process and Boszormenyi-Nagy's (13) (1973) identification of intergenerational loyalties deals with the conceptual aspects of these phenomena. Paul's operational mourning provides a specific technique for intervention.

Although some therapists (Hayley, Bandler, and Grinder, to name a few) advocate dealing with the "here and now," the literature has ample support for dealing with parents' relationships with their own parents (9, 13). Bell (14) states that parents' relationships with their own parents continues to be important in adulthood, especially in reciprocal emotional support bonds and influence on parenting. The author points out that the birth of a child necessitates a shift in roles and relations in all three generations: child, parent, and grandparent.

Strayhorn (15) states that people who have experienced the loss of a parent have an intense fear of abandonment or loss of love. As a marital partner, these individuals may respond by depressed withdrawal or vicious retaliation to any perceived threat of loss. Defenses used to cope with the threat of loss interfere with the couple's communication. According to Strayhorn, a spouse will often use a painful communication channel to ward off the fear of being unloved and abandoned.

These recent findings of Walsh (12) and Strayhorn (15) give credence to the early work of Erikson and Sullivan. Sullivan (16) emphasized the influence of the mother's mental health in the development of the child's sensitivity to frightening experiences. He believed that the mother's anxiety could induce anxiety in the infant through the interpersonal process of empathy. Erikson (17) identifies the importance of the establishment of basic trust by the infant based on the mother–child interactions. Trust and confidence are generated in the infant by the good management of the mother who is able to establish a mutual communication that allows the baby to read the meaning of her behavior and to inform her through its behavior.

Although these earlier theorists solely emphasize the role of the mother, Paul's clinical data documents the importance of the father's feelings as well. Anthony's (1970) studies of parenthood and his (1974) work with children at psychiatric risk reveal that neither the temperament of the child nor the parental characteristics alone had an independent influence on the child's development, but the two sets of factors worked together interdependently. He points out that "Although children evincing an amodal pattern of intensity, adaptability, regularity and mood were more vulnerable, all of them developed behavior disorders because of the modifying influence of the parental reactions" (18).

Therefore, we may safely conclude that, as hard as a parent tries to avoid, repress, or deny his/her own reactions to losses in the past, those reactions greatly effect his/her behavior and the subsequent functioning of the family system. Clinical data suggest that the concurrent death of a grandparent is correlated with higher incidence of family dysfunction.

IMPLICATIONS FOR THERAPY

Tomm and Wright (19) describe four major functions of the family therapist: engagement, problems identification, change facilitation, and termination. Operational mourning involves all four of these functions. A trusting and working relationship must be established by the therapist before any family member can be approached about his feelings regarding loss. The therapist must use her keen assessment skills in identifying problems. In none of the families discussed by Paul was the problem an unresolved grief reaction. In Paul's work, as in the work of many other family therapists (Bowen, Minuchen, Nagy, etc.), the family came for treatment because of "problems" of the "identified patient." Reading some of Paul's clinical excerpts, we see that it is often the parent of the identified patient who has experienced loss in the past. Therefore, the nurse therapist must carefully assess all family interactions and not focus solely on the problems of the identified patient role.

The third function of the therapist described by Tomm and Wright (1979) is change facilitation. The authors describe this function as "the core of the therapeutic process. It includes interventions aimed at altering interpersonal patterns of interaction and individual family members' behavior, thinking and experience. Efforts toward change are directed at replacing problematic patterns with adaptive ones" (19). Indeed, this is also the core of operational mourning. The directed inquiries by the therapist forces family members to recognize and express important affective content that has been denied and/or repressed for years. The honest and open expression and observation of such deep communication is the beginning of a change in interpersonal communication patterns. Each family member participates in the experience of becoming aware of the impact of the self on the other. Paul (10) states that in tracing the unresolved fixation points in the development of each member and their subsequent effect on the development of the family, each member acquires a perspective of the relevance of past experiences to the present.

Finally, operational mourning also deals with the termination process. From the beginning of treatment, Paul helps the family deal with the anticipatory loss of the therapist. The therapist should prepare the family for this loss, and at the same time she/he should help them develop more mature and reciprocal relationships among themselves. The importance of the empathic response by the therapist to the needs of the clients regarding loss is a key point in Paul's writings. He builds on Edelson's work dealing with termination of intensive psychotherapy. "The patient's ability to master the pain of separation and loss of the therapist is related to the therapist's level of empathic responsiveness to his patient" (10).

Paul (10) describes two types of psychotherapeutic empathy that are major implications for therapy: empathy on an associative level and empathy on an affective level. Empathy on an associative level occurs when the therapist responds to the verbal thought content of the client. It appears he is describing a cognitive process. Empathy on an affective level occurs when a therapist responds affectively to the emotional overtones the client is expressing. According to Paul, it cannot be fabricated and includes an "affective regression on the part of the therapist to a timeless feeling state."

Paul believes the resistance by the therapists and the clients to this primitive, yet powerful, communication of feelings is very common in both individual and family therapy. "The process of treatment, whether individual psychotherapy, conjoint marital therapy, or family group therapy, is fundamentally one rooted in affective transactions that transcend linguistic usage" (10).

As psychiatric nurses, we have been trained well in empathy on an associative level. Our trained ears quickly identify and clarify "themes" and "deep structures." However, what we often lack is training in empathy on an affective level. Though as Paul instructs, this cannot be taught in our usually cognitive way. It, like operational mourning, comprises primarily experiential rather than linguistic elements.

SUMMARY

The purpose of this chapter was to present Paul's technique of operational mourning as an intervention strategy for nurse-therapists working with families. Rationale for its use was given based on developmental theories and research with families. The implications of operational mourning were discussed for the family members as well as the therapist. It is hoped that this presentation will enable us to see that losses experienced by people that have not been resolved can and usually do lead to "fixity" in relationships. Conversely, fixed and rigid relationships in a family may be the result of unresolved disappointments, frustrations, and losses of the family members. Operational mourning can aid exploration and expression of such unresolved losses and increase the affective communication and empathy in the family system.

REFERENCES

1. Mauksch, I. G., & David, M. L. Prescription for survival. In M. Browning (Ed.), *The nursing process in practice*. New York: The American Journal of Nursing, 1974, p. 3.

2. Ackerman, N. W. *Treating the troubled family*. New York: Basic Books, 1966, p. 61.

3. Smoyak, S. *The psychiatric nurse as a family therapist*. New York: John Wiley & Sons, 1975.

4. Barnhill, L. R. Healthy family systems. *The Family Coordinator*, 1979, *28*(1), 101–108.

5. Paul, N., & Grosser, G. Operational mourning and its role in conjoint family therapy. *Community Mental Health Journal*, 1965, *1*, 339–340.

6. Jackson, D. The question of family homeostasis. *Psychiatric Quarterly*, 1957, *31*(suppl), 79–90.

7. Ferreira, A. Family myth and homeostasis. *Archives of General Psychiatry*, 1963, *9*(5), 456–463.

8. Minuchin, S. *Families and family therapy*. Cambridge, Mass.: Harvard University Press, 1974.

9. Bowen, N. Theory in the practice of psychotherapy. In P. J. Guerin (Ed.), *Family therapy: Theory and practice*. New York: Gardner Press, 1976.

10. Paul, N. The role of mourning and empathy in conjoint marital therapy. In G. Zuk, & I. Boszormenyi-Nagy (Eds.), *Family therapy and disturbed families*. Palo Alto, Calif.: Science and Behavior Books, 1967, pp. 187, 189–190.

11. Lindemann, E. *Beyond grief: Studies in crisis intervention*. New York: Jason Aronson, 1979.

12. Walsh, F. Concurrent grandparent death and birth of schizophrenic offspring: An intriguing finding. *Family Process*, 1978, *17*(4), 457–463.

13. Boszormenyi-Nagy, I., & Spark, G. *Invisible loyalties*. New York: Harper & Row, 1973.

14. Bell, N. W. Extended family relationships in disturbed and normal families. *Family Process*, 1962, *1*(1), 175–192.

15. Strayhorn, J. Social exchange theory: Cognitive restructuring in marital therapy. *Family Process*, 1978, *17*(4), 437–448.

16. Sullivan, H. S. *The interpersonal theory of psychiatry*. New York: W. W. Norton, 1953.

17. Erikson, E. *Childhood and Society*. New York: W. W. Norton, 1950.

18. Anthony, E. J., & Benedek, T. *Parenthood: Its psychology and psychopathology*. New York: Little, Brown & Co., 1970, p. 6.

19. Tomm, K. M., & Wright, L. Training in family therapy: Perceptual, conceptual, and executive skills. *Family Process*, 1978, *17*(4), 457–463.

20. Bowlby, J. Separation anxiety: A critical review of the literature. *Journal of Child Psychology and Psychiatry*, 1961, *1*, 251–259.

38

Evaluation of Clinical Performance

Francesca Farrar and Imelda W. Clements

In assisting the family in assuming the responsibility for changes in its system, the therapist will find interval evaluations in the therapist-family interactions helpful. This evaluation can aid in judging the effectiveness of his/her interventions and, whenever necessary, can assist in altering the therapy approach to aid the family members in working together more effectively. The following is an evaluation checklist using the nursing process devised to assist the therapist in performing this procedure.

A SELF-EVALUATION TOOL (1–4)

Directions: Place an X on the continuum at the point you think appropriate.
Criteria: Nursing Process

Expected Behavior	Achieved	Needs Improvement	Did Not Achieve
I. Assesses family's psychosocial needs.			
A. Understands rationale for the family approach.			
1. Understands systems theory as applied to family units.	____	____	____
2. Orients therapy toward eventual termination.	____	____	____

A SELF-EVALUATION TOOL (1–4)

Expected Behavior	Achieved	Needs Improvement	Did Not Achieve
B. Establishes the therapist-family alliance by therapeutic contract.			
1. Contracts with family for a certain number of sessions to work on specific problems.	_____	_____	_____
2. Audiotape consent form signed.	_____	_____	_____
C. Develops a collaborative working relationship with the family.			
1. Uses purposeful verbal and nonverbal interaction with family.	_____	_____	_____
2. Uses nonverbal communication when relating to children.	_____	_____	_____
3. Demonstrates good listening skills.	_____	_____	_____
4. Clarifies communication.	_____	_____	_____
5. Respects family loyalties.	_____	_____	_____
6. Explores negative reactions to particular therapeutic intervention.	_____	_____	_____
D. Acquires and interprets primary and secondary family data.			
1. Interviews with purpose.	_____	_____	_____
2. Selects significant data from interviews.	_____	_____	_____
3. Identifies causal relationship between precipating events and family problem.	_____	_____	_____
4. Selects primary data significant to psychosocial needs of the family.	_____	_____	_____
5. Obtains primary data from direct observation of verbal and nonverbal interaction.	_____	_____	_____
6. Selects secondary data significant to counseling of family from medical history and psychosocial history.	_____	_____	_____
7. Interprets and correlates primary and secondary family data based on previously acquired knowledge. (e.g. crisis intervention, systems theory, adult and child psychology, study of family, Quid pro Quo, etc.).	_____	_____	_____
II. Plans counseling sessions.			
A. Clarifies family problems.			
1. Obtains a complete and accurate account and development of the problem.	_____	_____	_____

Expected Behavior	Achieved	Needs Improve- ment	Did Not Achieve
2. Encourages family members to share their knowledge and experience of the problem.	⸻	⸻	⸻
3. Stimulates interaction between family members to expose relationship problems.	⸻	⸻	⸻
4. Identifies maladaptive interaction and family rules.	⸻	⸻	⸻
5. Clarifies the boundaries within the family and between the family and outsiders.	⸻	⸻	⸻
B. Identifies individual problems.			
1. Explores with family member how he/she preceives the problem.	⸻	⸻	⸻
2. Explores other family members' perceptions concerning an individual's problem.	⸻	⸻	⸻
3. Curtails the inquiry if blaming becomes severe.	⸻	⸻	⸻
C. Formulates family needs.			
1. Records an individual problem list that may affect the behavior of a particular individual including physical, psychological, and social problems.	⸻	⸻	⸻
2. Lists interpersonal family problems at the most relevant systems level.	⸻	⸻	⸻
3. Identifies the priority psychosocial needs and both the immediate and long-term goals.	⸻	⸻	⸻
D. Develops counseling plan.			
1. Identifies family strengths as well as weaknesses.	⸻	⸻	⸻
2. Sets goals.	⸻	⸻	⸻
3. Includes the family in problem identification, setting goals, and the counseling plan.	⸻	⸻	⸻
4. Formulates appropriate counseling strategies to meet the priority psychosocial needs to encompass both the immediate and long-term goals.	⸻	⸻	⸻
5. Formulates alternative counseling strategies to meet unfulfilled psychosocial needs.	⸻	⸻	⸻
6. Presents psychosocial rationale for planned counseling actions.	⸻	⸻	⸻

Expected Behavior	Achieved	Needs Improve- ment	Did Not Achieve

7. Initiates interaction and collaboration with other resources in development of the counseling plan. ____ ____ ____

III. Implements counseling session.
    A. Performs counseling actions.
        1. Validates psychosocial needs in the family. ____ ____ ____
        2. Performs counseling actions on the basis of psychosocial knowledge. ____ ____ ____
        3. Modifies counseling plan to meet family's changing needs. ____ ____ ____
        4. Supports modifications in counseling with data obtained by observation and communication. ____ ____ ____
        5. Uses interaction and continuing collaboration with other resources to facilitate counseling. ____ ____ ____
    B. Implements change facilitation.
        1. Influences the family to change. ____ ____ ____
        2. Refrains from introducing changes that exceed the capabilities of the family or its members. ____ ____ ____
        3. Assesses the family's capacity to change. ____ ____ ____
        4. Controls maladaptive patterns by restructuring family interactions. ____ ____ ____
        5. Demonstrates possible solutions by being a model if necessary. ____ ____ ____
    C. Removes inappropriate affective blocks.
        1. Encourages open discussion of the emotional turmoil of family members. ____ ____ ____
        2. Realizes that weeping is an adaptive tension release and is less destructive than the expression of anger. ____ ____ ____
        3. Provides support to family members. ____ ____ ____
        4. Slows the therapeutic process when an issue is too stressful. ____ ____ ____
    D. Initiates adaptive interaction patterns.
        1. Challenges maladaptive ideas. ____ ____ ____
        2. Emphasizes concepts that have adaptive potential. ____ ____ ____
        3. Encourages family members to try new behaviors in the sessions. ____ ____ ____
        4. Implements adaptive changes in behavior by changing the interpersonal boundaries between family members. ____ ____ ____

Expected Behavior	Achieved	Needs Improve- ment	Did Not Achieve

IV. Evaluates the counseling.
    A. Validates the effectiveness of counseling interactions.
        1. Validates the effectiveness through observation and communication.
        2. Analyzes the effects of own behavior on the counseling.
        3. Modifies counseling actions on the basis of the evaluation.
    B. Initiates termination constructively.
        1. Encourages disclosure of fears related to the termination process.
        2. Concludes therapy on a positive note.
        3. Reviews unresolved family problems.
        4. Expresses personal appreciation for family openness and for the opportunity to have worked with them to solve problems.

REFERENCES

1. Cleghorn, J. M., & Levin, S. Training family therapists by setting learning objectives. *American Journal of Orthopsychiatry,* 1973, *43,* 429–446.

2. Liberman, R. Behavioral approaches to family and couple therapy. *American Journal of Orthopsychiatry,* 1970, *40,* 106–117.

3. Tomm, K. M., & Wright, L. M. Training in family therapy: Perceptual, conceptual and executive skills. *Family Process,* 1979, *18,* 228–250.

4. Yura, H., & Walsh, M. B. *The Nursing Process.* Washington, D.C.: Catholic University Press, 1967.

Index